Ambassador of Nowhere

A Latin American Pilgrimage

Richard Gwyn is a keen explorer of Latin American maps, as attentive to small anecdotes as he is to the larger conflicts that define a society. His way of joining up poetry, political critique and autobiographical narrative is no less remarkable than his ability to make links between countries with very different traditions . . . To accompany this empathetic traveller, tragicomic chronicler and passionate scholar of an entire continent is a rare pleasure, as well as a beautiful demonstration that we only ever belong to a place if we keep our eyes open. .
– Andrés Neuman

Richard Gwyn journeys through the literature and landscapes of Latin America with the attentive gaze of someone on the lookout for the unexpected, and the conspiratorial air of one who makes close friends of perfect strangers. The 'Ambassador of Nowhere' deals in equal measure with poets and beggars, demystifies the colonial gaze of famous authors, and delves into the mysteries of Spanish with the wisdom of an interpreter of dreams. An existential pilgrim, Gwyn explores himself, too, and ends his Odyssey at his place of origin, by his father's side. The paradox of this solitary adventure is that its author becomes the best of travelling companions.
– Juan Villoro

A wonderfully rich and immersive tour through the lands and literatures of Latin America, but very much more than that. Gwyn explores translation and alcoholism, history, mortality and Welsh identity with the same acute and generous eye.
– Tom Bullough

With his customary ranging intelligence and elegance of prose Richard Gwyn here presents the rewarding and probing life of the peregrinating writer, flying back and fore between Wales and Latin America much like the migrations of Manx shearwater, which similarly bridges continents with ease. A series of informative, revealing and meditative journals – with poetry set very much at the heart – they remind us how Gwyn is one of the most companionable of writers and most perceptive of cultural guides.
– Jon Gower

Ambassador of Nowhere

A Latin American Pilgrimage

RICHARD GWYN

SEREN

Seren is the book imprint of
Poetry Wales Press Ltd.
Suite 6, 4 Derwen Road, Bridgend,
Wales, CF31 1LH

www.serenbooks.com
facebook.com/SerenBooks
twitter: @SerenBooks

© Richard Gwyn 2024

The right of Richard Gwyn to be identified
as the author of this work has been asserted
in accordance with the Copyright,
Designs and Patents Act, 1988.

ISBN 978-1-78172-777-5
Ebook: 978-178172-756-0

A CIP record for this title is available
from the British Library.

All rights reserved.
No part of this publication may be
reproduced, stored in a retrieval system,
or transmitted at any time
or by any means electronic,
mechanical, photocopying, recording
or otherwise without the prior permission
of the copyright holders.

The publisher works with the financial assistance of the Books Council of Wales.

Cover photograph: Richard Gwyn
Back cover photograph: Paulo Slachevsky @pauloslachevsky
All photographs unless otherwise attributed, are by the author.

Printed by Akcent Media Ltd.

Contents

The Map: A Prologue	9
PART I	13
PART II	123
PART III	215
Notes	330
Acknowledgements	340
Author Note	342

Fayan was on pilgrimage and he was lost in a snowstorm. He came upon the monastery where Dizang was Abbot. Dizang asked Fayan: 'Where are you going?' Fayan said: 'Around on pilgrimage'. Dizang said: 'What is the purpose of pilgrimage?' Fayan said: 'I don't know.' Dizang responded: 'Not knowing is most intimate.'
— *The Book of Equanimity*

Latin America is the insane asylum of Europe. Maybe, originally, it was thought that Latin America would be Europe's hospital, or Europe's grain bin. But now it's the insane asylum. A savage, impoverished, violent insane asylum, where, despite its chaos and corruption, if you keep your eyes wide open, you can see the shadows of the Louvre.
— Roberto Bolaño, *Por sí mismo*

The Map: A Prologue

At the age of nineteen, living in a student house in east London, I hung a map on my bedroom wall. Believing that I enjoyed a special connection or allegiance to Latin America, the map enabled me to practise a variety of sympathetic magic, whereby knowledge of the thing depicted might become reality through a process of imagination, just as our ancestors, wishing to invoke an antelope or bison, painted its likeness on the walls of their caves. A map is usually a means to an end, the end being an actual place we need to go. But maps do more: they move us beyond the normal terrain of cartography, into the realm of the imagination and of dreams, in other words, into the domain of fiction: maps offer stuff to dream with, the raw materials of the writer, as well as the traveller.

I was a student of anthropology, and was intrigued by the indigenous peoples whose worlds lay hidden within the vast territory represented by the map on my wall. I read chronicles of the conquest of the Americas and the terrible adventures of the conquistadors, as well as more recent histories and ethnographic studies. At the time I was doing a lot of LSD, which possibly facilitated the process of imagining things, but certainly didn't help me complete my studies, which I abandoned after my second year. Meanwhile, my enthusiasm for Latin American fiction was keen, but my reading haphazard. Gabriel García Márquez's *One Hundred Years of Solitude* had been a revelation, and the florid excesses of the Colombian's literary invention almost succeeded in making a Macondo of Dalston, where I was living at the time, the Ridley Road market evoking the sounds and scents of a kindred or parallel Caribbean. My bus journeys across the metropolis were enhanced by my reading of García Márquez, Vargas Llosa, and other writers of *El Boom*, as the wave of new writing from the region became known. Carlos Fuentes' *Terra Nostra* – a sort of phantasmagorical history of the Hispanic world, in which Queen Elizabeth I is married off to Felipe II of Spain – was a novel that I considered transformative at the time, but which now I would probably find unreadable. I plunged into the poetry of Pablo Neruda, César Vallejo, Nicanor Parra, and Octavio Paz, in translation, since I knew no Spanish then. Paz's *Labyrinth of Solitude*, in which Mexico is described as a place that is distant, strange and impenetrable to European eyes, also made a lasting impression. Despite this strangeness and impenetrability, I recognised myself in the works of these Latin American writers more readily than I did in authors closer to home.

However, the political regimes in place across much of the region, as well as a lack of funds, discouraged me from travelling there, and it was only much later that I visited America at all, North or South. My peregrination around Latin America, beginning in February 2011, was conceived as a quest for poems, to fill an anthology I had been commissioned to translate.[1] But when I first left London, exactly three decades earlier, and settled on the island of Crete, sharing a house with an Argentinian in exile, who, like me, had a Welsh father, I had no need of my map at all, and my itinerary during those early years was for the main part confined to the lands skirting the Mediterranean.

It was in Crete that I first read Borges, a confirmed lover of maps, whose story 'On Exactitude in Science' I reproduce here in its entirety:

> … In that Empire, the Art of Cartography attained such Perfection that the map of a single Province occupied the entirety of a City, and the map of the Empire, the entirety of a Province. In time, those Unconscionable Maps no longer satisfied, and the Cartographers Guilds struck a Map of the Empire whose size was that of the Empire, and which coincided point for point with it. The following Generations, who were not so fond of the Study of Cartography as their Forebears had been, saw that that vast Map was Useless, and not without some Pitilessness was it, that they delivered it up to the Inclemencies of Sun and Winters. In the Deserts of the West, still today, there are Tattered Ruins of that Map, inhabited by Animals and Beggars; in all the Land there is no other Relic of the Disciplines of Geography.

---

1. Published in 2016 as *The Other Tiger: Recent Poetry from Latin America* (Seren).

Borges attributes these words to one Suárez Miranda, in his *Viajes de Varones Prudentes* (Journeys of Prudent Men). The idea that those "Tattered Ruins" of the map, "inhabited by Animals and Beggars" are, indeed, the very fabric of the world we live in, and that the map has become the thing it was designed to represent, is a variation on the theme that obsessed Borges throughout his life, that of the other, the double, most succinctly expressed in his late fragment, 'Borges and I'. In that piece, again a single paragraph, Borges reflects upon his dual identity as both a first person 'I' and as his own doppelgänger, a "name on a list of professors or in some biographical dictionary", and acknowledges that, little by little, he is giving over everything to an ever-present other.

This pervasive sense of doubleness, of wandering through a corridor of mirrors, seems curiously apt in relation both to maps (which replicate a version of the world) and translation (which replicates a version of the word). Of all literary works it is, perhaps, the work of translation that most nearly replicates the reading of a map. From the outset, the translator attempts to interpret the map's legend, trace the contours of the escarpments and the courses of the rivers that populate the textual landscape. Translators need to be consummate map-readers if they are to come close to navigating a route through the landscape of their chosen texts. They must filter their words and phrases through a sieve of possible renditions, always juggling alternative meanings and readings, to imply and suggest and resist all at once, to dwell in a state of continuous uncertainty or ambivalence between what is to be translated and what must remain in silence. And the translator, like any reader of maps, or storyteller, needs to choose a point of departure.

The notes that I gathered over several years of intermittent travel across Latin America form the basis of this chronicle, but it is only now, as I put them in order, that I am able to reflect on the ways in which the writing of a book, much like the making or reading of a map, resembles, more than anything else, an act of translation. In the ever-shifting cartography of the writer, the vehicle for discovery is the work itself. And like Suárez Miranda in the Borges story, I found that, even as I travelled to new places, the world I set out to record was already scattered with fragments of the map with which I sought to navigate it.

The journeys I took to Nicaragua, Argentina, Uruguay, Mexico, Colombia and Chile, provided me with the opportunity to seek out poems that might best help me understand the worlds from which they arose. Also, inevitably, I began to enjoy the experience for its own sake; the exquisite tension of the unfinished journey. In this way I was able to take up and unfold the map I had abandoned over thirty years before on the wall of my room, in a house in London.

PART I

> God said:
> Love your neighbour as yourself.
> In my country
> he who loves his neighbour
> is dicing with death.
>
> Gioconda Belli, 'God said'.

Nicaragua, February 2011

I caught the early morning shuttle from Cardiff to Amsterdam and after a short stopover at Schiphol boarded the KLM flight to Panama City. I took my seat just as a dispute was warming.

In the aisle to my left, an obese man was arguing with a female cabin attendant about his seating allocation. It was not possible, he said, for him to sit next to a strange woman. The attendant responded that the flight was full, but she would see what she could do. The man was sweating and agitated, and although he seemed uncomfortable at being the centre of attention, he could not bear to do anything as perilous as sit in close proximity to a woman he did not know.

The cabin attendant was handling the situation with admirable restraint. I wonder, though, whether she acted with total disinterest when she placed the unfortunate complainant on the end seat of a row of three shaven-headed men, who had already, I observed, made a start on their supply of duty-free spirits. The men were speaking a Slavic language, I couldn't tell which at first, but eventually plumped for Russian or Ukrainian or Belorussian. They were East Slavs, at any rate.

The woman who had originally been allocated the seat alongside the men seemed only too happy to relinquish it to her increasingly perplexed replacement, on whom the injustice of the arrangement was certainly not lost. The spectre of a hundred bloody pogroms may have haunted him as he took his seat alongside his well-lubricated neighbours, but what could he do?

He had already asked to be moved once, and a second request would surely fall on deaf ears. He did protest, but without much enthusiasm; it was more of a mumble of dissent to the world at large than a proper complaint. By now the plane had begun to taxi, and he resigned himself to sitting and strapping himself in, all the while wearing an expression of stony martyrdom.

I settled into my book, and only took stock of my surroundings again an hour later, when we were cruising high above the earth's surface. I had an aisle seat, on the starboard or right hand side of the plane, and had a good view of the middle section, just ahead of me, where the earlier action had taken place. The man who didn't want to sit next to a woman had vacated his seat next to the depilated trio, and was standing in the passage near to the WC. As he was such a large man, he had to step back inside the cabin to make room whenever a passenger or crew member approached. He seemed as unhappy as before, but was now reciting words under his breath. Peering over, I saw that he held a small book outstretched before him. From time to time, however, he cast an angry glance in the direction of the troublesome Slavs, who, apart from being identically shaven-headed, sported tattoos on much of the surface of their visible skin, though only one, it must be said, had a tattooed skull. Across the aisle from me sat a young Central American woman who, like me, was travelling alone.

I was wondering about the man who had refused to sit next to a strange woman. There is nothing in the Torah, the Talmud, or elsewhere in the rabbinic tradition that prohibits Orthodox Jewish men from sitting next to women on public conveyances, but there is a longstanding belief – shared by fundamentalist adherents of Islam and Christianity – that men are unable to control themselves, or to resist 'evil thoughts' (*yetzer hara*, in Hebrew) in the close company of women. So it is, paradoxically, men who need protecting and women who carry the stigma as contaminant or corrupting vessels. I looked at the attractive Central American woman across from me, and wondered if I, too, were in danger.

The meal trolley was moving down the aisle as the three bald men progressed to the rowdy stage of their drinking. They were being told off for breaking into their duty-free supply of vodka, which, the flight attendant informed them, must be stored in the overhead lockers. They were allowed to order drinks with their meal, which was now being served, but apparently no more than two miniatures of spirits or two small bottles of wine per person, a limit which they, via their spokesman, a tall, hatchet-faced individual who managed a very basic English, thought unreasonable. Considering the already advanced state of their inebriation, the offer seemed quite generous, but that is not how it works. For the enthusiast, the more one drinks, the more one wants.

I watched a film, or maybe read, I can't remember. Perhaps I drifted off to sleep again after the meal, but at some point around the middle of the fourteen-hour flight a racket started up again in the centre aisle. The man I thought of as the leader (they struck me, not unreasonably, as being a criminal gang of some kind) was waving a large bottle of Grey Goose vodka around, so he must have plundered the supplies from the overhead locker, in defiance of the flight attendant's instructions. He and his companions were standing now, exchanging loud banter. The man who disliked being seated next to strange women was still outside the lavatory, his lips moving wordlessly and his head bobbing up and down like a mechanical doll as he scanned the sacred text that he held before him. Everyone else in the cabin was trying to carry on as though the drunken disturbance in the East Slavic row was not happening, but it very evidently was, and there was a spiky tension in the air. The flight attendant returned, accompanied by a male companion. The vodka was quickly stashed away at their approach, words were exchanged, apologies were offered, but once the stewards had gone the men started laughing amongst themselves. My neighbour across the aisle looked nervous, and seemed to want to start a conversation. She made a face in the direction of the East Slavs. She told me she had been visiting family in Europe, and was headed home to Panama, then enquired after me. I told her I was on my way to a poetry festival in Nicaragua. She nodded, unimpressed, and returned to her magazine.

It was around this point that the man I had designated the trio's leader decided it was time to get busy. Reaching inside the overhead locker, he retrieved a bag, and went into the lavatory, brushing past the man at prayer. He emerged wearing a gold lamé jacket, and began working his way down the far side of the cabin, apparently in search of single women. He edged backwards down the aisle, but seemed not to meet with any luck. Of the women who were awake, and whom he deemed worthy of his attentions, none responded with any enthusiasm to his pitch.

I wondered: *had he actually planned this?* Had he decided, at some point prior to the flight, that he would take the opportunity, during this long transatlantic crossing, to come on to some random woman, with the objective, no doubt, of having sex in the confines of the airplane toilet and thereby joining the ranks of the so-called mile-high club? Obviously, he must have thought, in order to be successful in this goal, he needed the sartorial bonus of his special jacket, since it is well-known that women of all nationalities will succumb gratefully to the advances of a shaven-headed man with an assassin's face, dressed in gold lamé and wearing – yes, I could see them now – snakeskin boots.

However, the rejections he received only added to the thrill of the chase and before long this bald Cossack was sidling up to my terrified Panamanian neighbour. He began the attempted seduction with some choice phrases of English, voiced in the kind of gangster drawl immortalised by the actor Robbie Coltrane in a pair of Bond films: All alone we travel? How can this be? Such a pretty girl ... and so on. She looked past her unwelcome suitor, straight at me, with an expression of desperation. I hated scenes like this. It was time to play the Victorian Father.

Can you leave her alone? I said, in a very British rendition of strained politeness. It's obvious she doesn't wish to speak with you.

Gold Lamé Man, who was squatting in the aisle between the young woman and me, swivelled on his haunches, fixed me with a bleary glare and snarled: Who you are? Her brother?

No, I said. Her father. Now, go away and leave her in peace.

You are her brother, he slurred, with the dogged insistence of the hopelessly drunk, ignoring both parts of my utterance. Respect, he said. The family is all. You protect your sister honour. This I do, in my country. You are good man.

Rather than being offended by my intervention, and my claim of kinship to the young woman – fairly improbable considering her strongly indigenous features – Gold Lamé Man now seemed intent on befriending her brother. Perhaps, following Grey Goose logic, he believed that this would enhance his chances of winning her over. However, I didn't wish to play this game, and am in any case, somewhat ironically, intolerant of drunks, and hopeless at dealing with them.

Look, I said. She doesn't want you, and I don't want to be your friend, so why don't you fuck off?

But my interlocutor's attention had been distracted; he had spotted another potential victim further down the cabin and was on his way, as if pursuing the most vital quest of his life. But as he headed down the aisle he was intercepted by the flight attendant, again accompanied by her male colleague and another, non-uniformed man, whom I took to be airline security. The two men steered him back towards his seat. They were discreet but forceful. Gold Lamé Man looked up at them belligerently, at the same time appearing to make gestures of submission. The two men withdrew, and there was – after a brief pause – an eruption of deep, manly laughter from the East Slavic row, and I could again see a bottle being passed from one to the other. Within seconds, the security man and the male crew member were back, the former carrying handcuffs. The two of them hauled Gold Lamé Man into the aisle, forced his arms behind his back and cuffed his wrists. He protested, but his comrades remained silent. The two airline staff dragged him towards the front of the plane. Shortly afterwards, the plain-clothes man returned, and told his two companions, in English, and in a voice loud enough to reassure nearby passengers, that their friend was being detained and would be handed over to the local police on arrival in Panama City. Any further disturbances from them and the perpetrator would meet the same fate as Gold Lamé Man.

I considered, without the least compassion, the prospect of waking, hungover, in a Panamanian police cell, and reckoned that Gold Lamé Man probably deserved it. I also pondered the cultural significance of what had taken place on this flight thus far. The vignette played out before my eyes by the Orthodox Jewish man and the East Slavs seemed to epitomise, in microcosmic form, how the historical conflicts of the Old World were carried over into the New, as they have been, uninterruptedly, for the past five hundred years. Thus two worlds meet, in a constant, uneven interaction, bringing all the bias and prejudices of the one to nest in the other, which already contains its own sorrowful litany of racial and social turmoil.

I swallowed a sleeping pill and slept for the remainder of the journey, waking as the plane banked steeply to a vision of the wide ocean and the entrance to the famous canal far below, granted a celestial view of the phalanx of oil tankers that crowded the waters below us, like small toys in the paddling pool of the immortals. A three hour wait in the dreary terminal followed, and finally, after a further delay, my third flight of a long day; the connection to Nicaragua.

At Managua airport, the guests to the International Poetry Festival were filtered off, our passports taken from us, and we were bundled into the so-called VIP waiting room, with sofas and a wide-screen TV. The room was functional and smelled of cleaning product. I chatted for a while with a friendly Argentinian poet, before stretching out on the sofa to watch a movie about nazi zombies, or zombie nazis. Within minutes I was asleep.

★   ★   ★

My first experience of Central America is framed in memory by the image of twin palm trees swaying in tandem beneath a full moon.

It was well past midnight when our bus, packed with a diverse throng of poets, arrived in the colonial city of Granada and we were dropped off at our respective hotels. I found my way to my room, unpacked, and sat for a while by the open window, which overlooked a small swimming pool cocooned beneath a giant bougainvillea, its blossoms fluorescent in the bright glow cast upward from the pool's underwater lights. I sat and let it all soak in, hypnotized by those swaying palm trees at the pool's edge. I knew it was a cliché, but I was too tired to resist.

The next morning, in the hotel foyer, I noticed a sign warning clients of the law against child prostitution. The sexual abuse of children is a profitable business in Nicaragua, as in so many parts of the nominally developing world. No doubt the country's president, Daniel Ortega, long accused by his stepdaughter, Zoilamérica Narváez, of serially abusing her from the age of nine onward, sets the example. Depressed by this, and beset by an obscure anxiety, I took a walk with my new friend, the Argentine poet Jorge Fondebrider, whom I had met the previous evening in the VIP waiting room at the airport, where we – the guests at Granada's International Poetry Festival – had waited for several hours for our passports to be processed.

Together, we paid a visit to the festival bookshop. Housed in a white marquee, it displayed a selection of works from across the Spanish-speaking world. Jorge impressed me with his comprehensive knowledge of Latin American poetry: he even proposed a fellow Argentine I might wish to translate, plucking an edition of the poet's work from the stacked shelves. You'll like this, he informed me, although at this stage Jorge knew next to nothing about my tastes in poetry. Outside the bookshop, on a large placard listing the sponsors of the festival, I was surprised to see the words 'Embajada de Gales' ('Embassy of Wales'). Since Wales is not a nation state, it does not possess embassies or ambassadors, least of all in Nicaragua. The idea, however, was appealing, and lent a fictitious aspect to my being here, in a covertly ambassadorial role. As things turned out, it was also strangely prescient.

Although I had been invited to Granada in my capacity as a poet, I had another agenda, as a translator, and aimed to attend as many of the readings as possible in order to find potential recruits for the anthology of Latin American poetry I was planning. I was only partially successful in this aim, being reminded yet again, as I often am, that I don't much enjoy poetry readings; in fact much of the time I actively dislike them, an aversion that extends, naturally enough, towards poetry itself. In this I am not alone. "I, too, dislike it," wrote Marianne Moore, famously, and "many more people agree they hate poetry" – as Ben Lerner writes in his curiously compelling essay, *The Hatred of Poetry* – "than can agree what poetry is." "I, too, dislike it," he continues, echoing Moore, "and have largely organized my life around it and do not experience that as a contradiction because poetry and the hatred of poetry are inextricable in ways it is my purpose to explore."

In my own list of grievances against the spectacle of the poetry reading, I could cite the depressing drone of the 'poetry voice', with its grating and gratuitous high rising tone at the end of lines, as though each utterance were a vaguely mooted question which no one, least of all the poet, could be bothered to answer; or the bravura and heroic declamation of the overtly political poem, a specialty of many performance poets, as well, I soon discovered, as of the would-be revolutionary poets at this festival, most of them Central Americans; or the stupefying self-importance of a certain breed of versifier convinced of their own brilliance – usually men – who will always and inevitably run on beyond the ten or fifteen-minute slot allocated them, so crucial are their insights, and so piffling, by comparison, the creations of any reader who might follow them on the programme. All of this without even considering the offence inflicted by the poems themselves ...

There may be a paradox in poets hating poetry readings, but it is one I can celebrate alongside the Colombian poet Darío Jaramillo, who was present at the festival in Granada, and who claims, in an essay, that the majority of poets who read at public events, quite apart from having no talent whatever for writing, are also unable to read their work effectively. However, he concedes, in a self-deprecating tone, that despite his own reluctance to go to poetry readings, he always commits the distressing error of appearing as the reader of his own poems when invited to do so. "The outcome of all this," he writes, "if it were possible, is more pathetic still, in that I make myself available to take part in this ridiculous montage with other poets, to share not only my own part in the collective ridiculousness, but to share my own ridiculousness with the ridiculousness of the person next to me."

I feel likewise, and the only remedy for the gloom into which I routinely descend when obliged to attend a poetry event is the exhilaration I experience when, once in a while, I witness a reading that proves an exception to the rule, and the poet blends literary skill with performative genius, prompting me, temporarily, to forget my antagonism towards poetry readings and poetry at large.

On leaving the festival bookshop, Jorge and I strolled through the market in Granada's central square. There was very little local produce, but an abundance of Chinese manufactured plastic goods. All of this seemed very strange, as I had read that the textile industry accounted for more than half of Nicaragua's export revenue. We fell into conversation with a Guatemalan woman who ran a well-stocked stall of brightly coloured bags, mats, skirts, jackets and rolls of fabric, all of which she had brought with her from her own country. She told us of a women's cooperative that had recently been set up in Granada, whose members produced handicrafts and ceramics for the tourist market, but was not sure where it was located. I bought a tee shirt at another stall, with NICARAGUA emblazoned across the front. It was, the label informed me, Made in Honduras.

I was growing increasingly uncomfortable about my ignorance of Nicaragua and its history. I knew that in 1979 the Sandinista revolution had overturned a corrupt and cruel dictatorship, led by Anastasio Somoza: I was living in London at that time, and had held a typically uninformed allegiance with the revolutionaries, no doubt amplified by The Clash and their 1980 album, *Sandinista!,* but I knew little of what had really gone on in Nicaragua during the revolution and immediately after, nor indeed why the Contra war, as Ronald Reagan's intervention during the 1980s was called – when an army of US-sponsored mercenaries attempted to impose a counterrevolution – came to an end.

Even in the centre of Granada, which was showcasing an international poetry festival, signs of penury and suffering were abundant. Child beggars followed us around, cheerfully but persistently, and women – many of them very young – openly solicited for sex. I had read that Nicaragua suffered the greatest levels of poverty in the western hemisphere, after Haiti. If revolutionary Sandinismo was for the people, why were the people so poor? In left-leaning European circles back in the eighties, the Contras had been seen as the embodiment of reactionary evil, whereas the brave Sandinistas were represented as the progressive apostles of land reform and greater social equality in a country traditionally divided by a wealthy landowning elite and the impoverished rest. Was this an accurate picture? If the Sandinista revolution was in the first instance a good thing, where had it all gone wrong?

Salman Rushdie visited Nicaragua in 1986 – seven years after the revolution – and briskly published an account of the trip, *The Jaguar Smile*, which he later described as "a period piece, a fairy tale of one of the hotter moments in the Cold War." In the book, his attitude is one of sympathy towards the Sandinistas, informed to some degree, as he readily admits, by his own experience of growing up under the legacy of the British Empire in India. He is acerbic about the interventionist policies of the USA, and especially the role of the CIA in Central America, describing how the agency operated through its cynically titled "UCLA's: Unilaterally Controlled Latino Assets." During 1986-8 President Reagan awarded the CIA a budget for operations in Nicaragua of around $400 million, with another $300 million being spent on "buying off Nicaragua's neighbours."

Rushdie is convincing on the idea that for many Nicaraguans, Sandinismo meant having a sense of home, because during the Somoza regime they had none: all the land was owned by the dictator and his cronies. "They were," he writes, "inventing their country, and, more than that, themselves." Reporting on a field trip he made with a Sandinista government team to hand out land rights to peasant farmers, he recalls: "The campesinos came up and received their land titles, informally, with little fuss. It seemed natural to be moved."

Rushdie's account is enthusiastic about the essential justice of the Sandinistas' cause, and of the radical change they were attempting to effect in their country. However, he has few delusions about the likely eventual outcome of their revolution. On his meetings with Daniel Ortega ("that odd mixture of confidence and shyness"), he is cautiously respectful, but the interviews reveal very little about the man who went on to betray the revolution he then so ardently espoused. Rushdie's portrayal of the leader is certainly lacking the full endorsement he offers to Sergio Ramírez, the vice-president and an internationally acclaimed novelist, with whom he is personally at ease, and can drink rum and talk literature. Meanwhile, he seems dumfounded by the poet-priest Ernesto Cardenal, whose support for Cuba was unconditional, and who viewed freedom of the press as "cosmetic".

In the years following Rushdie's trip, things went downhill for the Sandinistas. Although they avoided outright defeat, the Contra War of the 1980s succeeded in destabilising the country, and caused severe economic hardship. In the general elections of 1990, Ortega lost to the press heiress Violeta Chamorro (whose lavish jewellery offended Rushdie when he met her on his 1986 visit) and although she and her liberal successors ran the country with coalition governments for the next fifteen years, Ortega returned to win the 2006 elections with a watered-down version of Sandinismo, and has maintained power in various rigged plebiscites ever since. Sergio Ramírez, disgusted with the way things were turning, officially retired from politics in 2008, while Ernesto Cardenal remained a constant but ultimately ineffective critic of Ortega's leadership until his death in March, 2020. Thus Nicaragua completed its transformation into the sort of run-down shadowland it was when I visited in 2011 – and which it continues to be today – hanging onto the coat-tails of whichever major power brings investment, currently China. There was recently a plan to build a rival canal to Panama's, which would cut the country in two, effectively destroying the large freshwater lake from which the country takes its name (and which is home to many rare species, including the unique white freshwater shark). While that plan has been temporarily shelved, following the withdrawal of the main Chinese backer, environmentalists point to the devastation that would be wreaked on the ecology of the entire region by such a vast operation, as well as the inevitable disruption to the inhabitants of the coastal area, made up almost entirely of indigenous Miskito and African-Caribbean people. In the meantime, Ortega has been accused of profiteering from land grabs associated with the project.

While Nicaragua's political evolution was of particular interest to me, I was also aware that, in historical terms, the USA viewed Central America at large as an asset or purview over which it maintained utter dominance. The series of conflicts that engulfed the countries of this region throughout the twentieth century cannot be studied in isolation. Each of them exists – in one form or another – with the say-so of their giant neighbour. This was certainly the opinion held by Jorge, whose view of the region's politics, as I soon discovered, was coloured by the experiences of a family member. He told me a story that has haunted me since, and whose resonances echo across Central America, Colombia and Mexico, with their endless succession of mass killings – and more recently, to Ecuador. Jorge believed that US intervention, which had taken the form of support for repressive regimes in Guatemala, El Salvador and Honduras, as well as financial and military backing for the Contras in Nicaragua, came to an end not only because of a change in policy after the Cold War, but also because public opinion in the United States had already been influenced by the increasingly ugly forms of repression that had taken place in the name of the Free World; in particular, as he explained, following a notorious massacre at El Mozote, in nearby El Salvador.

His brother, Jorge told me, was a forensic anthropologist on the Argentine team Equipo Argentino de Antropología Forense (EAAF) that investigated the mass murder of civilians at El Mozote. The details, as I discovered, were bleakly shocking.

On the afternoon of December 10th, 1981, units of the Atlacatl battalion of the Salvadoran army – trained in the United States at American military bases, and armed and actively directed by US military advisors operating within El Salvador itself – appeared in the small town of El Mozote, having clashed with guerrillas nearby. The Atlacatl battalion had a single purpose: to eliminate the rebel forces in the Morazán region of northern El Salvador. However, the people of El Mozote were not supporters of the left-wing guerrillas; they were predominantly evangelical Protestants, some of whom may have sold food to the guerrillas, but who did not in any significant way make them welcome. This detail was no deterrent to the officers of the Atlacatl battalion and their men. During the course of the following day they destroyed El Mozote utterly, torturing, murdering and burning the bodies of around one thousand victims, many of them children. The younger women, and girls as young as ten, were raped before being machine-gunned. The children's throats were slit and their bodies hanged from trees. It was a slaughter executed with terrible thoroughness.

When news trickled through to the wider world, the massacre was investigated by the journalists Raymond Bonner, of the *New York Times*, and Alma Guillermoprieto, of the *Washington Post*, and their reports caused an outcry in American liberal circles. However, the US government's response, when the news first broke in January 1982, was to deny the massacre, and claim that the reports by these two journalists were exaggerated – if not actually fabricated – and biased by their left-wing views. Bonner was suspended as a *Times* reporter shortly afterwards, the paper's executive editor, A.M. Rosenthal, a committed anti-communist, claiming that he lacked "journalistic technique," a roundabout way of saying that he disagreed with the political perspective offered by Bonner's report. Alma Guillermoprieto visited the site of the massacre in person: "We began smelling it from Arambala [a nearby settlement]. These kids started leading me down paths and pointing to houses and saying again and again, 'Aquí hay muertos, aquí hay muertos.' The most traumatizing thing was looking at these little houses where whole families had been blown away – these recognizable human beings, in their little dresses, just lying there mummifying in the sun. We kept walking, got to El Mozote. We walked down these charming and beautiful roads, then to the centre of town, where there was this kind of rubbly place [the sacristy] and in it, a stupefying number of bones."

It was not until the Argentine forensic team submitted their report, eleven years after the massacre, that the true extent of the horror became known, and what took place at El Mozote, long the subject of speculation and official denial, was eventually revealed, and supported by irrefutable evidence. The *New Yorker* magazine, for only the second time in its history, devoted an entire issue to Mark Danner's report, 'The Truth of El Mozote', but it was only in December 2018, thirty-seven years after the massacre, that a court in El Salvador finally recognised that the events of the El Mozote massacre constituted war crimes and crimes against humanity. Even given that concession, it seems unlikely, at the time of writing, that any of the perpetrators – or those who remain alive – will ever be brought to justice.

Jorge told me that the outrage caused by the final confirmation of the massacre prompted the end of US support for right-wing paramilitary groups across Central America, but of course, by the time of the *New Yorker* piece in 1993, the Berlin Wall had come down, so the threat of a Marxist state in Central America was no longer of such consequence.

Since El Mozote, Jorge's brother, Luis, and his team at EAAF have been kept busy in Latin America, Africa, the Middle East and Europe, exhuming corpses and identifying dead children by the ownership of a particular toy clasped in the hand – a doll here, a little wooden horse there – for well over three decades and are in greater demand than ever, Mexico alone providing enough scenes of torture, beheading and murder to keep the organisation in work for many years to come, even if such killings were to stop now.

A few days after my conversation with Jorge, we went on an excursion to a coffee plantation on the slopes of the Mombacho volcano, to the south of Granada, and continued on a walking tour through the cloud forest. Jorge and I got talking with our guide, and for a brief interlude, as we sat looking down on Lake Nicaragua, he let his guard down. Although we were high on the mountainside, and he was with foreigners, he glanced around us while speaking, as though used to being on the alert to any eavesdroppers, and then explained that the education system might be taken as a symptom of all that was wrong with the country. Before the Sandinista revolution, he said, in the days when he was at school, you learned, as he put it, the old way; the educational system was religious and very strict, and you received traditional schooling along conservative, Catholic lines.

During the early years of Sandinismo and the Contra wars, he went on, students learned in the classroom about Leninist theory and how to dismantle and reassemble a Kalashnikov. In mathematics classes, – as he had discovered while helping his son with homework – pupils would be set sums such as: "I have three grenades; if I throw one how many remain?" "I have two machine guns, and my comrade has three: how many machine guns do we have between us?" Nowadays, he told us, the kids don't even go to school; they hang around on street corners, drinking rum and smoking marijuana. Before, Somoza stole everything from us, but left us with hope. The Sandinistas too have stolen everything from us, including hope.

★ ★ ★

I was sitting in my hotel room before going out onto the plaza on the final night of the festival. Outside, a gentle wind was ruffling the bougainvillea that adorned the wall across the patio, and the twin palms were swaying obediently above the spot-lit swimming pool. I needed to change my shirt. It was seven in the evening, and the heat was stifling. The temperature had nudged forty degrees that afternoon and although the breeze had taken the edge off the furnace since darkness fell, it still seemed, to my European sensibilities, a trifle warm for February. In half an hour I was due to go on stage and read poetry to over two thousand people, across the square from my hotel.

Outside, in the tropical night – in defiance of our guide's account the previous day – I could smell the unfamiliar aroma of hope, or something like it. The crowds milling around the plaza, the rural poor, had brought food and drinks for the occasion. Little stalls had sprung up, selling nacatamales and quesillos. Children had shimmied up the statues by the fountain, and were perched in trees in order to get a better view of the stage. For the past week people of all ages had been listening to poets declaim ecstatically or bravely, flamboyantly and with excessive gesticulation and emotion, and the crowds kept coming, joyously chanting the words: *Viva la poesía!* (Long live poetry!) For all my inbuilt scepticism, I was in an unusually good mood, and certainly didn't feel that awful sense of desolation that so often accompanied my attendance at poetry readings back home, sure in the knowledge that the poet is the practitioner of a moribund art, a ghoul of the literary night, guiltily stealing a few minutes of drinking time from the thirsty punters in the back room of some dingy pub. The festival had severely tested the limits of my misanthropy, which I was now beginning to regard as something of a First World indulgence.

On the one hand it felt as though we were being whipped up into a kind of populist frenzy, spurred on by a revolutionary fervour which was at odds with the climate of political oppression that was and is the current reality in Nicaragua; on the other hand, the audience at this festival were participants in the country's rich tradition of activism and wanted desperately to believe in the inherent value of poetry as a weapon of protest. Although, with many of the poets, rhetorical intent prevailed over and above talent or craft, there was nevertheless something deeply moving in the prevalent mood at Granada as we were urged towards poetry as though it had some innate curative or shamanic properties, or even spoke for the Sandinista movement itself, before the whole thing fell in on itself, morphing into the sorry show run by Daniel Ortega and his inner circle today. The dreams of the original Sandinistas, including Ernesto Cardenal (one-time minister of culture and education) and the former high society débutante and ex-guerrilla Gioconda Belli – with both of whom I would be sharing the stage tonight – had been cynically undermined since the heady days of the revolution back in the early eighties, but at least in 2011 the festival was still going strong; at least the people supporting it had something, however fragile, left to cheer about.

The poetry festival in Granada was my first introduction to large-scale literary events of this kind, and although I would go on to attend several such gatherings in Mexico, Colombia and Argentina in subsequent years, and would continue to be amazed at the enthusiasm generated by poetry as a political force in Latin America, Granada was in many ways the strangest and most perplexing of them all. It awakened in me a sense of utter confusion concerning the role that poets might have in a modern society. Such a question rarely seems to have any significance at all in a country like the United Kingdom, whereas here in Nicaragua poets have often been regarded as spokespeople for a better future, heralds of a fairer world. Nowhere was this difference more apparent than in the procession we had carried out on the third day of the festival. The poets were accompanied by hundreds of masked and garlanded dancers and performers, carrying a hearse in which was laid out the coffin of 'poverty and despair' – such was it titled. We made our way down to the shores of Lake Nicaragua, stopping every few hundred metres for readings, in which we poets declaimed our verses, and then we all witnessed the tossing of the symbolically charged coffin into the lake. In the light of more recent developments, one wonders whether our hopeful disposal of poverty and despair in the waters of Lake Nicaragua was not a little premature.

In 2018, a wave of anti-government protests was met by savage reprisals from the state security forces, including a new group of armed thugs known locally as las turbas (the mob). Daniel Ortega seems to be leaving much of the PR – and of government – to his widely vilified wife and vice-president, Rosario Murillo, who in an astutely phrased political judgement, deemed the protestors "criminals" and "vampires in search of blood." Murillo, who attended a girls' convent school in Tiverton, Devon, and a Swiss finishing school before dedicating herself to revolution, knows that of which she speaks. During 2018 alone, more than three hundred protestors – a conservative estimate – met their deaths at the hands of the Nicaraguan security forces and las turbas, many of the victims being deemed "enemies of the revolution." One cannot hope for the Ortega-Murillo dictatorship – for such it has become – to end well.

In December 2018, Alma Guillermoprieto, the journalist who first reported on the El Mozote massacre in the *Washington Post*, and who has braved the most arduous assignations across Latin America for over forty years, delivered the annual Robert B. Silvers lecture at the New York Public Library. She concluded with these words:

> My colleagues and I who reported on the triumph of the Sandinista revolution never expected that forty years later we would be writing about how Daniel Ortega, the Sandinista leader who was president from 1985 to 1990 and has been president again since 2007, has become increasingly like Anastasio Somoza, the dictator he helped overthrow. Or about how his companion, Rosario Murillo, has acquired all the eccentricities of a dictator's wife – the crappy poetry readings, the spiritual séances, the crazy makeup, the offering of her own daughter for her husband's bed. And now the grotesque couple has officially sponsored the killing of more than three hundred students and other demonstrators by the Sandinista police and brand-new paramilitary forces since protests began in April 2018.

In 2019 the International Poetry Festival at Granada was cancelled, the organisers releasing a press statement that explained their decision: "Taking into account the terrible situation that Nicaragua is going through, which has left more than 500 dead, more than 600 incarcerated, thousands of disappeared and tens of thousands of exiles, this Directive considers that there is no favorable environment for any festive activity."

Since then, matters have only worsened. Obviously the poetry festival did not go ahead during the COVID pandemic. But in November 2021 Ortega won his latest rigged election, after first having all the main opposition leaders arrested. The wave of persecution began in May of that year, when one political rival, Cristiana Chamorro, was put under house arrest and banned from running for office, allegedly for money laundering. Over forty other political adversaries were then arrested, including rivals and critics such as Berenice Quezada, Dora María Téllez, and María Fernanda Flores Lanzas, the lawyer and activist Ana Margarita Vijil, and two opposition candidates; Juan Sebastián Chamorro and Félix Maradiaga. In September, an order was put out for the arrest of Ortega's long-time critic (and his former vice president), the novelist and winner of the Cervantes Prize Sergio Ramírez, on the grounds of inciting hatred and conspiring to destabilize Nicaragua. In an interview with the Chilean newspaper *La Tercera*, Ramírez said that "Ortega has no limits. His strategy is to hang on to power whatever the cost. He is a military dictator."

In a familiar contemporary twist, Ortega's government has also been running a social media disinformation campaign for the past three years on Facebook, Twitter, and TikTok, in an effort to denigrate the opposition. Such campaigns have, of course, become common enough, at least since pro-Brexit campaigns on Facebook urged UK voters to leave the European Union in June 2016 and similar interventions influenced the US elections later that year. But on this occasion the disinformation was too blatant even for Facebook, which announced in a public statement that the Nicaraguan campaign was "a coordinated effort to corrupt or manipulate public discourse by using fake accounts to build personas across platforms and mislead people about who's behind them."

Following the elections in November 2021, which President Biden called a "pantomime," the Ortega-Murillo dictatorship has received offers of backing from the usual suspects: Cuba, Venezuela, and Russia. In language that recalls a bygone era, Ortega has castigated his US critics as "Yankee imperialists." Meanwhile, everyday life for Nicaraguans continues to deteriorate, with many leaving the country for Costa Rica, or else following the trail north toward the United States. Many of these exiles do not progress farther than Mexico, where they become the victims of people traffickers, the latest casualties in that country's interminable drug war. I cannot help but remember our guide's words on the slopes of the volcano: they have stolen everything from us, including hope.

> We have a house in South America.
> Here are the dogs with no owner,
> the river, palm trees, summer,
> the little tangled bush
> of wild roses,
> slanting light in autumn.
> Here's where old clothes end up, silence,
> non-matching glasses,
> the most long-lived members
> of different races, made siblings
> by chance, by an oversight of death.
>
> Daniel Samoilovich, 'The House in Tigre'.

Argentina – Uruguay – Argentina, September 2011

The next trip that I undertook in my quest to find poems for the anthology – to feed the elusive tiger of its title – could not have begun more differently from the one to Nicaragua, back in February of the same year.

At Heathrow's Terminal Five, I was surprised to find the place teeming with uniformed soldiers, who were clearly not in the service of Her Britannic Majesty. There were around fifty of them, wearing the blue berets of the United Nations, and they were speaking Spanish with Argentine accents. But what were they doing on a scheduled flight? Didn't the UN have its own planes? And when did you last see the uniformed troops of another nation state marching around on mainland British soil? Had this happened, I wondered, since the thwarted French invasion of Pembrokeshire, in 1797?

The soldiers boarded first, along with the rich, the infirm, and families with small children; then it was my turn. The British Airways official glanced at a screen and informed me I had been upgraded to BA Club World, starting price £3,000 one way. "Have a nice flight," he said, pleased with his own munificence. I smiled graciously and made my way onto the plane.

In the cabin I was planted between a supermodel and a star polo player, the pilot even emerging from his cabin to chat with the latter. In this elite enclave, separated by our individual reclining seats, we didn't greet each other or speak at all, except to order stuff from the flight attendant.

Once I had eaten, and declined the offers of this or that vintage wine, the lights went down, the seat turned into a bed, and I lay in my little cubicle and watched a film about a sixteen-year old psychopathic killer with an elfin face, untidy hair, and a heart of gold. Then I slept – which I seldom manage to do on long flights – for six hours. All told, it was a most welcome contrast to my transatlantic flight earlier that year, from Amsterdam to Panama.

Passing through immigration at Buenos Aires' Ezeiza airport, I was intrigued by the long list of articles that one is prohibited from bringing into the country. Obviously, as a nation whose economy is dependent on livestock farming, this must be a concern, but I was especially stuck by an item prohibiting the importation of semen. Since most adult males are carriers of semen, at least in its potential or unexpressed form, they should, if any logic prevails, be prohibited from entering the country. But they let me in, and I promised, silently, that I would be keeping my sperm to myself.

On a more serious note, I was also acutely conscious that the last time I visited Buenos Aires, to attend a publishing conference in 2005, my niece, Nicola, who was living in the city at the time, was abducted by a gunman, immediately after we had dined together, on my first night. The memory of that trip, and the trauma of Nicola's ordeal and her brave but perilous escape from her captor, weighed heavily on me as I passed through customs.

This time around, on my first evening, I attended a reception at the Embassy of The Netherlands, held in honour of the Dutch writer Cees Nooteboom, who, like myself, was a guest of the city's International Literature Festival, FILBA. After the European summer, I found it hard to acclimatise to the tail end of the southern winter. The trees were bare along the boulevards, and there was no birdsong. I tagged along with my friend Jorge Fondebrider – whom I had met in Nicaragua, and who had wangled the invitation for me here – and Inés Garland, a writer of beautifully crafted short stories.

The ambassador was an erudite, cultured sort, and he and his wife conveyed an immaculate sense of decorum in making small-talk, a facility that usually eludes me. What a skill it is, I reflected, to talk about almost any subject without ever once saying anything that might be construed as controversial or defamatory. The feints, deflections and pirouettes of diplomatic chitchat combine to make an art form in itself. I determined to make more effort in acquiring such skills, but knew in my heart it was something I would be incapable of emulating; certainly not to the standard practised by this ambassadorial couple.

On leaving the reception, as we walked through the diplomatic quarter, Jorge pointed out an impressive building which, he told me, was named the Palacio de los Patos – the Palace of the Ducks – and that the phrase 'quedarse pato' which literally translates as 'to be left a duck', refers to a person who has had, and subsequently lost, a fortune. I recalled that in the game of cricket a 'duck' refers to an innings in which the batsman fails to score any runs. The Palace of Ducks was divided into numerous apartments, many of which were once occupied by upper-crust Porteños[2], and of families who had come down in the world, largely as a consequence of the economic crash in the late 1920s. In other words, it was the collective home of people who had lost their properties, and could no longer afford to have a whole palace to themselves; however, they made sure the surroundings were glamorous enough to remind them of their former elevated status, and to forget their penurious circumstances. It was a reminder, too, of the immense wealth that was once the birthright of many such Argentinians, and that during the first third of the twentieth century, theirs was considered one of the richest and most progressive countries in the world, and the elite social life of Buenos Aires imitated and rivalled the Parisian salons of earlier decades.

Victoria Ocampo was one of the great patrons of the arts at that time, as well as a fine essayist. She published Borges' early

2. Porteño: an inhabitant of Buenos Aires

stories in *Sur*, the magazine she founded, and she hosted and promoted writers and artists from around the world on their visits to South America. Among others, Igor Stravinsky, Aldous Huxley, André Malraux, Indira Gandhi, Drieu La Rochelle, Antoine de Saint Exupéry, Rabindranath Tagore, Albert Camus and Graham Greene were guests at her house, the Villa Ocampo. Lorca's *Romancero Gitano*, among other works, was published by its press, as were the first Spanish translations of Dylan Thomas, Yukio Mishima, Jack Kerouac and Vladimir Nabokov. Victoria maintained a lasting friendship with Virginia Woolf, who, like her, struggled to find her place in a hostile intellectual climate of male hegemony; their correspondence has only recently become available, and was published in Argentina in 2020.

Three days into the festival, along with Nooteboom and his wife Simone, the Japanese writer Minae Mizumura, and Inés, who acted as chauffeur, we drove through the leafy suburbs to visit Victoria's one-time home in affluent Béccar. We were served lunch, and then received a guided tour from the house manager, the slick and well-informed Nicolás Helft, who, after the tour, invited each of us to select a back copy of *Sur* from a packed bookcase, as a gift of the Foundation (I chose a 1961 issue that contained the Spanish translation of a short story by Nabokov, 'Scenes from the life of a double monster', as well as poems by Gregory Corso and Lawrence Ferlinghetti). The house itself was spectacular, even if the interior rather resembled a mausoleum, with rooms kept as they were when the place and its owner enjoyed their greatest renown; the piano at which Stravinsky played bears his framed photograph, and Victoria's study is just as she left it. The grounds, filled with great trees and green lawns, once spread down to the Río de la Plata, several blocks away, and though now considerably less extensive than in the estate's heyday, were still impressive. The odour of privilege wafted down the corridors and up the stairways, causing me to feel slightly dazed. It's hard to place this discomfort, but I reflected afterwards that simply by being here, on a private visit, we were partaking of that elitism, and I wondered whether it were possible, having brushed against their ghosts, ever to be entirely detached from the illustrious dead of such a building.

Victoria Ocampo was something of a tyrant, and those who crossed her often lived to regret it. She also possessed a vicious sense of humour. On returning from a trip to London in 1964, and having become, in her mid-seventies, an ardent Beatles fan, she invited friends around, played her new LP, and tried to get Borges (who once referred to her as "the quintessential Argentine woman") to put on a wig modelled after the coif of John Lennon. "You," she gestured to him, "put that on!" Borges, ever reserved, refused, and she chastised him: "Usted, che, con lo empacado que es nunca va a llegar a nada" (You, you're so stuffy, you'll never amount to anything).

I sat in her chair and meditated on the state of Being Victoria, and for a brief moment felt the thrill of something like burnished glory.

In harsh contrast to the rarefied air of Villa Ocampo, the next day I visited a shanty town – a so-called *villa miseria*, or slum – to the south of the city, in Barracas 21/24, a barrio without running water or electricity, and with only the most basic of social amenities. I went there with Pablo Braun, the FILBA director, and co-founder, with Paz Ochoteco, of *Fundación Temas*, which seeks to improve, in small but significant ways, the living conditions of children in barrios such as these.

We drove to the outskirts of Barracas 21/24 (the numeral affix reducing the place to a statistic) where there was a heavy police presence. The police, Pablo told me, did not enter the ghetto, except in occasional concerted actions against criminal gangs; they left the place to get on with life in its own lawless way.

Paz was waiting for us. Pablo parked up and we got into her car, one that the inhabitants of Barracas 21/24 would recognise. Unfamiliar cars, I was told, would be vandalised, or the tyres removed, at the very least. Strangers were not welcome. We loaded up a couple of cases of books, which we were delivering to the school as a gift from Pablo's bookshop, Eterna Cadencia.

Fundación Temas, with Paz at the helm, provided help in the provision of schooling for the younger children, a kitchen with free meals, and a boxing club. The idea for the boxing club was inspired by the work of the sociologist Loïc Wacquant, who wrote about a similar club in Chicago (and whose ideas influenced the makers of the HBO series *The Wire*). As Pablo explained to me, Wacqaunt argued that the discipline of boxing, within a defined context where the rules were clear, channelled a good deal of the natural aggression of deprived and ghettoized kids, and provided a focus away from the easy distractions of drugs and crime. There was very little infant schooling for the children here because the facilities did not exist. Forty per cent of the children in this barrio received no junior school education, and a half of those who did never reached secondary school.

The Río Matanza (meaning 'slaughter') that flows – though 'flow' is hardly the word for the sluggish progress of its viscous and putrid effluvia towards the sea – is reportedly the most polluted river in the western hemisphere. Upstream, a leather factory producing luxury goods spews out contaminating chemicals. A disused railway line runs between the makeshift shacks.

In the tiny office of Fundación Temas, beside the gym where the boys and girls were boxing – more than half of the members of the boxing club are girls – was a poster of Che Guevara. It was the only time I had ever seen this poster in a place where it made any sense.

Paz told me that if you ask the kids in this barrio where they would like to go when they grow up, they will reply 'Buenos Aires'. They do not consider themselves a part of the city to which they allegedly belong: downtown is a foreign world to them and most of them have never been there, even though it is only a few kilometres away. I learned that the footballing genius and celebrity addict Diego Maradona grew up in a place like this.

I had promised to write something for the festival about my impressions of Barracas 21/24 but found it very hard to do so. Apart from the fact that such slums exist – itself a crime against humanity – I had difficulty comprehending the extent of the poverty and deprivation in a place like this, and the effect it must have on a young person as she or he grows up and sees no way out other than through drugs or crime. There were health issues also. Western Europe and North America have a problem of obesity among the children of the socially disadvantaged, and I wondered if the same were true here. Paz told me that child obesity was on the increase, even amongst the very poorest families in Argentina. In one of the great paradoxes offered by the new global economy, deprivation and the excessive consumption of fats and sugars are not mutually exclusive. The multinational junk food outlets only profit from the addiction they have created.

★   ★   ★

On another day when I have nothing programmed at the festival, I arrange a trip up the Tigre delta. After an early breakfast I take a train to Tigre, where I meet up with Inés, who will be my guide for the day. Here, a complex of waterways is broken up by hundreds of small, wooded islands, many of them inhabited. The whole, vast area is a web of small estuaries, and the graveyard of three centuries' worth of shipwrecks and abandoned dreams. As late as the 1870s the delta was the haunt of pirates, some of them women, including the infamous Marica Rivera, who, with her band of bloodthirsty followers robbed and murdered travellers, although she also acquired the status of a kind of Robin Hood figure, occasionally distributing her booty among the poor.

Willows grow abundantly along the riverbanks, and Inés tells me that the people who live on the islands have a reputation for a kind of wistful lethargy, a condition known locally as 'mal del sauce', which might be translated as 'weeping willow sickness.' I imagine it as the sort of listless melancholy that afflicts a person who spends too many hours gazing at the slow passage of water.

To illustrate the effects of weeping-willow sickness, Inés explains that, historically, the people of the islands collected reeds for a living: mosquitoes might swarm over the workers' backs as they toiled in the heat of the day, but such was their lethargy that they could not be bothered to brush them off, even when their backs became covered in festering sores. I am both confused and beguiled by stories such as these, even though I suspect that they exaggerate a particular characteristic – in this case the evocative 'weeping willow sickness' – in order to make a point about a group of outsiders or social outcasts. I also know that Inés has written an internationally acclaimed novel, *Piedra, papel o tijera* (Stone, paper, scissors) – not yet translated into English – about the community of islanders, and is watching me curiously, awaiting a reaction to her lavish account. She is invested in the place, and its people, who in many regards were still regarded as outsiders, long after the wealthy incomers from Buenos Aires started to build holiday homes on the islands and employed the locals as housemaids and gardeners.

Setting out from Tigre, we take our seats on a chugging river boat, its wheelhouse perched on the prow, a return trip that lasts around three hours, and we pass dozens of islands, the ones nearer the town of Tigre being quite densely populated. Private jetties adjoin the grounds of luxurious summer dwellings, and on some of these packs of dogs keep a noisy lookout. Further out, and across the Paraná itself, the island homes become more isolated, and eccentric in design. The island people are dependent on the delivery of goods by boat, and the children go to an island school. The delta seems to me like a fictional place, a story invented by the people of Buenos Aires to reassure themselves that – in addition to the brutal reality of shadow places like Barracas 21/24 – there is also a green, sylvestral, otherworld that co-exists alongside the hectic life of the metropolis.

★   ★   ★

Back in the city, the festival is warming up for the arrival of the headline guest, J.M. Coetzee. This event deserves special attention, as it allows me to observe the way that a society other than my own indulges in the act of literary adulation. I have already witnessed how, in Nicaragua, where every other person claims to be a poet, the idea of poetry, if not its most eloquent execution, is central to cultural identity, and I am curious to know how Argentina, or rather Buenos Aires, with its sophisticated literary tradition, compares.

Prior to Coetzee's arrival – he is flying in from Australia to do just the one event – the festival director, Pablo, tells me he is driving to the airport himself to pick up the Nobel laureate, but he is nervous, as Coetzee is famously taciturn, and Pablo wonders how he might start up conversation with him. The 2011 Rugby World Cup is in progress – I stayed up to watch South Africa beat Wales by a single malignant point a couple of nights earlier – so the solution seems obvious. Coetzee is a rugby fan, Pablo muses, as we stand in the foyer of my hotel, and so am I. Do you think I should chat to him about the World Cup? I think that's the only way to go with Coetzee, I reply, sagely, although I know very little about the man. What else would you talk about? Pablo seems relieved.

Coetzee's event is the festival's grand finale, in the theatre of the MALBA Arts Foundation, on the last night of a long week. I take a seat in the front row, hoping to catch some of the charismatic fallout from the great man, and am approached by a security guard who tells me that the first two rows are reserved for guests of the funding organisation. I reply that I am a guest of the festival, and stay in my seat. The guard moves off, hesitantly, unsure what to do about me. Half the seats in the front two rows then remain empty, even though there are dozens of people outside who have been refused tickets, sitting on the steps in the foyer, watching the proceedings on a big screen, and (as I learn from Pablo) hundreds more who have been told the event is sold out. Sitting at the front, I hear the photographers being told that they can snap away only during Coetzee's introduction, but not once the reading has begun. After considerable delay – a feature of all such events in Argentina – there are the usual overblown introductions, the first quite brief, the second far too long, both of them excessively sycophantic, and finally Coetzee emerges from the wings like a tall and elegant rock star, a slightly more reverend Eric Clapton, wearing a dark grey suit, white shirt and red tie.

He makes a brief introductory statement in faltering Spanish, and then reads a story, set in Spain – this was several years before he made the decision to publish all his new works in Spanish editions simultaneously with or prior to the English originals – and perhaps he chose one with an Hispanic theme for the occasion, believing there is not a lot of difference between one Spanish speaking country and the next (a notion bound to rile any Argentine) and it contained, for the sake of authenticity, a couple of Spanish phrases, one of which was 'vaya con dios,' which no one says unless they're a character in Cervantes or at least a hundred years old. The story lasts half an hour, or forty minutes, I can't be certain as I doze off briefly mid-way, and it's about a man called John (which is Coetzee's name) visiting his mother, who lives in a village in Castile, and looks after a bunch of cats as well as the village flasher – yes, she has made her home available to the local exhibitionist – because he is going to be taken away by social services, and the mother steps in and says she will look after him. I'm not sure that this is the way things work in Spain, but we can probably let it go in the name of poetic licence. In any case, I enjoy the parts of the story I am awake for. When Coetzee has finished, we all clap for a long time.

I wonder, though: did the environmentally concerned Coetzee need to travel thousands of air miles to read it? Because that is all he does: read a story. He does not take questions, but sits down, centre-stage, and signs books for his abundant fans, who queue patiently (a very difficult task for Porteños) before being shepherded, one at a time, before the maestro (as he was addressed in the introduction) and then trundle off, clutching their books as if they were holy relics. I wonder, ungraciously, how much he is getting paid to do this. I wonder if he is doing any sightseeing while he is here, and then remember Pablo saying that he was pretty much going straight back to Australia. He certainly won't be tasting the famous Argentinian steaks as he is a vegetarian, or possibly a vegan; nor will he be partaking of the fine Argentinian wines, as he does not drink alcohol.

Coetzee stands in a very upright manner. There is, in fact, something quintessentially upright about him. Nooteboom – who knows him personally – tells me this is related to a self-abnegating Afrikaaner Protestant streak (although he did attend a Catholic school, so perhaps got the worst of both worlds). In any case, he is not a man to let his hair down. According to another reliable source (i.e quoted on Wikipedia) he "lives the life of a recluse," and "a colleague who has worked with him for more than a decade claims to have seen him laugh just once. An acquaintance has attended several dinner parties where Coetzee has uttered not a single word." The Wikipedia entry also states that he has expressed support for the animal rights movement. Because he rarely gives interviews or readings, signed copies of his books are highly valued.

Despite his saying that he is pleased to be here, Coetzee does not really give the impression of being overjoyed by the occasion. He is more like a pontiff bestowing a blessing on his devotees, with great dignity and reserve. And the notion occurs to me that there are two Coetzees, one of them scribbling away, locked in his cell, wherever it is he lives, Adelaide or thereabouts, and the other version, the one I am witnessing, a phantom Coetzee, who is dispatched very occasionally by the real Coetzee to commune with his public, a doppelgänger dressed like a banker, reluctantly engaged in the contemporary phenomenon of the book signing, that bizarre ritual in which members of the reading public are able to pretend that they have a personal relationship with the author, some of his greatness trapped in the trail of ink on the title page. I am almost certain Coetzee, or his emissary, hates the experience.

The next morning, I walk into the hotel's breakfast room, and there is John Coetzee. It is early, as I have planned an excursion. A couple of other early risers are seated by the buffet display, otherwise the place is empty. Coetzee is sitting in the corner with his back to the wall, dressed in jeans and a black gilet, reading the newspaper. He is alone. I sit down, a couple of tables away, and observe him discreetly. After taking a bite of his medialuna (a diminutive, glazed version of the croissant) he licks his fingers, delicately, cat-like, and slowly, carefully, turns the page of his paper. At once I feel a wave of sympathy for the man, the compassion that is sometimes brought on by watching another human, or animal, eat. Eating is a social activity; watching men who cannot cook – men who are widowed, and whose spouses always cooked for them – eating alone at restaurants in Spain or Italy or Argentina, is a sight I find uncommonly moving. Sharing food, and giving to eat, can be an expression of love or pity. Eating reduces us to the status of any random creature, displays us at our most vulnerable, our most fragile. Watching Coetzee eat his medialuna is a thousand times more revealing to me than witnessing him give a reading to a theatre-full of enthralled fans, and I instantly warm to him. It can't be easy, being J.M. Coetzee.

Before I leave Buenos Aires, I pay a visit to the Museo de Bellas Artes, where I hope to see some paintings by Cándido López (1840-1902), an Argentinian painter who took part in the War of the Triple Alliance (1864-70) and lost his right arm in the conflict. Although right-handed, he taught himself to paint with his left hand and produced a number of sprawling battle scenes, developing a naïf style that pre-empts L.S. Lowry. Many of his paintings depict the regimented lines of troops preparing for battle, and the horrific aftermath of combat, corpses and body parts littering the wide and desolate spaces of his canvasses.

The War of the Triple Alliance pitched Argentina, Brazil and Uruguay against Paraguay. Something of an uneven contest, one might think, although at the start of the conflict Paraguay, led by the dictator Francisco Solano López, had a larger army than the other three put together. It was perhaps the bloodiest of all the bloody wars to afflict South America in the nineteenth century, and when it was over Paraguay was utterly laid waste. According to some sources, Paraguayan losses alone, due to the conflict and disease, were as high as 1.2 million (90% of its pre-war population) though more conservative estimates suggest a 'mere' two thirds of the country's males, causing a gender imbalance that had a lasting impact on the country's socio-political development.

The causes of the war are still disputed by historians. The Paraguayan leader, Solano López, had expansionist ideas, certainly, but the British encouraged him in his acts of aggression towards the Atlantic coastline in the hope that he might establish a port to supply the Empire with cotton, which was in high demand due to the shortages brought about by the American Civil War.

★ ★ ★

I have a couple of free days before the next stop on my agenda, an international poetry festival in the city of Rosario, three hundred kilometres north-west of Buenos Aires, and I decide to spend them in Montevideo: the Uruguayan capital is reached by a ferry hop on the quaintly named Buquebus (pronounced bookie-boos) to the port of Colonia del Sacramento, followed by a short coach ride. When I arrive at the Ibis Hotel, situated on the waterfront, Manu Chao's *Clandestino* is playing in the lobby. Manu supposedly stands for the rights of the dispossessed, the homeless, illegal immigrants, the excluded, the marginalised; in other words, everything that a global hotel chain does not. I sit in the lobby while waiting for my room to be cleaned, horrified at the casual incongruity between this rebel music and my shiny plastic surroundings. Up next on the sound system is Manu's hero and inspiration, Bob Marley, who has been given this kind of treatment for decades now. And this, I reflect, is how consumerist culture works; it sucks in all opposition, chews it up and spews it out in a new guise, in this instance as a once familiar but now curiously neutered and trashy musak. And although these are the same recordings that I listened to, aged seventeen, on an old mono record player, when *Natty Dread* was first released, and was spellbound by its unique vitality – especially coming in the midst of the dreary epic rock era, characterised by such acts as Emerson, Lake and Palmer, Yes, and Genesis – the songs have somehow become re-configured, recycled as hotel mood music, and it feels as though my experience of being in the world has become flattened and sullied and I will no longer be able to listen to this music without the memory of these new, blandly emasculated versions super-imposed on – no, replacing – the songs I hold dear in memory.

As I ascend in the lift to the sixth floor, and enter my clean, well-lighted room, I am plunged into a deep and intractable melancholy. I am feeling sorry for myself, which is sometimes a by-product of solo travel, and feeling sorry for oneself is, I acknowledge, only one step away from wallowing in self-pity, an expression employed in the English-speaking world in order to reduce ordinary everyday sadness to an act of moral torpor; but this appropriation of the music of rebellion feels hugely offensive, as though – I am in a mood to exaggerate – everything of value, everything we held sacred in the shining pantheon of youth, has been lost. Once I have dumped my luggage I wander out again and away from the sea, up into the side streets, where I find a grocery store and buy a carton of cheap wine. The storekeeper tells me the wine, which costs only a few cents, is riquísimo – very delicious. It is turning into an afternoon for exaggerations, mine and those of others. I return to my hotel room and drink the wine out of a plastic cup. It is a cloyingly sweet and scented rosé, with a bouquet of air freshener, but has a high alcohol content, and I finish the carton quickly, then descend to the bar and order a cold beer, to erase the taste of the wine, and a rum, just because. Since arriving in Montevideo, I have felt like an actor in a bad movie, to a score of the Greatest Hits of Bob Marley – or worse still, a clone of myself, a hologram, like one of the characters from Bioy Casares' novel *The Invention of Morel* – and I am worried by my actions, as indeed I should be. Such beginnings, in the past, have often led to a downward spiral, when the seeds of self destruction enter the heart, no bigger than a grain of sand …

And this destructive urge, the desire for self-annihilation, is not confined to the recidivist drunk: it strikes anyone who has ever felt that quiet sliding out of control, the slow-motion impending disaster that the smallest, slightest disharmony begins to offset; the careless (or not-so-careless, scathing or bitchy) remark; the forehead bumped against the edge of the open window; the accidental verbal spillage, foot placed firmly in it; the unforeseen riposte, the threat made, the words that appal, and the music of Bob Marley drifting cynically across the foyer of the budget chain hotel, knowing there will come a moment at which you take a step that cannot be retrieved, definitively.

You have just one more drink, one more than you actually want, in a vain attempt to recapture a sensation, a sense memory, that is lost somewhere in the haze of euphoric recall, or reconstructed memory, which are the same thing; a memory that is always elusive and almost certainly not accurate, a kind of longing created on the misremembered detritus of the past. And you confabulate with yourself, you talk yourself into this ever more tediously repetitive narrative; you drink that one extra glass in order to be able to reach back and experience again those blissful moments that quite possibly never were, but whose reality you cling to as though it were a lifeline. You remain at the bar until it closes, and then you stagger into the lift again and return to your time capsule on the sixth floor.

The next day, chastened by the salt air carried on the South Atlantic breeze, I wander into the centre of Montevideo. A wide thoroughfare, the Rambla, curves around the southern edge of the city, bordered by the Río Plata, which you would be forgiven for thinking of as the sea. In the midday sun – it is the start of spring here, but like a July day in the UK – assorted citizens are sunbathing on the low parapet at the edge of the sidewalk: below them is a drop of a few metres and then a narrow beach and the river. Many passers-by clutch a maté gourd and a flask. Uruguayans and their maté are notoriously inseparable; a stimulant and antioxidant, more bitter than coffee, with a fresh, grassy aftertaste, maté is ubiquitous, including among the young, with whom it has been reinvented as a fashion accessory and identity marker. If you add a mobile phone, sunglasses and a pack of Marlboro, Uruguayan hipsters have quite a lot to lug around with them. I am walking briskly, attempting to rid myself of the vestiges of a hangover, but also conscious of the tempting waves of lethargy emanating from the sun lizards.

Half way into town, in an abrupt switch of allegiance, the Rambla Argentina turns into the Rambla Gran Bretaña, and I pass a large bust of the onetime British ambassador, Sir Eugen Millington-Drake, described on the commemorative plaque as "a loyal friend of Uruguay."

Millington-Drake was ambassador during the standoff between British and German naval forces in the early days of World War Two, when the cruiser *Admiral Graf Spee* was eventually scuttled in Montevideo harbour. The *Graf Spee* posed a major threat to Atlantic shipping and had already sunk numerous vessels during 1939-40. Convinced by false reports of superior British naval forces approaching his ship, its commander, Hans Langsdorff, ordered the vessel to be blown up, and on 20 December 1940 laid himself out on the ship's ensign togged out in full dress uniform, and shot himself in the head. The Powell and Pressburger film, *The Battle of the River Plate*, which, for me, reeks of the dismal

Sunday afternoon TV of a 1960s childhood, perfectly conveys the cliché of English sangfroid up against Teutonic fanaticism. Apparently, a part of the *Graf Spee* still remains visible above the surface of the water in Montevideo harbour at times, but I didn't see it.

As I enter the old town, I am greeted by the kind of graffiti that lifts the spirits:

EL INFINITO NO TIENE ACENTO (The infinite has no accent). I am not sure the phrase means anything, but it sounds as if it should. Two boys are collecting junk with a horse and cart, a picturesque reminder of earlier, less frantic times. It must be said, Montevideo feels laid-back after the hectic whirl of Buenos Aires.

The following day I take myself to the National Gallery, where I am treated with great kindness by the librarian when I tell her I wish to look at materials on the painter Juan Manuel Blanes (1830-1901). Blanes is the most influential of Uruguayan painters, whose work contributed significantly towards the myth of national identity. He made his name as a portraitist, working to commission for the Provincial Governor of Salto before producing – like his younger Argentine colleague, Cándido López – a number of large scale battle scenes from the serial civil conflicts that beset Uruguay and neighbouring Argentina and Brazil over the 1840s and 1850s; but it is his paintings of gauchos, often deeply idealised, lassoing horses (the word lasso is from the Spanish 'lazo', a knot or loop) or else sprawling indolently on the sparse turf of the Pampa, with maté gourd at the ready, that interest me.

I study Blanes' gauchos, the original paintings where I can, although many of these are out on loan or else in private collections, and in the books of reproductions sought out and delivered to me by the helpful librarian. I am struck by this calculated creation of a fiction, the need for these images to serve a purpose: the readymade gaucho as a cypher for a national type.

Gauchos were usually mestizos (that is, of mixed European and indigenous ancestry), although some were black, or mulatto, a term still used in Spanish, as once it was in English, to indicate mixed African and European ancestry. In Argentina, drawing on their ballads and legends, a dedicated literature of the gaucho – la literatura gauchesca – became an important part of the cultural tradition.

The idealisation of the gaucho depends in large part on the dichotomy between the Europe-facing, urbane sophisticate (intellectual, Francophile, effete) of the city-dweller from Buenos Aires or Montevideo, and the rough and ready, fleet-footed gaucho (son of the soil, land-locked, macho) a conflict that is addressed by many writers, most notably in José Hernández's epic poem, *El gaucho Martín Fierro* (1872) and Ricardo Güiraldes' novel *Don Segundo Sombra* (1926). Borges, too, who was fascinated by the gaucho and gauchesca literature, included glimpses into the lives of these men in such stories as 'El Sur' (The South), in which a group of gauchos confront the protagonist – a convalescing literary type – in a small rural canteen when he foolishly allows himself to be provoked by one of them into a knife-fight. This theatrical conceptualisation of the gaucho prevails in Uruguay also. There is in fact a Museum of the Gaucho and Currency (Museo del gaucho y de la moneda) in Montevideo – an odd pairing of themes, you might have thought – containing, according to a Tripadvisor review, "impressive displays of spurs, stirrups, knives, bolas, and other items used by gauchos," as well as collections of historic coins. However, I will not have time to investigate as my plane leaves tonight; I am returning to Argentina.

*   *   *

At Montevideo airport, the flight for Rosario is announced only thirty minutes before it is due to depart. There is an immediate scramble, as three dozen of my fellow passengers, who have been sitting or else strolling about the departures lounge, looking confused, as have I, rush for the designated gate, which, however, remains stubbornly unattended for a further fifteen minutes, at which point the announcement, and the scramble, is repeated.

We eventually take off, flying north-west towards Rosario, in the province of Santa Fe. The city was the home, before his self-imposed exile in France, of the Argentine novelist Juan José Saer, whose masterpiece, *El entenado* (the stepson) is one of the most extraordinary novels of the late twentieth century.

Published in Spanish in 1983, and in English as *The Witness* seven years later, in a superb translation by Margaret Jull Costa, the novel describes the life of a cabin boy on an exploratory Spanish voyage up the Río Paraná in the early colonial period. The ship's crew, foraging on shore, are attacked by warriors from an indigenous tribe and all except the narrator are slaughtered, cooked and eaten in a drunken feast which soon morphs into an extended orgy. The boy, however, is saved, and adopted by his captors as a kind of sacred trophy, remaining with them when village life returns to normal, daily routine following a remarkably ordered and even prudish restraint. It transpires that every year, whenever the tribe's warriors attack and capture their enemies (whom they invariably cook and eat), and celebrate their orgies, they keep one captive alive as a 'witness', who wanders the village in a state of terror and disorientation until the collective hangover ends, whereupon the captive is bundled into a canoe and sent downstream. During their sojourn with the cannibals, these witnesses are given food and treated with kindness, but they take no part in village life and are rarely if ever spoken to, nor are they included in any of the tribe's activities.

The cycle is repeated over the ten years the boy spends among his adoptive people, and while the other witnesses are all sent away, the boy remains. Eventually, the tribe's members spot a new expedition of Europeans, and despatch the boy downriver in a canoe. Although the witness – now a bearded young man – has forgotten most of his Spanish, he does reveal enough for the invaders to locate and massacre the people with whom he has spent the past decade. The witness returns to Spain, and settling back into a Christian way of life, is apprenticed to a friar-scholar who teaches him Latin, Greek and Hebrew. Having acquired the skills of literacy and developed his intellect, he decides to capitalise on his celebrity status, and after a chance encounter in a tavern, joins a theatre troupe, giving popular performances of his "life among the savages of the New World." Thus, after a fashion, he encapsulates the postmodern experience, living out, as simulacrum or parody, the experiences of his youth, complete with replica 'savages'. The second-hand nature of his life in Europe causes him to reflect more deeply on his life among the Indians, and the precariousness of their world view, in which "everything seems and nothing is ... and the appearance of things is situated above all in the field of non-existence."

Amassing a fortune from his tours with the troupe of travelling players, the witness retires to the countryside with a clutch of his own adopted children and spends his last years writing the account that we are reading. Now an old man, he reflects, in one passage, on the moment, all those years ago, when his captors, while remaining courteous to the cabin boy himself, are about to eat his shipmates:

> I think that was the first time – aged all of fifteen – that an idea with which I am now familiar first occurred to me: namely that the memory of an event is not sufficient proof that it actually happened, just as the memory of a dream that we believe we had in the past, many years or months before the moment in which we remember it, is not sufficient proof that the dream took place in the distant past rather than the night before the day on which we recall it, or even that it occurred before the precise moment we state that it has occurred.

You dream a dream, and even as you are dreaming it, you have the sensation that you are re-dreaming a dream you had many years before. It then seems as if the world you enter in dreamtime is a continuum that exists with or without your participation, and when you dream you simply tip into it, become a witness to whatever happens to be occurring in the ongoing theatre of sleep. It combines the impression, so familiar in dreams, that events simply happen to one, with the realisation – which constitutes so-called lucid dreaming – that one is still able to stop the dream, or change its direction, should the need arise. But – and this seems crucial – you also seem to remember part of the dream landscape from previous dreams, and you waken with a feeling of déjà vu, as if you had just returned from a familiar place. Now, what is that? Is there a dream territory that exists outside of human consciousness? Sometimes, it is as if that place exists neither in reality nor in dream, but some place in between.

★   ★   ★

The next day, waking in Rosario, after breakfast in my hotel, I take a walk and try to find the building where Ernesto 'Che' Guevara was born, and which now houses the offices of MAPFRE, a Spanish-owned insurance and finance group. I have a dim view of insurance companies, and I am sure Che's contempt for them would have far exceeded my own. But since they are taking over the world, it makes sense that they should start with the first home of that emblem of global revolution, Che Guevara. Opposite the building, a rather run-down hostel is named after him.

Che was not from Rosario, he was just born there, by accident, before his parents – who both inherited considerable wealth – moved to Córdoba, in central Argentina, where he grew up. But Rosario claims him as its son as it is good for tourism and the building where he was allegedly born has been declared a national treasure. In fact, he was born in a local hospital and only spent a few weeks in this rather luxurious building. Che's parents falsified the date of his birth from May to June 1928, as his mother was pregnant when she married Che's father, and the false birth date looked a little more respectable.

In his teens – despite suffering from severe asthma, which he always stoically resisted – and as a student of medicine in Buenos Aires, Che became a keen rugby player, a sport, like polo, associated with the upper classes in Argentina. Che's social conscience was awakened by his reading of Marx and by travelling. He set out on long excursions, first by bicycle, later by motorbike – as recounted in the book, and subsequent movie, *The Motorcyle Diaries*, in which Che is portrayed by the actor Gael García Bernal, who, I am assured, manages a convincing Porteño accent, no mean feat for a Mexican – and driven by both an insatiable curiosity about the way that others lived and a desire to improve the material conditions of the most wretched of the earth. The rest is so well known it has entered the realms of myth.

Rosario has a reputation as a haven for bohemian types. I find it relaxed and friendly, the kind of place a person ends up and, without thinking about it too much, forgets to leave. The poetry festival, too, is genial, a very different kind of buzz from the more frantic ambience of the Buenos Aires literary circuit. While in Rosario, I eat a lot of fish, and meet some interesting younger poets. I am particularly impressed by Jessica Freudenthal from Bolivia, and the Mexican Luis Felipe Fabre, both of whom I recruit for my anthology. Jessica's poem 'Family Tree' recounts the turbulent recent history of a Bolivian dynasty marked by suicides, drug overdoses and suspicious airplane crashes, even naming one relative who was responsible for the capture and murder of Che Guevara himself; while Luis Felipe's poems reflect the kind of tense precarity that I associate with the best of the new Mexican writing. I hang out with Luis Felipe and a small contingent of hard-drinking poets, Niels, Markus and Jerry, and spend a couple of nights out far too late clubbing with them, including a visit to a drag show. My notebook reads: "my last but one epiphany in a gay nightclub, in a provincial Argentine city, at a quarter to three on a September night, when a very convincing drag queen – convincing on stage but not so much under the harsh glare of the streetlight, where she joined us for a cigarette after her set and entered into laconic conversation in a husky growl – enchanted me with a rendition of 'Over the Rainbow', a song that moves me occasionally, although never before quite so pitiably, to a state of wretched melancholy. It had been raining, and there was a breeze blowing in from the river. I should have had an early night, especially after those two days in Montevideo, followed by further indulgence with my new friends in Rosario, and I felt as though I were hanging on by a thread ..."

Apart from this single entry with its 'last but one epiphany' – what on earth might the final one have been? – I failed to keep up my notebook in Rosario. By the time I caught my return flight to London, I had become weary of literary events. On the plane, I struck up a conversation with my neighbour, a Greek bee expert, or melittologist, who had been attending a conference in Buenos Aires. He told me that bees have been around for at least thirty million years, and that they are able to recognise individual human faces; that when bees are deprived of pollen, they nibble on the leaves of plants that have not yet flowered, using their proboscises and mandibles to cut holes in the leaves, causing the plant to flower early, but that if you replace a flower with the image of a flower, the bee will be fooled, and will attempt to extract pollen from the image.

> I went out into the street in flames
> and without myself,
> what was left were shreds of gazes:
> the world was my eyes
> and my eyes
> me ...
>
> Julio Trujillo, 'Ten Tequilas'.

Guadalajara, Mexico, November-December 2011

Guadalajara, Mexico's second city, is capital of the state of Jalisco, the home of tequila and mariachi. It hosts a famous Book Fair, the *Feria Internacional del Libro*, the outstanding fixture in the Spanish-speaking world's literary calendar. In November 2011, two months after my trip to Argentina and Uruguay, I was invited to the city as a guest of the festival.

Following the first of my events, quite by chance, I met the poet Juan Gelman, whose work I had long admired. Revered as one of Latin America's finest poets, Gelman came to the attention of the world's media after a long campaign to find his granddaughter, Macarena, whose parents – Gelman's son and daughter-in-law – had been murdered by the Argentine military regime in 1976. The remains of his son, Marcelo, who had been tortured, shot dead and buried in a barrel filled with cement and sand, were found thirteen years later, in 1989, by the EAAF, the same forensic team that had unearthed evidence of the El Mozote massacre. Marcelo was twenty at the time of his death. The child's mother, Maria Claudia García, had also been killed, shortly after giving birth. She was nineteen years old and her body has never been found. Like others whose parents had been murdered by the regime's agents, Macarena was adopted as a newborn by a supporter of the military junta, in her case a Uruguayan police officer and his wife, and she grew up unaware of her true parenthood. In 2000, Juan

Gelman's sustained search homed in on Montevideo, and after DNA testing, Gelman and his grandchild were reunited, in an extraordinary tale of vindication in the face of a heinous crime.

In the festival's Green Room, Gelman, a resident of Mexico since 1990, was chatting to the Nicaraguan novelist Sergio Ramírez, who has courageously fronted up to the corrupt and oppressive Ortega regime, the pair of them knocking back tequilas. I joined them, somewhat sheepishly, after being introduced by a mutual acquaintance, and listened to Gelman as he explained which poets I might include in my anthology. I was used to receiving this advice (though not normally from such elevated sources as Gelman) and made a mental note of the names, some of whom I had read, and a couple I had already discounted. I could not stay long, however, as I had arranged to have dinner with a friend, but felt a nervous thrill at quaffing tequila with these titans of the left and drank several shots in quick succession. Ramírez and Gelman had a head start and were in full flow, and I began to experience a familiar sense of disconnection, as if I were living in a no-man's-land between the addict self described in my book *The Vagabond's Breakfast* – which I had just revisited at its Mexican launch, upstairs in the auditorium – and another, parallel self, who lives and then writes about his own life as though it were happening to someone else. All the while a sentence was playing in my head, and it expressed an almost visceral fear, but I could not recall the precise words, nor even know from whence they came. A deep sense of claustrophobia crept over me as I made my way out of the Green Room and into the night, relieved to breathe again, despite the exhaust fumes and dense pollution floating on the Guadalajara air. And then the words of the poem, by the Mexican poet Julio Trujillo – or rather, my translation of them – bounced back: *Out into the street in flames, and without myself ...*

On joining my friend, Andrés Neuman, who was waiting for me in the restaurant of his hotel, across the way from the Book Fair, my sense of displacement eased, since his company almost always cheers me up: I would even say that Andrés acts a sort of antidote to my more negative impulses. So it came as something of a shock when, after we had ordered food (but no more alcohol) and as though in the normal course of conversation,

Andrés mentioned a mass execution, carried out by a narco gang, that had taken place in the city, only a few days prior to the opening of the Book Fair. I was astonished that I did not know about this, but acknowledged that the local authorities were probably not keen on publicising news of a massacre on the doorstep of the literary festival. Andrés told me that the timing of the murders, and the dumping of the bodies not far from the Fair, might be interpreted as a message of intimidation: there was a rumour circulating amongst some of the writers here that the assassins murdered twenty-six people – or at least left twenty-six bodies in three trucks – precisely because the Book Fair was celebrating its 25th Anniversary. 'It's as if,' he told me, 'they were saying *congratulations on your quarter centenary, here's twenty-five plus one.*'

I had no idea if the cartel bosses really conceived their act of mass murder in this way, as a taunt or threat to the Book Fair, and nor did Andrés, but it certainly made for a better story. It was chilling to think that these two worlds existed side by side; the cultivated and generally speaking enlightened world of the International *Feria del Libro* on the one hand, and group executions by narco thugs on the other, all within a few streets of each other. It felt as though these two worlds should never meet, except perhaps in a Roberto Bolaño novel.

Later, after Andrés had walked with me back to my hotel – and set off back to his own, ignoring the advice of the festival administrators (which he had relayed to me) that guests should not walk the city streets alone at night – I checked online, and a report from CBS news confirmed the account he had given me: "The bound and gagged bodies of twenty-six men were found dumped before dawn Thursday in the heart of the picturesque city of Guadalajara, a sign that full-scale war between drug cartels may have come to the metropolis." The bodies were found, the article continued, "about a mile from the site of the Guadalajara International Book Fair, which opens on Saturday ... The fair's website said it was expecting more than 600,000 visitors from around the world."

Early the next morning, I received a call from the hotel's reception. A man's voice informed me that he was waiting for me in the lobby, and that he had come to take me to the town of Zapotanlejo, an hour's drive from Guadalajara, where I was due to visit a school. I had no idea this trip was on my agenda, since, having arrived late at the festival, I had not put aside time to study my programme in detail, and then I could not find it. A little paranoid after last night's revelations, I wondered if I might be the target of a kidnapping. The argument that I would be of no possible financial interest to any kidnapper was quickly discounted because, firstly, however financially strapped I might have felt myself to be, there were millions in Mexico who would regard me as wealthy, and, secondly, it was not unheard of for kidnappers to seize the wrong person. I made a quick phone call to my official festival minder and learned that the man in the hotel lobby was not a kidnapper, and that the event at the school was on my agenda, which I had somehow mislaid.

Originally from Yucatán, in the south-east of the country, Fabio was a middle-aged man of Mayan stock, with strong, kindly features. He addressed my many questions attentively. Fabio taught history at the Zapotanlejo regional high school, where I was due, he told me, to give a talk to the students on the writing life, a topic which always aroused in me the strongest sense of impostor syndrome. On the way, as we chatted, Fabio filled me in on some details about the killings of the previous week, as well as background on the perpetrators. It had come as a huge blow to the city, he said, because Guadalajara and the state of Jalisco had, until then, been comparatively free from attacks of this kind – compared, that is, to other regions of Mexico. Fabio offered me an alternative, and more plausible explanation of the massacre than the one speculatively offered up by Andrés the previous evening. It would appear that the Zetas (the Milenio Zeta cartel) were seeking revenge for a recent massacre in Veracruz, carried out by the Sinaloa cartel against some Zetas. Who are these Zetas? I wondered. The Zetas, Fabio explained, were originally a group of renegade commandos from the Mexican army, led by Arturo Guzmán Decena, who had been a high ranking officer in the security forces before opting for the significant boost in salary that might be gained by switching sides. They were called Zetas after Guzmán's military codename, Z-1. Guzmán, Fabio told me, was shot down inside a restaurant in Tamaulipas in 2002, but the Zetas had continued to thrive after his death and were now, with this massacre, no doubt making a play for the state of Jalisco. This was clear from the message they had left with their twenty-six victims the previous Thursday. The cartels, Fabio explained, usually leave threatening messages – their 'calling card' – on or around the corpses they abandon in their wake. The victims in this attack all had the words 'Milenio Zetas' written on their bodies, in oil. It felt like a major shift, said Fabio, as though the people of Guadalajara might no longer expect to live in the relative peace they had enjoyed in recent years.

Zapotlanejo means the place of the Zapote a soft tropical fruit (*tzapotl* in the Nahuatl language). It was a bright, exceedingly warm day, and I was by now a little nervous about meeting the students at the Prepatoria Regional or High School, as I hadn't had time to prepare any notes, and I was experiencing something, as I imagined, of the fear of the toreador about to enter the ring. However apprehensive I may have been, the reality was far less bloody than a corrida.

After being escorted onstage by two female students dressed gorgeously in traditional costume, introduced by the headmaster, and then again by the literature teacher, Rubén, I spoke fitfully to the hundred or more assembled teenagers, revealing, no doubt, how little I knew about anything of significance, and read a couple of poems. I then decided to open up to the floor, a rather dangerous move considering the reluctance of teenagers – at least some of those I've worked with elsewhere – to be seen reacting positively under such circumstances. But these kids humoured me with a bombardment of questions, the most astute coming from a youth in a hoodie who asked: "how do you know, when you get to the end of a page, that the words you have chosen are the right ones?"

Most of the other kids laughed at him, and I sensed that he was probably the class clown, or possibly, which didn't necessarily negate the first diagnosis, the class rebel without a cause, but I replied that this was the single most important question that a writer faced every day and, citing something about the right words in the right order, complimented him roundly on his question, addressing him as *joven*, 'young man', a term employed ubiquitously in Mexico, regardless of the age of the addressee. This raised a cheer, and all the kids who had laughed when he posed his question were then booed by those who were friends with the hoodie kid. From this point on, the questioners were clearly divided between those who were booed and those who were cheered, depending on their alignment with the hoodie kid's original supporters. I was impressed by the huge Welsh flag that acted as a backdrop to the stage, and which displayed an indignant-looking red dragon. I learned that it had been specially made by the students, and after my talk we posed in front of it for a photo shoot.

Following this performance, Fabio and Rubén took me to a nearby place of historical interest, where the first major battle of the Mexican War of Independence had taken place two hundred years earlier. Near an ancient bridge, Puente de Calderón, a hundred thousand insurgents, under the rebel priest Miguel Hidalgo y Costilla, were defeated by six thousand Royalists, which perhaps suggests that one should never let a priest command an army. There, beneath the scorching sun, Rubén explained to me the details of the conflict, and as I clambered through the scrub to take a picture of the famous bridge I wondered out loud if there were rattlesnakes hereabouts, and was assured that there probably were.

While at the park, we happened upon the local chief of police, known personally to the schoolteachers; a short, muscular man with several gold teeth, who was out walking his dogs, a large Alsatian with slavering jaws and an incongruous Yorkshire terrier. We fell into conversation and, following my companions' questions about a recent news story in which this man had featured, he gave us an account of the raid, which he had led, immediately after the dumping in Guadalajara of the twenty-six murdered men. It involved neutralising a drug manufacturing laboratory and had resulted in many arrests and a number of deaths. The police chief's narrative style was relaxed and self-effacing, but the events he described were terrifying. When they had finished, he told us, the ground outside the laboratory was strewn with the bodies of those who had fallen in the assault, along with hundreds of spent cartridges. You could barely see the ground, he said. He seemed a mellow-mannered, thoughtful fellow, but I would not have wanted to get into a gunfight with him.

"Mexico is a land of many faces," Fabio remarked to me, as we walked back to his car, providing the answer to a question I hadn't actually asked.

> The days keep taking away the things that I have loved.
> With secret steps, behind my back
> they vanish. Little things,
> provisional things. The things
> I supposed were mine.
>
> Jorge Fernández Granados, 'Things'.

Cardiff, Wales, 2012-13

In December that year, returning to Wales from Mexico, I was forced to make a decision about the future, which, however, bore about it the indelible shadow of the past.

For many years, I had been living with the Hepatitis C virus. At that time, the disease was notoriously difficult to treat, and many carriers of the virus died as a result of liver failure. Back in 2007 my own liver had become so decompensated as a result of this illness that I needed a transplant; the liver graft allowed me to expect at least a few more years of life, but it was a temporary solution, and it would only be a matter of time before the virus began to wreak damage on my new, implanted liver, just as it had on the original organ. I was invited to join a trial for a new drug, Telaprevir, a so-called protease inhibitor, which had been used successfully with ordinary Hep C patients, but whose efficacy with post-transplant cases was unknown. If I didn't volunteer for the trial, it would be two or three years before the drug became widely available, by which time I might be too ill to respond to treatment. Volunteering for the trial seemed to be the only sensible course of action, even though it meant enduring a further round of treatment with Interferon and Ribavirin, an especially unpleasant and intrusive drug therapy, with which I had been treated, unsuccessfully, some years before, and which was included in the treatment plan alongside the new drug, on a sort of belt and braces approach.

However, as was now apparent, there was a new problem, or rather, an old one had returned. Despite the evidence of two decades of destructive drinking and drug abuse in an earlier life, which had led to homelessness, vagrancy, innumerable hospitalisations, incarceration in three countries, a sectioning, several ruined relationships and untold miseries, I had convinced myself I would somehow be able to enjoy moderate, controlled drinking. After quitting shortly before my fortieth birthday, in 1996, and enjoying fourteen years of productive sobriety, during which time I helped raise our two daughters with my wife, Rose, I casually picked up a drink one evening in Bratislava, while on a translation residency in the Slovak capital, in September 2010. The foaming tankard of Pilsener would surely do no harm, I reasoned; I had never been much of a beer drinker, after all ...

Thus speaks the logic of addiction. It had taken me half a lifetime to get sober, but only a single distracted moment to pick up a drink. In the months that followed, I not only continued to drink, on and off, but dedicated myself to a study of websites and scholarly articles that 'proved' that alcoholism was either illusory or misunderstood; that alcoholism, in contemporary parlance, was not even a thing, and that whatever it was it certainly shouldn't be called alcoholism.

In the TV series *Catastrophe*, the character played by Rob Delaney, sober for some years, decides he wants to drink again and in one scene we find him googling: "Is alcoholism a myth?" I too did that. I dug up articles in medical journals and elsewhere to corroborate my newfound conversion to the belief that addiction to alcohol was a state of mind rather than an irreversible, lifelong condition. And, naturally enough, I found what I was looking for. Even the term 'alcoholism', I learned gratefully, was up for grabs. The most recent edition of the American Psychiatric Association's diagnostic manual referred to the condition as *alcohol-use disorder*, which had replaced the older *alcohol abuse* and the much more dated *alcoholism*, which has, apparently, been out of favour with researchers for decades. I felt vindicated. I continued to nurture my desire to be right about alcoholism, even though, paradoxically, I knew that I was wrong; but I had to present some kind of a case, in order to inform all the people that I had previously told I was alcoholic and could not drink that it was now OK for me to drink, that I was, effectively, 'cured'. This state of cognitive dissonance has been encapsulated by Leslie Jamison, in her memoir *The Recovering*, when she describes her own decision to return to drinking after a lengthy spell of abstinence: "I was either calling my past self a liar for saying I was an alcoholic, or making myself a liar now by saying I wasn't."

However I chose to justify it, and even disregarding my qualms about the term 'alcoholism', my decision was flawed on at least two counts: first, and most significantly, I still had Hepatitis C, and even moderate drinking was not only inadvisable, but in my case, life-threatening; secondly, despite my years of abstinence, I discovered that my body reacted to alcohol in exactly the same way that it always had; if I took one drink, I would, sooner or later, want many more. That's how it works, how it had always worked. But I ignored the evidence and continued insisting to myself that I could, if I tried, drink like a 'normal person', even though I had very little understanding of how a normal person drank. As I write this, I am bewildered by the sheer force of this obsession, and by the persistence of the delusion that I might be able to drink like other people I knew. Such is the nature of addiction — a disease defined by denial — that once I had decided that I was going to drink again, an implacable determination to abide by this decision set in, as though it were a kind of sacred mission.

For long periods of 2011 I remained abstinent, but there were occasions, especially when I travelled, that I drank to excess. During the trips I have described, to Argentina, Uruguay and Mexico, I drank heavily, and on a daily basis. So much so, that when, in December 2011, I was invited to participate in the trial to treat my Hepatitis with Telaprevir, my liver function tests (LFTs) returned well over the threshold for participation, and I was told that unless they fell below a certain limit, I would not be eligible to join the trial. This was a serious setback. Although Hep C patients are prone to widely variable LFT results, I knew that my drinking was the real reason for the high reading.

The specialist nurse on the liver team at the Queen Elizabeth Hospital asked me to return to Birmingham in late February and take another blood test to check if my LFTs had reduced to a level whereby I could be a candidate for the trial. I was extremely worried, since I knew that I could not afford to lose this opportunity – my last chance, most likely – to be rid of the virus. The month passed without incident, including a return trip to Nicaragua, to attend the festival at Granada for a second time. Rose, who had never been to Central or South America, came with me. While there, we met up with an old friend, the Scottish poet Tom Pow, a supportive and cheerful presence, and we were put up at a stylishly renovated hotel owned by Violeta Chamorro, who had succeeded Daniel Ortega as President between 1990 and 1997, and whose embattled family – two of her children were Sandinistas, another a 'Contra' – was a microcosm of the conflicted state. Rose and I made friends among the cosmopolitan crew attending the festival and I gathered new material for my anthology, notably from younger poets such as the Dominican Frank Báez, the Colombian John Galán Casanova, and the Ecuadorians Edwin Madrid and Aleyda Quevedo Rojas. I stuck to water and the sorrel cordial, Flor de Jamaica, rather than Flor de Caña, Nicaragua's famous rum. On returning to the UK, I had a second blood test, and learned that my liver function had returned almost to normal. My relief was tempered by shame: it felt as though I had gotten away with it by the skin of my teeth, even that I had been culpable of a kind of deception. I was offered a place on the trial and vowed to myself, once more, never to drink again, but, alas, I didn't entirely believe me. Although my intentions were clear, a minuscule hope, a tiny grain of sand, remained lodged in the depths of my reptile brain, insisting that once I was through with the trial, and hepatitis-free, I would be free to drink again.

I decided to keep a treatment journal, and discussed the idea with the specialist nurse, M, a kind and perceptive woman, who thought that keeping a journal might be helpful for the purposes of the trial, which had the daunting title of *Open-Label, Phase 3b Study to Determine Efficacy and Safety of Telaprevir, Pegylated-Interferon-alfa-2a and Ribavirin in Hepatitis C Genotype 1 Infected, Stable Liver Transplant Subjects*. The trial was taking place with volunteers from half a dozen hospital research centres across Europe.

During the initial stages, I had to be resident in Birmingham, close to the Queen Elizabeth Hospital, for daily blood tests. I stayed at the University Conference Centre, a shabby, institutional building from the 1960s that smelled of floor polish and school dinners. The treatment involved me learning to inject myself with Interferon, a drug that hinders the replication process of the virus, while enhancing the body's immune response. The new drug, Telaprevir, I ingested orally with high fat foods, late at night, which inevitably made me nauseous.

According to the trial information booklet, the potential side effects of Interferon, taken alongside the antiviral Ribavirin, included chills, fever, joint and muscle pain, as well as depression and suicidal ideation. Even without these last, the combined medication is guaranteed to make you feel extremely unwell. If all went to plan, the new drug, Telaprevir, would clear up my Hepatitis C within a few weeks; but since I had agreed to the full term of the trial, I could look forward to a year of weekly Interferon injections, whether the treatment with Telaprevir was successful or not. However, at the time, it seemed a fair deal. I was so grateful to have made it onto the trial I was prepared to undergo almost any discomfort. At the conference centre I tried to work in my room, and in the mornings went swimming at the university pool, but after three days became too tired for such exertions. Fatigue, anxiety and nausea were the most noticeable initial reactions to the treatment.

Hepatitis C is measured by viral load – the amount of virus contained in the blood. Mine was very high; but then again, it was of a vintage, and had been maturing since the late 1970s. I injected the Interferon subcutaneously, in the area around the belly button. Preparing the syringe was a painful reminder of an earlier life, and one which I did not much enjoy.

In March I was due to curate a two-day literary event, *Fiction Fiesta*, to which I had invited Jorge Fondebrider, who was living in Paris at the time, and Andrés Neuman – whom I had last seen at the Guadalajara Book Fair in November – as well as a handful of Welsh writers, the publishers Christopher MacLehose and Charles Boyle, and *The Independent*'s literary editor, Boyd Tonkin (back then I regularly reviewed books for the newspaper). I had invested a lot of time and preparation in this event, and it was all set for the second weekend of the drug trial. The Fiesta was established in order to share my love of Latin American writing with a local audience, and I had teamed up with a friend, the Cardiff entrepreneur Nick Davidson, to use his pub, The Promised Land, located in the city centre, as the venue for the weekend. As the date approached, and the side effects of the treatment kicked in, I felt truly wretched, but was unwilling to cancel the festival, which had already been publicised. The event drew a good audience, packed into the welcoming ambience of The Promised Land, and Nick and I decided afterwards that we would seek to repeat the Fiesta on an annual basis.

On the Monday morning following *Fiction Fiesta* weekend, less than two weeks into the trial, I received some good news. My viral load, which stood at five million on the first day of the trial, had fallen to a mere 622 by the seventh day. The Telaprevir was taking effect. It was a spring day of sunshine and pristine skies. I took my two Argentine guests up to Hay-on-Wye to visit the bookshops, and we enjoyed a pub lunch in Kilvert's Inn. Afterwards, we followed the old road across the Black Mountains, past Gospel Pass and Capel-y-ffin, making an unplanned stop at the village of Cwmyoy, where, from the road, Andrés had spotted the crooked tower of the church and let out an exclamation of surprise; the tower, he said, could have been that of the church in Wandenburg, the setting for his novel *The Traveller of the Century*, the launch of which we had been celebrating at Fiction Fiesta. We reversed back along the road and drove up to the village, inspected the church and walked around its ancient graveyard. From there, we took a detour into Herefordshire and visited Kilpeck Church, with its strange, pagan sculptures. As Andrés and Jorge gazed at the Sheela na gig carvings, I noticed two hares in the field adjoining the church; they were boxing, as they do, dancing on their hind legs, and breaking away to leap and tear around the field in diminishing circles. I recalled a line from a poem: "The man who tells you he has thought of everything has forgotten the hare." Watching the magical creatures act out their ritual, on a freak summer's day in March, I was able to detach from my own discomfort, which seemed a small thing compared to a sight as wondrous as dancing hares.

My treatment diary tells a sorry tale of restless nights and days blighted by fatigue. Insomnia is a vicious circle, the anxiety it generates invariably resulting in further sleeplessness. Apart from the insomnia, the diary lists other ailments that flourished as side effects of the aptly-named Interferon, including persistent fluey symptoms and shortness of breath, due to anaemia. I was unable to move about much without becoming increasingly fatigued. I didn't leave the house for days on end, and felt nauseous, faint and dizzy. When I gave myself the interferon injections in the stomach, there was livid bruising around the umbilical area.

Although constantly tired, I found that I was less morose if I set myself specific tasks and tried to get a certain amount of writing done each day. For brief spells I could use my work as a way of distracting myself from the discomfort I was enduring. On Monday 16th April, I noted a conversation with Dr O, in which I told him of the surprising outbursts of tearfulness, and the sense, as I put it, that the normal protective skin between myself and the world had peeled away, leaving me feeling raw and exposed. However I managed to work on some translations of Joaquín O. Giannuzzi, the poet that Jorge Fondebrider had recommended to me on our first day in Nicaragua, the previous year. If I could work in the morning I might get two or three hours done. If I delayed, or went out, I always became too tired to work in the afternoon and needed to rest. Increasingly, I became forgetful; I made a mental note to do things, and the next minute I had forgotten all of them.

Throughout April and into May, I continued to suffer from anaemia and was frequently lethargic and drained of energy. Climbing a flight of stairs was an effort. I developed a rash across my chest, a great red weal that seemed to me like a physical manifestation of my inner rage. I itched all over, and lathered myself with unguents and lotions which, however, had little effect. The problem was systemic, brought on by the drugs I was taking. Then, on 8th May, I received the news that the Hepatitis C was no longer detectable, which provided a much-needed lift. However, three weeks later, in consultation with Professor D, my consultant, I was reminded that a person can be Hep-C-undetected at this stage and yet relapse after treatment. The Professor told me that this was because of the difficulty of measuring the virus in very low quantities. The virus could hide out, he said, in the liver itself. If one were able to test all the blood in the patient's body, then theoretically one could determine the virus' total absence, but otherwise it was not 100% accurate. In my imagination, I envisaged my body drained entirely of blood, leaving a pale, emaciated sack of skin, as a huge glass tank beside my deflated body filled with crimson fluid. A white-coated assistant stood by, reciting figures to the Prof, who recorded them on a clipboard.

One day in June, while resident again in Birmingham, one of the nurses remarked in an offhand way how Guinness, strong in iron, was known to help with anaemia. Grateful for the permission, as I chose to interpret it, I ordered a pint of the black stuff at lunch, along with a bowl of vegetable soup, in the university staff bar. I justified it by telling myself I was getting nothing of substance down me and the anaemia was affecting me so very badly. It seemed to help, and the Guinness felt most wholesome. I repeated the dose at supper, nursing the pint glass in my hands as if it were the holy sacrament. The following morning, M, the specialist nurse, commented that I had a much better colour. My blood was "a lovely shade of beetroot," she said. I had no desire to drink more than a pint at a time, so could not see any harm in this, but was conscious that I was probably deluding myself.

"Addicts often suffer from self-deception, which has many faces or guises. Rationalization, denial, and minimalization are some of the more familiar forms", writes the philosopher Peg O'Connor in an account of her own alcoholism and recovery, *Life on the Rocks*. My rationalisation of a pint of Guinness was just such a moment. The very fact that I could congratulate myself on the lovely beetroot colour of my blood only confirmed the quality of my delusion. O'Connor also makes the point that we problem drinkers "may believe we can control our drinking while at the same time believing we cannot. We have plenty of evidence showing we cannot control it, yet we remain firmly in the saddle of our belief that we can. We also believe that this will be the last time we drink, all the while inhabiting a sense of the inevitability that we will use again. And most obviously, many of us would say, 'I knew that I was an alcoholic, but I knew I was not an alcoholic.'" In ways like this, addicts spend much of their time and energy trying to solve an existential crisis that could be averted simply by abstaining. What is required is surrender to the bare fact of one's addiction, and accepting life on life's terms, without recourse to a convenient anaesthetic. Only with that acceptance and surrender can the fires that feed the addicted self be extinguished, and other selves found to replace it.

My treatment proceeded in troughs and – after the initial elation at finding myself free of the Hep C virus – increasingly lower peaks. The 'rage' of which the patient information leaflet initially warned me – and which Rose and I had joked about, imagining scenes of cartoonish fury – now no longer seemed so funny, and the crimson weal on my chest spread to my face, so that whenever I stood before a mirror my red and blotchy countenance peered lugubriously back at me. The doctors continued to be concerned with my low white cell and platelet counts, but these were not quite low enough for me to be taken off the trial. I was in a dilemma, since it would seem as though the virus had departed, and yet I was still taking the medicine that was making me ill. It was only because I had agreed to undergo the whole trial that I was continuing to comply with the increasingly arduous demands it made of me. I later discovered that I was the only volunteer on the Birmingham trial who successfully stayed the course.

As I continued with the treatment, past the six month point, and through the summer, I remained anaemic and run-down, with continuing insomnia and an intense restlessness in my limbs, as though an electric charge were being driven through my body. I was in an almost constant state of anxiety; and the extreme fatigue brought about by sleep deprivation was affecting my mental health.

*   *   *

During the year of my treatment for Hepatitis C, I paid regular visits to my father in Crickhowell, where I had spent my childhood. A widower for several years, he no longer took the long walks in the hills that he had previously enjoyed, and that we had once taken together. Indeed, he barely ever left the house. He could walk, with difficulty, but was not the sort of man who could easily accept being seen in a wheelchair in the community where he had spent his working life as a doctor. This reluctance to show vulnerability is something I had long associated with him, and I imagined it was a quality that he acquired through coming to adulthood during wartime. His stoicism with regard to suffering was a hallmark of his character, but that did not prevent him from grumbling about almost any trivial aspect of contemporary life. He would take a petulant pleasure relaying, in forensic detail, the phone conversations that he endured as a victim of diverse utilities providers. The intrusive nature of these unrequested service calls drove him to distraction. He would pass on the content of such interactions to me, adumbrated with his imagined responses – which he was far too polite to actually deliver – uttered as exasperated asides. "And how has your day been?" *(None of your damn business)*; "Is it alright if I call you by your first name?" *(No it is not)*; "Can you can spell that please?" *(For the love of God, it's written there under you nose, otherwise you wouldn't be calling me ...).* He liked being addressed correctly and abided by standards of civility current in the 1940s, which he saw no advantage in exchanging for – in his eyes – sloppier practices that promoted a false sense of intimacy. In spite of this, he had a sharp and wry sense of humour, which often took me by surprise. During these visits, amid the litany of everyday complaint, he would recount stories, some of which I had never heard before, others describing events at which I had myself been present.

One of my father's regular gripes over the years was with the church, or more specifically, with religious dogma. A lifelong agnostic, he had reluctantly endured outings to Sunday worship while we were children, in part to appease our mother, but mainly to enact the role of stalwart of the community that came with being a country doctor in those days. As children, my siblings and I were permitted to attend tea parties at the Rector's house, at which the Reverend Cyril James showed us slides of his visits to one or other African country where he had carried out good works on behalf of the Anglican ministry; but Father's contempt for the clergy, whom he saw as largely parasitic, was otherwise unremitting. I recall one story that neatly reflected this attitude. I must have been thirteen years old, and it was Christmas Day. The phone rang – as it so often did at inopportune moments – and my father picked up. It was clear from the change in his demeanour that this was a professional call; his brow furrowed and he adopted a characteristic pose that indicated thoughtful abstraction, staring at the ground while slowly stroking his chin. It transpired that he was talking to PC Austin, the village policeman, whose voice I could hear blaring from the receiver. There was a hippy colony (as such communities were then called) up on the Llangynidr mountain, and one of the residents had descended on Crickhowell that morning, claiming he was Jesus Christ. Given the day, this might have seemed an innocent enough delusion, especially for one who, according to PC Austin, was "all drugged up on LSD or some such", were it not for the additional information that the hippy – "a tall, bearded chap, with hair down to his waist" – was half naked and wielding an axe. The constable was wondering whether the doctor might come along to the churchyard, where a colleague was attempting to restrain the man, in order to carry out the necessary paperwork for a sectioning order. My father spent a while taking this in. "The fellow has an axe?" he mused into the receiver, at length, his eyes scanning the ceiling as though in pursuit of an invisible insect: "He's in the churchyard, you say? And claims he is Jesus Christ? ...Well, Constable, given these details, I rather think this is the Rector's domain ... give him a call, would you?" Then: "Yes, of course, I'll come along and attend to the paperwork." My father replaced the receiver, smiled at me, and went into the hallway for his coat and hat. "I'm sure dinner won't be ready for another hour or so," he said. "Let your mother known I'm out on a call."

During the period of my treatment, I wasn't well enough to take my usual hike in the hills before dropping in on him, so Father and I would sit in the front room of his bungalow and watch television, or rather, we would almost exclusively watch the rugby union internationals he followed throughout his life as a keen Wales supporter. It was on one such visit, after watching a Six Nations game in February 2013, that I strolled along to the local confectioner and tobacconist shop, Jehu's, across the road from the war memorial in the town centre.

It has always seemed to me that my dependency on alcohol had an antecedent in my childhood addiction to sugar, and visits to Jehu's shop were the concrete expression of a singular passion for sweets; fruit salads and blackjacks (four a penny in old money); barley sugar sticks; and best of all, those thin wormlike strands of sweet coconut-flavoured pretend tobacco, wrapped in waxy paper, called Spanish Gold, which I am certain could not be sold to children today. Old Mr Jehu, the shopkeeper, had very bad teeth – a solitary gold specimen gleamed suspiciously amongst them, much to my fascination – and no doubt he had been on the real Spanish Gold all his life. But the pretend stuff obsessed me, and fitted in with my career plans at the age of six or seven, which consisted of running away with Janet Morgan to a place called the Spanish Main, where we would become pirates and sail wooden ships, and do other exciting pirate stuff, all of which we rehearsed in the school yard at Saint Edmund's primary school, opposite the church of that name.

So, on this visit to my father, I returned to the shop for the first time in many years, to buy real cigarettes, and was served by a man a few years younger than myself (the original Mr Jehu's grandson, Ed) and I at once recalled a former self standing in the same spot, surveying the rows of confectionery. The years slipped away. I was using up my entire shilling allowance on sweeties. Old Mr Jehu was looming over me, displaying blackened stumps and national health specs and addressing me as "the young doctor", while stuffing a white paper bag with teeth-rotting goodies. There was something both daunting and spectral about his presence before me, dressed in a scruffy charcoal suit. Old Mr Jehu always worried me, and his insistence on referring to me as "the young doctor" conveyed a terrible sense of predestination. I couldn't be other than that which I had been born to become, the young doctor, who would eventually replace the older doctor that was my father.

I remembered a particular visit to Jehu's. I must have been around five years old. I had picked up a box of matches while we were in the shop and our nanny, Kathleen, spotted them on the way home, perhaps I even showed them to her. Now that I think about it, the gesture becomes clear: I showed them to Kathleen and told her they were a present for Mummy. The memory stands out because I knew at the time that what I had said was not true; they were not a gift for my mother. Although not properly speaking a pyromaniac, I did like playing with matches; I loved the spark they made when struck against the rough edge of the box or against the red brick of our house. The idea that the matches were a present for my mother is the first conscious lie I remember telling.

I wonder too, while on the subject of fire, at my early discovery of alcohol, and its role in the writing life, an association explored brilliantly by Olivia Laing in *Trip to Echo Spring*, her study of alcoholic American writers. From a young age, my relationship with alcohol was influenced by my reading. Although I started drinking in secret from the age of seven, my attachment to the bottle was refined, or at the very least compounded, by my discovery of 'serious' literature, a few years later. Perhaps the two discoveries were made simultaneously.

When did the link between the enjoyment of literature and the consumption of alcohol become concretely established? I believe I can pinpoint the precise moment of this discovery, during an English class, aged fourteen, while studying Eugene O'Neill's play *A Long Day's Journey into Night*. As part of our instruction we were taken to see Lawrence Olivier in a 1971 performance of the play at the National Theatre in London. I was impressed, as we all were, by Olivier, in the role of Edmund, but even more so by his recital of a prose poem by Baudelaire:

> Be always drunken. Nothing else matters: that is the only question.
> If you would not feel the horrible burden of Time weighing on your shoulders and crushing you to the earth, be drunken continually. Drunken with what?
> With wine, with poetry, or with virtue, as you will.
> But be drunken.

I was profoundly affected by this, and encouraged by Baudelaire's endorsement to get drunk on wine and poetry, choosing to ignore that uncomfortable, and frankly incomprehensible "virtue". In preparing a school essay on the play, my research led me to the discovery that Eugene O'Neill's brother Jamie (the model for the dissolute character of Jamie Tyrone) was "an alcoholic by the age of twenty-one." When I read this, I found the idea of being an alcoholic by the age of twenty-one perversely attractive. What was it in those words that inspired such a delicious, tremulous fear? What terrible hubris could lead one to sacrifice one's future, one's entire life, in the pursuit of drunkenness? Was it associated with the notion that twenty-one was a watershed age, when one received the mythical 'keys to the door'? Was there not something wonderfully subversive about this embracing of disaster, of entering the citadel of adulthood in an already irremediably damaged state?

I can remember, from around the same period, a boy at school telling a group of us, in an awed tone, that he had stayed for a week at a friend's home over the summer, and how the boy's mother, divorced and alcoholic (that terrible pairing of adjectives) slept with a bottle of whisky at her bedside. I tried to picture my own mother acting in this way. Such was the civilised restraint of my parents' lives that the image was impossible to conjure. And yet, in the abstract, it seemed dangerously seductive. I was aroused by the thought of this boy's mother, whom I imagined by turns as young and attractive, or else as ruinously addled and depraved – like Bette Davis in *Whatever Happened to Baby Jane*, a film I had watched on television – sprawling in drunken abandon on the unmade bed, a half-empty whisky bottle on the bedside table. Even this bizarre fantasy, and others like it, made me want to drink.

I cannot fully understand why I wanted to transgress in this way, but I know that I felt attracted to a place where certain moods and music and works of art and literature led me; somewhere dark and mysterious, tinged with the prospect of danger. Later in life I would find these places had manifest form in the cities to which I travelled, and I was drawn ineluctably to the darkest, most insalubrious drinking dens, without having to seek them out. Instead, they found me.

Driving back home to Cardiff after visiting my father that time, I attempted to distinguish between the things that actually happened in that mythical sweet shop, and the things that my memory had conferred upon the place over the interceding years, including my visits there in dreams. I was reminded again of Saer's *The Witness*, when the old man, who was once a cabin boy, reflects that the memory of an event is not sufficient proof that it actually happened, and it is the same with the sweetshop, the incident with the matches, and the seedy bars – or sanctuaries, as I considered them – that I was to frequent in adulthood, all of them real places that had infiltrated my personal dreamscape. In the present, however, they existed neither in reality nor in dream, but some place in between.

★   ★   ★

Around this time, as the drug trial entered its final months, I attended a talk at the university where I worked, by the poet and translator Adam Thorpe, titled 'My nights with Emma B', in which Thorpe, whose manner of delivery I found both stimulating and refreshingly self-effacing, reported back on his three years spent in the throes of translator-sickness, that peculiar ailment that has one hooked up, at times almost against one's will, to some other writer's creative process – something with which, while working on *The Other Tiger,* I would become familiar, although in my case the other writer's creative process, rather than pertaining to one individual, was multiple, and necessitated my adjusting to a disparate range of voices. In our work, we translators must enter and inhabit the work more thoroughly than any other reader if we are to produce versions that are both reflective of the original, as well as contextually informed and sensitive to the needs of the present.

Alexis Nuselovici (Nouss to his friends), who was at that time a professor at the university, and who introduced Thorpe's talk, threw down the challenge that "untranslatability was the stuff that *Madame Bovary* was made of." Perversely, I reflected, it is that very problem of untranslatability, in any work, that will often most appeal; the lines on which you feel certain to come unstuck. Conversely, at least with regard to the anthology upon which I was then embarked, the most transparently 'translatable' poems are not always the best choices for inclusion. As Susan Bassnett has commented: "Translating poems that seem to be very straightforward and easily understandable in the source language all too often end up as banal in English. Translating the apparently simple is, in a different way, as tough as translating a very complex text, for the effect of simplicity is only achievable with considerable skill, and a translator needs comparable skills." Those particular skills, as I discovered, are perhaps the most underestimated in the translator's repertoire.

During his talk, Mr Thorpe kept me thoroughly engaged for an hour, something of a miracle considering how difficult it had been for me to concentrate on anything for more than ten minutes at a time over the past year. He stressed the key aspects of a successful translation: accuracy (i.e. matching the source text), style, and music – most especially rhythm. I particularly approved of his emphasis on the element of rhythm, which he described as "the most appallingly difficult aspect of translation." Thorpe is a poet, and he understands better than most that rhythm is perhaps the singular most essential component of the creative process, something which Flaubert knew very well. As for the Death of the Author – or his Absence, a question predictably raised by a critical theorist in the audience, Thorpe was unforgiving towards the notion that Flaubert, as a novelist, was in any way absent from the work. "Nonsense," he said. "I could smell him in every word. The text is saturated with him. He was a bluff, gruff companion."

Returning home from the lecture, I remembered something I had recently read, and pulled down my densely-annotated copy of W.G. Sebald's *Rings of Saturn*, where we learn of Flaubert's "fear of the false which ... sometimes kept him confined to his couch for weeks or even months on end in the dread that he would never be able to write another word without compromising himself in the most grievous of ways ... He was convinced that everything he had written hitherto consisted solely in a string of the most abysmal errors and lies, the consequences of which were immeasurable."

Flaubert believed that the relentless spread of stupidity in the world had invaded his own head, and the resulting sensation was one of sinking into sand. According to Sebald's friend Janine Dakyns, sand possessed enormous significance in all of Flaubert's work. Sebald puts it like this: "Sand conquered all. Time and again, Janine said, vast dust clouds drifted through Flaubert's dreams by day and by night, raised over the arid plains of the African continent and moving north across the Mediterranean and the Iberian peninsula till sooner or later they settled like ash from a fire on the Tuileries gallery, a suburb of Rouen, or a country town in Normandy, penetrating into the tiniest crevices. In a grain of sand in the hem of Emma Bovary's winter gown ... Flaubert saw the whole of the Sahara." The Blakean synecdoche of this image sets the heart racing. It gives a glimmer of the kind of inclusive, detailed understanding of the world that so fascinated and appalled Flaubert.

As I was to discover in my own translations of the poets included in *The Other Tiger*, immersion in the work of others produces, cumulatively, a kind of inner upheaval; a confusion brought about by plenitude, for which the metaphor of sinking into sand might well be appropriate. Given the scale of the task I had given myself, namely, of mapping an entire continent's poetry, I had to impose limits, otherwise I would drown, in sand or otherwise. I had decided early on that I wanted to compile an anthology of poems, rather than of poets, and did not wish the book to be laid out chronologically by author, or by country. I therefore decided that the book was going to be themed by topic rather than by nationality or date of birth, these topics being approximately: home and the immediate environment; childhood and family; animals and the natural world; the social and political world; love, sex and the body, and conflict, illness and death. Since my intention was to focus on poetry of the late 20th and early 21st centuries, I decided to limit my selection to living poets, as I was keen to discuss my translations with them wherever possible. Consequently, I wrote to all of the poets whose work I wished to represent, or else, in many cases, met them in person, so that I might, to borrow Thorpe's phrase (and at the risk of some exaggeration) "smell them in every word." Once the translations were done, the poets would receive my versions and were invited to comment on or question them. Many of those who knew English took up this opportunity, raising interesting and sometimes perplexing choices for the translator, or else pointing out small but often crucial details of vocabulary or representation. In all of this, however, remained the certainty that the translator's voice – in this case my own – would intrude upon the work. While one might take steps to prevent this personal voice or habit becoming over-intrusive, it is bound to be there, as Ezra Pound famously proved in his own work as a translator. It is for this reason that I put my translation through the filter of other readers' responses; where possible, and where their command of English was adequate, the poets themselves, as well as through trusted and patient translator friends. But this could not prevent the appearance of my own voice, or personal habit.

The reading of a poem is itself a kind of translation, an act of intimate decipherment. In this sense we are all translators, because a translator is – as Borges pointed out – "a very close reader; there is not much difference between translating and reading." Nor, for that matter, is there much difference between reading and writing. Nor even between reading and travelling. Or writing and travelling, whose synergetic relationship I had already discovered. As Lydia Davis has put it: "to translate is also to read, and to translate is to write, as to write is to translate and to read is to translate. So that we may say: To translate is to travel and to travel is to translate." As it turned out, my selection of poems from Latin America came about through just such a confluence of travel, reading, and writing, and the translations that ensued formed a part of the continuum.

> The beggars emerge from ancient catacombs
> Or from remote cathedrals that raise their domes
> Between hospices and hospitals.
> As they go by they wound and poison the landscape
> And the people give way at their passing
> As if they were parting a sea ...
>
> Juan Manuel Roca, 'Landscape with Beggars'.

Colombia, July 2013

Four months after completing the drug trial, and now Hepatitis-free, I took my first trip to Colombia. The taxi driver on the ride from Bogotá's El Dorado airport was talkative, keen to impress on me his view that despite the reputation his country had acquired over decades of conflict and kidnappings, there was a longing for change among the people of Colombia; a desperate desire, he said, for peace. His loquaciousness, not unusual in taxi drivers, revealed an attitude that I soon found to be common amongst Colombians, although it was often concealed, at first, behind a carapace of suspicion, as if they were all too accustomed to strangers, both from within the country and without, posing a threat of some kind: it was an attitude that signalled a striving for recognition, and a wish for the nation to be shed of its role as the world's pantomime villain. The taxi driver really wanted me to believe him when he said the country was changing.

The city spreads out chaotically along Septima, the main artery from which all else devolves. We stopped at my hotel, and I tipped the driver over the odds, relieved at how little he charged, relieved that I didn't have to begin my stay here – as sometimes occurs after a long flight – by haggling, or with the feeling that one has been mugged on the ride into town.

At the time of my visit, there were already proposals being put forward to hold a national plebiscite on the question of an amnesty for the FARC (Revolutionary Armed Forces of

Colombia) which was eventually held in 2016. President Juan Manuel Santos was the principle proponent of the deal, and had built his political career on it. Contemplating Santos' photo on the cover of the Spanish edition of his book *La batalla por la paz* (The Battle for Peace), published in 2019, I discern in the face the same saurian aspect – as though squeezed through the sphincter of incredulity and reborn on a TV evangelist – as those proffered to photographers by the UK's ex-prime minister, Tony Blair, a man, like Santos, once upon a time the bearer of half a nation's hopes. It therefore comes as no surprise to learn, from the book's cover blurb, that Santos and Blair co-authored a book, *La Tercera Via* (The Third Way), adapting Blairite political philosophy to a Colombian context. The book's contents are summarised by the subheading: 'The long journey to put an end to the war with the world's oldest guerrilla army', a war that had displaced more than six million and cost the lives of around a quarter of a million people. In many ways Santos' achievement was remarkable, and yet his referendum failed to achieve a majority in favour of peace with the FARC, as we shall see.

There is a telling anecdote early in his book when Santos is deliberating between a career in politics or journalism (his family owned *El Tiempo*, Colombia's leading daily). Seeking counsel from prominent figures in both spheres, he claims that he received this advice from Alfonso Palacio Rudas, a journalist and ex-government minister, who told him: "There's a difference between having influence and having power ... you don't simply want to influence things, you want to make them happen, that is your temperament." Politicians have this knack of making themselves sound as though they were concerned only with the common good. The photographs in the book show Santos in the company of the famous men of his time – and they are all men– an elite club of the powerful, whose actions have determined the course of the lives (and in many cases, the deaths) of countless people: Santos with Fidel Castro; Santos with Nelson Mandela; Santos with his mentor and ally Tony Blair; with Hugo Chávez, with Felipe González, with Bill Clinton, with Barack Obama, with President Nieto of Mexico, with Pope Francis – and finally, with Donald Trump, both men grinning like imbeciles. Santos writes with a single-minded clarity of the ways he set out to bring peace to his country, and refuses to submit to the fact of his plebiscite's defeat. But all this happened later.

The state of Colombia at the time of my visit, in July 2013, might not have elicited great optimism among the masses still crowding into Bogotá from the outlying provinces, displaced by the ongoing war with the FARC, but there were at least stirrings, suggestions that things might indeed be beginning to change, as my taxi driver had suggested. The guerrillas had been pushed into the remotest parts of the jungle, and — whether or not this was a good sign is debatable, but it was broadcast as such — there was a heavy police and army presence in Bogotá itself.

Like everywhere else in the world, but more so, in Colombia the comforts and privileges of the few are considerable and well-protected. In all but the very smartest areas, patrolled by private security companies, you will, in Bogotá, come across the most desperate beggars imaginable. I don't know why this is, the homeless shouldn't be on a sliding scale of depravity and wretchedness, but somehow the street-dwellers of Bogotá seem more lamentable than elsewhere, even India. Perhaps the miserable climate of the Colombian capital makes their plight seem more intolerable, and perhaps my own rather pensive mood coloured my perception, but the beggars of Bogotá are often so moribund that they are too far gone to put out a hand in supplication or mutter an appeal for charity; many of them simply sprawl out flat on the pavement, or hang onto a post or railing, gurning at the world that passes them by. The victims of poverty, rampant drug abuse and despair, these sorry individuals, filthy, caked with grime, shoeless and utterly beyond concern, stagger around the streets like zombie revenants from one of the more wretched precincts of purgatory.

On my first excursion from the hotel, as I passed by a newly opened *Dunkin Donuts*, one of them stared at me briefly, glazed, uncomprehending, covered in the filth of centuries, clothed in colourless rags, and to my shock I realised that this ancient vision was actually a young man, probably in his early twenties. He brought to mind Juan Manuel Roca's poem, 'Landscape with Beggars':

> The good people wonder
> Why a tattered rabble of beggars
> Block their prospect of the lilies.
> If they don't receive their ration of manna,
> It's due to their savage custom
> Of blighting the landscape and the view.
> More ancient than their profession
> The beggars emerge from ancient catacombs
> Or from remote cathedrals that raise their domes
> Between hospices and hospitals.
> As they go by they wound and poison the landscape
> And the people give way at their passing
> As if they were parting a sea
> Which they stain with taunts and devastation.
> A procession of smells and a procession of dogs
> Go past with the wretched hordes. Town mayors
> Watch them with watery eyes
> While spooning out soup as thick as lava.
> The priests seek them out like food
> From a kingdom in another world
> And describe to them the quarries of hell,

> Although they seem to have lived there forever.
> They are of another race, another country,
> The beggars are dark strangers
> Who live on the invisible frontiers of language ...

As I transcribe this poem, I am reminded of a line from a speech given by President Santos in November 2016 at the London School of Economics, when he quoted Nelson Mandela as saying that the quality of a society should be measured by how it treats its weakest members. I wonder how many of these – the lost, the abused, the rejected and the downtrodden, who haunt the city streets of Bogotá, of Bombay and of Birmingham (England or Alabama) – can truly be saved from the desperate straits into which circumstances have driven them.

★ ★ ★

On my second day in the capital, along with Jorge Fondebrider, with whom I have been reunited, I visit the poet Darío Jaramillo for lunch at his apartment. I first met Darío at the festival in Nicaragua, two years earlier, where he gave me a couple of his books. I have included three of his poems in the anthology I am preparing; furthermore I am hoping to translate and publish a volume of his poetry in the UK.[3] Hopefully this invitation will help me get to know him better. As I have said, I like to know something of the lives of the poets I translate, especially those still living. Darío, a supremely courteous and generous man, is certainly alive, but only by a hair's breadth, having lost much of his left leg to a car bomb attack in 1989, while working as director of the cultural programme of the Banco de la República (the national bank of Colombia), a job he continued to hold for some years afterwards. A cruel irony of this outrage was that Darío was not the intended victim of the attack; this was the car's owner, an official of the bank who had refused to sell a prize racehorse to a cartel boss, an offence for which the car bomb, by the logic of those lawless days, was considered reasonable payback.

3. Published as *Impossible Loves*, Carcanet (2019).

Jorge and I arrive early at Darío's place, so we take a stroll around the neighbourhood. I catch sight of a bar named 'Minos', and since I cannot forego an opportunity to pursue a connection with the island of Crete, where I lived for three years in my twenties, we cross the road and go in. It is a small, unpretentious place, with room for only two or three tables. I speak to the barman, who is also the owner. He has a vaguely Greek air to him, so I ask him if, indeed, he is. No, he answers, he is not Greek, but he called his bar 'Minos' out of an interest in classical mythology. Then, as if in afterthought, he adds, 'and because Colombia is a labyrinth.'

The conjunction of the Old World and the New is something that has interested me since the beginning of my travels in Latin America, and I am curious to know what of the Old World its migrant peoples – those whose families originated in Europe – wished to import, or retain, and what they preferred to leave permanently behind. Since much of modern Latin American culture has its roots in the Mediterranean, including the term 'Latin' or 'Latino', I wonder what the affinities are, real or imagined. After all, if one wishes to make a fresh start there is no need to import anything, other than for sentimental reasons; and, of course, it is not only European culture whose traces are discernible here. Many immigrants to Colombia come from the Levant and the Middle East, Syrians and Lebanese especially (Shakira's family, to name one famous example), all of whom, regardless, are referred to incorrectly as 'Turks', as in *One Hundred Years of Solitude*, with its 'Street of Turks.' But my brief exchange with the owner of the Minos bar intrigues me, because of his referring to Colombia as a labyrinth (of which Bogotá is the elusive centre) and it pleases me to imagine this man as the Minoan overlord of his tiny domain. I wonder whether I might return to the bar when I have more time, and quiz him about the labyrinth, over a coffee.

We walk back to Darío's place for our lunch appointment. The day is wet and windy. Gabriel García Márquez – Gabo, to Colombians – who grew up on the gentler, warmer, Caribbean edge of the country, was horrified by the perpetual cold and drizzle of the capital when he moved here as a young man.

Despite having lived for much of my life in Wales, a country not blessed with fine weather, I feel likewise. Gabo unwittingly contrives to cancel my dinner appointment for the following day with an old acquaintance, the novelist Juan Gabriel Vásquez. Vásquez messages me to say that he has received an urgent request from the octogenarian writer to visit him at his home in Cartagena. Rumours have been circulating about the old man's health for some time now, and he feels it would be imprudent not to go; after all, he adds, one doesn't turn down a summons from Gabo.

A couple of nights later, returning to the hotel after dinner with Darío in another part of town, the taxi-driver was unable to find his way to our hotel, a not uncommon occurrence in this city. It was night-time and at every other street corner there was a police detail and, in some places, an armoured car and substantial military presence, as the taxi-driver took multiple turnings, doubling back on himself twice. Bewildered by the sheer number of armed men out on the street, I guessed it was supposed to be reassuring to the population at large, but to me, with my limited experience of conflict zones, it had the opposite effect; it seemed heavy-handed and oppressive. On another occasion, Jorge and I having been invited to lunch with Piedad Bonnet in one of the more affluent suburbs, our hostess was so concerned about the long delay to our arrival that she had been about to call the police, for fear that we had been abducted. These things do happen, she told us, as if by the way, when we finally arrived at her house after a two-hour taxi ride, much of it in circles. Piedad, a woman with an unusually dark sense of humour to counterbalance a residual melancholy, is one of Colombia's most eminent poets, and the author of a best-selling memoir, *Lo que no tiene nombre,* (literally 'That which has no name'), in which she recounts the events leading up to the suicide, in New York, at the age of twenty-eight, of her son Daniel, who suffered from bi-polar disorder. In her apartment hang a few of Daniel's paintings; large, vivid works, troubled and troubling, but with a vital, visceral impact. Daniel clearly had a gift. It is Piedad who tells me, as we sit one afternoon in an upmarket tea-room frequented by women of the Colombian upper classes, of the practice local assassins sometimes perform on their victims. She explains with a terrifying bluntness, which I can only imagine stems from her own grief and despair: "these guys," she says, "the ones whose works are scattered around our country, they are not simple assassins; they are artists of death. They slit the throat (she gestures) and pull out the tongue, out front, like so. They call it 'the necktie' (la corbata)." Piedad's delivery is deadpan throughout.

★ ★ ★

In contrast to Bogotá's perpetual cold and drizzle, Medellín, known as the city of eternal spring, is bathed in sunshine. On the drive from the airport I am struck by the swathes of colourful flowers growing wild along the wayside, and on sale at the many stalls that line the road. This is the first impression Medellín makes on me: an abundance of flowers. Which is sadly ironic, considering that the city is still best known to the world as the home and field of operations of the most famous narco boss of them all, Pablo Escobar. As an example of the emerging popularity of *turismo oscuro* or dark tourism, there is even an 'Escobar tour' available to punters, which includes, among other treats, a visit to his very own torture chamber, where el patrón's enemies were subjected to unspeakable torments. I do not sign up.

The city's international poetry festival is the largest in the world. The main events, held in an open-air amphitheatre, regularly record audiences in excess of two thousand. The poetry might attract large numbers, but it is the political import of poetry as a weapon of resistance that, as in Nicaragua, is so remarkable to the foreign visitor. Unlike Nicaragua, the motivation here is focused, articulate and compelling, and the target is the ongoing conflict, its origins stretching back to *la violencia*, a decade of civil strife that began in 1948 with the murder of the liberal politician Jorge Eliciécer Gaitán – chronicled in Juan Gabriel Vásquez's fine novel *La forma de las ruinas* (*The Shape of the Ruins*) – and which has wrecked so many Colombian lives ever since.

This year the festival has as its tagline 'A thousand years of peace'. In an interview with the Spanish newspaper *El País*, on 5 July, 2013, the festival director, Fernando Rendón, is quoted as saying:"There are few Colombians alive who have known a period of relative peace. And since we haven't known peace, we have a deep desire for a time without conflict, a time of reconciliation." Rendón's big idea, therefore, which he has been pursuing since setting up the festival in 1991, is that poetry has a role in energising Colombians in a mass movement for peace. His ambition is echoed by the poet Juan Manuel Roca:"Poetry, amidst the war that we are living through, provides a kind of spiritual resistance." I can see how that might be, if, for example, we consider those British poets who successfully mobilised a greater awareness of the suffering brought about by organised violence on an industrial scale in World War One. To this end, the festival has gathered together poets from forty-five countries around the world who will perform their work in a hundred and fifty locations in the province of Antioquia, of which Medellín is the capital.

We foreign writers have been assigned a minder, or escort, whose task is to ensure that we turn up to our events, and who will sometimes act as the reader of the Spanish translations of our poems. The minder will accompany us every day of the festival. I am in the hands of Santiago, a slim and sceptical young man, who dishes out pithy verdicts on the state of the world with a sardonic smile. I rather like him. He and his colleagues have to spend a week attending to the needs of the poets and their accompanying egos, which can't be an easy task, at least in certain cases. Despite this, some minders form regular friendships with their charges.

The events at the festival auditorium are packed with listeners of all ages. Residents of the province of Antioquia attend for free. Starting at four in the afternoon on this, the first full day, the poets take it in turns onstage, in panels of four or five, and, rising above the marijuana fumes that occasionally drift across from the seated audience, they read or declaim their poems. At my first event I am on a panel with Juan Manuel Roca, whose work has impressed me with its imaginative repertoire and underlying sense of menace. His poems go down very well with the audience. Indeed, the applause becomes louder as the evening progresses, and the panels continue, one after another, for six hours. I am filled with warmth and respect for the Colombian people: withstanding a poetry recital of such epic proportions demands astonishing powers of endurance. On another day, a rainstorm intercedes mid-performance, and the organisers make an announcement, calling the readings off, but the audience take matters into their own hands, cover their heads with jackets and plastic bags, and chant loudly for '*Poesia, Poesia*'. It is an impressive display of people power, and since that is what the whole thing is about, the show is allowed to go on.

One day, with Jorge and the Irish poet Moya Cannon, I visit Santo Domingo Savio, until recently an area of the city riven by gang warfare, and once reputed to be the most violent place in South America. It has been largely redeveloped, although the ascent by cable car still allows for a view of countless corrugated-iron shacks, plastered across the slopes of the barrio. Graffiti abounds in every open space. The graffito below a huge banknote painted on a wall suggests that a "thousand poor die for each 1000 peso banknote in the idle republic."

We have come to visit a stylish library, designed by the architect Giancarlo Mazzanti, built in 2006-7 with Spanish money, and consequently known as 'the Spanish library'. The staff are welcoming, and show us around the theatre, which forms a part of the library complex. There are dedicated spaces for children to read books and play 'intelligent' games, but there aren't actually many kids around, apart from a couple of pubescent chancers who try tapping us for money in an almost deserted playground on our way in. While the urban redevelopment is impressive, one wonders at the absence of the young people for whom it was designed, as well as at the fact that, not long ago, projects aimed at social improvement, were in large part overseen by a drug lord named Pablo Escobar, for which reason the poor in such neighbourhoods regarded him – as some still do – with an attitude approaching adoration.

One evening, a few days in, after expressing a wish to get away from the company of poets, Santiago and I ascend the hill behind our hotel and step into the city's underbelly, by way of a small square called Parque Periodista. Santiago tells me that the square's name refers to a journalist who was murdered by police, although someone else tells me that it refers to 'any old journalist' rather than a specific one. Despite my research, I never get to the bottom of the park's name. However, I do find, on a website for visitors to Colombia, a description, in English, that sums the place up quite neatly: "Parque Periodista is the hangout of Medellin's bohemian underground … [it] can be sketchy at times because of drug-dealing in the area, but can also be one of the city's most exciting places because of the colorful variety of people that come there. The youth gathered at the square cannot be described. It's an ever-changing cultural mixture of punks, potheads, rockers, hippies, junkies, rappers, dealers, 'grillas', drunks, gays and even the occasional transvestite, regularly joined by university professors, poets and musicians."

In the square, we meet up with some of Santiago's friends, and a couple of the other minders from the festival, including the irrepressibly cheerful Valeria, who has brought her hippy mum along. Also present is Valentin, a long-limbed and ethereal Russian dancer, who performed a strangely bewitching dance at the festival's opening ceremony, and one of the African poets, a flamboyant Senegalese woman who claims to be a shaman and a princess. We are a motley crew.

The Parque Periodista resembles other urban meeting places around the globe where the young and disaffected hang out at night to drink and do drugs. I have stayed away from such places for some years now, and feel unusually self-conscious. I needn't have worried. A young woman, a friend of Valeria's, asks me how long I have been in Colombia. Six days, I answer. She claims not to believe me, as she had assumed – on what basis I cannot imagine – that I must have lived here, as she puts it, 'for years'. It is flattering to learn that I have slotted so seamlessly into the seedier side of Medellín night life. At one level this is what the traveller wants, not exactly assimilation – that is never quite possible, nor always desirable – but a sense that one has attained a degree of invisibility; because the real vocation of the traveller, especially one with literary ambitions, is that of a spy. You want to be able to observe without being too closely observed yourself. Espionage, after all, is the profession most closely related to the novelist's, a conceit explored extensively by the Spaniard Javier Marías, in whose narratives the clandestine observational practices of undercover agents become the vehicle for forensic examination of his human subjects.

As part of the agenda at Medellín, the poets are expected to do outreach work, both within the city and the province of Antioquia. One of these excursions takes me to the colonial town of Santa Fe, to give a reading and to meet local writers.

I am accompanied on this trip by a Colombian poet, a Mexican poet, our driver, an official of the festival (who is there to liaise with the local dignitaries) and Santiago. Shortly after arrival at Santa Fe, we are presented with a fruit cocktail drink, made of watermelon, mango and pineapple, with a dollop of strawberry ice cream, the kind of innocent, sugary thing that in my childhood used to be called a knickerbockerglory, and perhaps still is. We are then driven in a moto-taxi, also known as a tuk-tuk – this one was a kind of lawnmower with a bench for passengers – down to the Puente de Occidente, a famous bridge over the River Cauca, constructed by the engineer José María Villa (1850-1913), a local lad made good, who won a scholarship to the New Jersey Institute of Technology and assisted in the building of the Brooklyn Bridge. José María Villa never quite managed to oversee the entire building of the Puente de Occidente, since he was – as his Wikipedia entry puts it – 'carried away by alcoholism' and his German assistant saw the project through.

The poetry recital, in the enclosed patio of the town hall, is attended by the solidly Christian townsfolk of Santa Fe, who express vocal appreciation of a poem of mine that references a statue of the Virgin Mary, and applaud loudly every time God is mentioned (even ironically) in the poems read by my Colombian colleague, the splendidly named Robinson Quintero. After our reading, a pair of musicians play folk songs for half an hour, which brings the evening's entertainment to a melodious close.

We are about to go for dinner, but on our way out, Robinson and I are confronted by a Belgian resident of the town, who has attended the recital, and insists we visit his home, in order, he says, to show us the work he does with local orphaned children. The children do not actually stay here, the Belgian tells us – there is an orphanage nearby – but the walls of his home, an airy colonial building, are plastered with photographs of children, many in a state of semi or total nakedness, and I wonder out loud what particular service he is providing for these poor kids. He becomes defensive, and I pick up a very bad vibe from him. I ask him, to his face, if he thinks it's OK to display these photographs, and enquire how, precisely, he 'helps' the children. He tells me "it's not what you think," and shuffles away, disgruntled, then returns and shows me other photographs of the children, with clothes on, at work in his studio, drawing and making clay models. This seems to justify – to his mind, at least – his role in the community, but the visit leaves a bad taste in my mouth. I am silent during dinner, unable to enjoy my food, and yet unsure, in my role as a guest of the town, how exactly to express my discomfort at what I believe I have just witnessed.

After supper, we head out of the restaurant, and someone passes around a porro, or spliff. We pile into the cabin of the truck, and for the rest of the evening, during the drive back, I zone out to the accompaniment of loud ranchera music. With a grinding of gears, we first climb the serpentine road from the valley of Santa Fe toward the high cordillera, and then descend at breakneck speed towards the city. When the lights of Medellín finally appear before us, so long has the journey taken, that it feels as though we are returning from another world, a more ancient and more innocent world, but one, nonetheless, tainted by the onset of an insidious corruption.

Over lunch the next day, Roca asks me what my impressions had been of Santa Fe. I tell him about my encounter with the Belgian, and say that otherwise the place had seemed a kind of paradise. In a remark reminiscent of the history teacher Fabio's synopsis of Mexico as a "land of many faces" two years before, Roca replies: "Colombia is a land of many paradises, but also of many serpents."

★ ★ ★

On 2nd October 2016, Colombians voted to reject the peace deal signed by their president, Juan Manuel Santos, and the FARC leader Timochenko. By the slimmest of majorities (50.2 against 49.8 %), the people of Colombia voted 'no' to the amnesty. Many wanted the guerrillas to suffer the punishment they felt was their due. The following day, in the *Washington Post*, Nick Miroff regarded the vote as an anti-establishment cry from the heart: "Like the Britons who chose to break with Europe,

Colombians opted for uncertainty over the assurances of their leaders, panning the heavily promoted peace accord Santos had signed with FARC leaders in a lofty ceremony less than a week earlier." The deal's defeat, Miroff went on, "is the latest example of a popular backlash that has bucked polling data and defied elite opinion. The government's agreement with FARC had taken nearly six years to negotiate, winning the support of the United States, the United Nations and Pope Francis." It would not be long before the USA voted in its own avatar of this trend in the form of Donald Trump, ushering in a presidency from which the country may never fully recover.

Santos – who was awarded the Nobel Prize for Peace in 2016 – claimed, a month after the referendum, that voters were influenced by the lies of the 'no' campaigners, "encouraging citizens to vote with anger and for reasons that had nothing to do with the central question." Following the Brexit vote in the UK, and the election of Donald Trump to the White House, this result seemed to conform to a global pattern; a settling for the familiar comforts of prejudice and nationalism over those of reconciliation and inclusivity. Fear of the other was on the rise again, whether directed at the enemy within or the migrant hordes queueing at the gate. It felt as though the shutters were coming down around the world.

> To walk is to advance one step after another. It's the only thing there is. Across a neighbourhood, down the streets, through the suburbs; one step above a scrap of earth, and some stones, one step skipping the line that divides two paving stones. And another step. At the end sometimes I arrive home. Home is not the place where I live.
>
> Ariel Williams, 'Discourse of the teller of worms'.

Argentina, August-September 2013

I am headed to Patagonia, the land of the Big Feet (Patagones) – the earliest European visitors believing this remote land to be inhabited by giants. But first the train east, to London, and as I sit by the carriage window we pass the site at Reading where the music festival is in full swing, the very place, many years ago, that I experienced my first LSD trip. The blues guitarist Rory Gallagher and his band were performing during my maiden psychedelic voyage, of which my only memories are being hit on the head by an empty beer can, as the fans at the back of the crowd tried to get those at the front to sit down – and of my insisting, throughout the night, that my name was Gaston, adapting my behaviour to fit this imaginary French person. I have no idea why I did this, but then again I have practically no sense either of being the seventeen-year-old who attended the festival; nor do I easily identify with him – he is as remote to me as Caractacus. Why, I wonder, do we insist on the illusion of a single self, across the decades, rather than of multiple, shifting selves?

On this trip, I am accompanied by an enormous blue suitcase. Currently it is fairly light, as it contains only a few copies of my own books, which I will, over the course of our travels, sell or more likely give away, and they will be replaced by books written by other people, since one of the aims of the excursion will be to collect more poetry for my Latin American anthology. How different things are now compared with my twenties, when I carried barely a thing on those feckless adventures, by foot, across Greece, France and Spain. And yet, even though it is no longer true, I still maintain the illusion that I am travelling light.

I am accompanied on the journey by three other poets from Wales; Mererid Hopwood, Karen Owen and Tiffany Atkinson, and by Nia Davies, a poet herself, who will shortly become the youngest-ever editor of the magazine *Poetry Wales*, but who, for the purposes of this trip is joining us on behalf of the translation agency, Wales Literature Exchange. We are due to undertake a tour of the Welsh-speaking communities of Patagonia. But first, Buenos Aires. Arriving at the Ezeiza Airport at eight in the morning, we are greeted by Jorge Fondebrider and Inés Garland. I am embarrassed by my enormous suitcase.

It is Sunday, and I want only to sleep. I am exhausted after the long flight, and have the impression that my fellow travellers feel much the same way. However, despite our jet lag, we are led by merciless Jorge on a day-long tour of the city. First we visit the Centro Cultural de Recoleta, where we are lodging, to drop off our luggage, then take a walk through the barrio and its famous cemetery. We lunch at El Palacio de la Papa Frita (the palace of the fried potato), in which, upon arrival, we are ushered to our table by a tall and ancient character in a faded grey suit, a man who bears a striking resemblance to the actor Vincent Price in his later, more camp or dilapidated roles, and who acts as custodian of the doorway, seemingly his only function. I feel that I know him, and although I possibly visited the Palace of the Fried Potato on a previous visit to Buenos Aires, the sensation of déjà vu is not limited to this man, nor to this venue, but extends backward in time to all the miserable gatekeepers and wardens I have known over the years, and perhaps even to those before my time, such as the Cambridge Beadle in Virginia Woolf's *A Room of One's Own*, who expresses "horror and indignation" when the author has the temerity to walk across the grass rather than follow the gravel path across the quad.

In the evening, we attend a concert in La Boca, where we listen to a tango trio, led by the bandoneonista Julio Pane, the bandoneón being a variant of the concertina, used in Argentina and Uruguay and named after the German instrument dealer Heinrich Band (1821-60). German sailors and Italian immigrants brought the instrument to Argentina in the late nineteenth century, where it was incorporated into local bands, and thus, eventually, became identifiable as key to the sound tapestry of Tango. One of the first pieces played by Señor Pane's band is Astor Piazzolla's *Suite Punta del Este,* which I recognise from the film *Twelve Monkeys,* where Piazzolla's score was adapted (or re-composed) by Paul Buckmaster. In this way Hollywood thrives, by absorbing and reproducing, in a more gringo-friendly form, everything it comes into contact with.

Here in Buenos Aires, a large number of women – those who are not prepared to put up with their own faces over the passage of the years – go in for surgical modification of one kind or other. Someone tells me later that under Argentine health insurance schemes, women are entitled to one facelift per year, thereby officially endorsing the culture of surveillance by the male gaze. After two or three of these operations, the victim of this facial remodelling begins to acquire the flattened features of a pug dog. Nowhere before have I seen such a preponderance of botox-filled and otherwise refurbished faces as are present in this theatre tonight.

I am assaulted midway through the concert by an attack of Restless Leg Syndrome, (also known as Willis-Ekbom disease), a genetic condition caused by reduced levels of dopamine in the basal ganglia of the brain, in which the entire body becomes a tightly coiled spring. The rasping music, contrapuntal overlapping melodies, a jostling of musical tropes one after the other, discordant and argumentative, complements or even incites the jerky, neurotic spasms running through my lower limbs and I decide that I like the concept of this type of 'progressive' tango more than I enjoy the actual music. Indeed, the overall effect of Señor Pane's musical offering is rather like an assault on the central nervous system by popping candies, those tiny sweets that cause small explosions on the tongue, and are carried by delinquent neurons into the raging bloodstream. To exacerbate my physical discomfort, Señor Pane has an irritating habit of getting up between songs and delivering a commentary, at once patronising and self-deprecatory, on the concert itself, even making the rather sad suggestion that people are not clapping hard enough. If a performer stoops to this kind of self-indulgence, it is probably time to leave.

Eventually I get up and move. I cannot sit still and need to stretch my legs. I am currently treating my condition, or rather smothering it, with alternating or combined doses of codeine and Tramadol, either of which would release the endorphins necessary to calm my twitching limbs. But I have not taken my medication today and nor do I have any on me. Due to the long hours in flight my body is in any case disoriented, so I go to sit at the back of the hall and kick my legs and reflect, logically enough, upon the nature of the *duende* (translated literally as imp, goblin or sprite) that uniquely Latin concept of the creative impulse, to which García Lorca dedicated an inspired essay, 'Theory and function of the Duende', and I think, as I sit there twitching: you must remember to listen to your duende, and to pay attention to this ancient imp of inspiration, "dark and quivering", as Lorca says, otherwise you will forget how to listen to anything at all. And if you forget how to listen, then your duende will flee in disgust, and you will be left with nothing. Sitting at the back, I notice rather more people walking out of the show than any musician would wish to witness during a performance. However, those remaining do applaud enthusiastically at the end, as prompted by Señor Pane.

The day culminates with dinner at an Italian place near to the Centro Cultural in Recoleta. During the meal, Jorge asks Mererid and Karen why they write in Welsh. Perhaps it is an innocent question and Jorge is unaware of the deeply troubled waters he is entering, but I have my doubts. Mererid answers by inverting the question to ask why she would write in anything other than her mother tongue. We are all very tired by this point, and I can sense the tension rising. Karen, whose views on both the language and Welsh independence are no secret, is silent. Welsh, I interject, since I know Jorge better than the others, and wish to defuse the ominous atmosphere raised by his question, is a living language, nor is the decision to write in Welsh some kind of contrarian whim, as it might be to write in Esperanto or a fictional language such as Martian. Jorge concedes the point.

The following day we have a busy programme of activities which begins, for me, with a newspaper interview followed by a conference at the Centro Cultural de España, during which Mererid speaks eloquently about the history of the Welsh language and poetic form and I give a rather rambling talk on Welsh poets of the mid-twentieth century; David Jones and the two Thomases – R.S. and his more famous namesake Dylan (who, I have learned, is the second most widely translated English language poet of the twentieth century, after T.S. Eliot). This is followed by trilingual readings, masterfully hosted by Jorge. That night we return to the Palace of the Potato Chip, where I am beset by an unforeseen attack of inner rage. I cannot quite comprehend this in myself, and my frustration in not identifying the source of my anger – apart from the usual insomnia and compulsive twitching – is consumed by a deeper self-criticism, self-loathing even, and a severe questioning of the whole edifice of literary enterprise and its accompanying paraphernalia; public readings, interviews and the endless outpouring of words, words, words. I drink too much Malbec, which, given my regular intake of prescription opioids, does nothing to help. This state of mind makes for less than ideal preparation for the following day's events, when Tiffany and I are due to launch new bilingual poetry collections at the Eterna Cadencia store in Palermo, one of the loveliest bookshops in the world, a place in which my own verses, as I read, sound like a feeble chirruping against the silent symphony of great works that line the walls around us.

*   *   *

Finally, we take our leave of Buenos Aires, and board a morning flight south to Puerto Madryn, where we are booked into the Hotel Gran Madryn, which is anything but grand; rather, it is shy and homely. Puerto Madryn reminds me a little of some or other Welsh coastal town transplanted to the south Atlantic. I am curious to learn more about Patagonia, and hope to like it, despite the summary dismissal of the place offered by Jorge Luis Borges to Paul Theroux, who travelled here over forty years ago,

Borges saying, "It's a dreary place. A very dreary place," and suggesting Theroux stay a few more days in Buenos Aires instead. But my room at the hotel presents a view of the ocean, and I am delighted to observe a pod of whales cavorting in the distance while, in the foreground, young Argentine boys practice rugby on the beach. My relief at being away from the metropolis is enhanced by the salty freshness of the wind, and the clear light of the antipodean spring. In his book *Gwalia Patagonia,* Jon Gower, an intrepid world traveller, somewhat hesitantly enjoys Puerto Madryn, also. He invites the reader to "think Skegness on the edge of the Kalahari," and continues: "Harsh and desiccated in the arc-lamp heat of summer, in the winter, whipping winds keen over the dried landscape as if wailing for the souls of all lost tourists." But, he concedes, "this place, windswept and on the very rim of the Atlantic, can very swiftly feel a bit like home."

In the afternoon, Fernando Coronato, a local historian of Italian heritage married to a galesa – a woman of Welsh descent – shows us around the Museo del Desembarco in Puntas Cuevas, the exact site where the first one hundred and fifty-three Welsh pilgrims disembarked from the clipper ship *Mimosa* on July 28th, 1865. The emigrants were seeking a new life, away from the intolerance they endured under English linguistic and religious hegemony. But neither did these migrants especially wish to become Argentines. Jorge Fondebrider spells it out in the chapter dedicated to the Welsh in his own book on the region: "To suppose for one second that the Welsh who arrived in Patagonia in the mid-1860s travelled there in order to become Argentines would be utterly naive. The Welsh came in order to continue being Welsh, without the inconvenience of having England for a neighbour, and at the same time imagining that Argentina would not be bothered by the loss of a substantial chunk of territory."

However, despite their stubborn insistence on remaining Welsh, the immigrants did not harbour expansionist colonial ambitions, and their relations with the indigenous population, while mutually suspicious at first, were crucial to their survival; they would not have managed had they not befriended the local Tehuelche people, who taught the newcomers how to find fresh water and hunt guanaco, a native camelid closely related to the llama, alpaca and vicuña. But all this lay ahead; the first days and weeks were extremely arduous, as the new arrivals sought to establish their settlement and find ways of acquiring sufficient food to secure their continued existence through the southern winter.

We are given a tour of the museum, and then descend to the beach where we see the caves in which, Fernando explains, the settlers spent their first nights, many of them making these damp, rocky recesses their homes for months to come. Later that evening we are welcomed by the Asociación Cultural Galesa (Welsh Cultural Association) of Puerto Madryn, in Tŷ Toschke, where they also hold weekly Welsh language and cookery classes. Our hosts are quietly proud of their cultural inheritance, in a way that blends their identities as both Welsh and Argentinian.

I was sceptical, at first, about what seemed to me the essentially nostalgic nature of Welsh Patagonia. I felt that the affiliation with the mother country had developed into a kind of collective fantasy, and there was a strong sense that the idea of Wales that many Welsh Patagonians entertained was very far removed from the reality that, for instance, my daughters grew up with in the multicultural environment of contemporary Cardiff. Theirs was a pastoral and romanticised vision, lodged conceptually in ideas of hearth, home and *hiraeth* and, geographically, in the hinterland of rural west and north Wales. The Welsh language was key to this, the glue that held the concept together, and the identity package was tempered by an Argentine nationalism that brought the Welsh population in line with the rest of the country. I was confused and slightly ashamed by my ambivalence towards the Welsh Patagonians: they were, by and large, kind and generous people without great financial resources, trying to get on with their lives, and I had no right to make uninformed judgements about them. To compound my discomfort, my spoken Welsh was rusty, to say the least, never having acquired fluency, and neglecting to speak the language for some years; consequently I was more at ease speaking Spanish with the locals.

Our ethnic allegiance is a matter of chance – we have no say as to which ethnicity we are born into – but our cultural identity is a matter of choice. As for race, the very idea, at least as I understand it, is a myth, and even ethnicity is a can of worms. Perhaps cultural identity is all we need to consider, and that too, at times, presents a headache. We have a heritage, both in our genes and in our culture, and they are by no means the same thing. An Ancestry.com test has revealed that 83% of my DNA is a blend of Welsh, Irish and Scots, and the remainder is 7% Jewish, 6% German, 3% English and 1% Scandinavian. Thus I might choose to represent myself, if I were a tourist brochure, as a hybrid of predominantly Celtic provenance, with a dash of Jewish melancholy and a flash of Germanic steel. The cultural affiliation I have made, however, is with the land of my birth. The extent to which any of the DNA material becomes absorbed into my chosen identity is up to me. I cannot escape the pure randomness of this inheritance, just as I cannot escape the current significance of my cultural identity, here in a place where 'being Welsh' has been grafted curiously onto the fact of 'being Argentine', or rather, the other way around. My companions must also align themselves within these rather arduous confines. I suspect that Mererid and Karen have no trouble at all adapting. Tiffany, who was born in Berlin to English parents, who speaks no Welsh, but has been resident in Wales for twenty years and is considered an honorary Welsh poet is, despite being made welcome, more of an outsider than any of us in this hybrid and yet strangely exclusive world.

Jorge, the prime agent in organising the tour, has titled our joint adventure 'Forgetting Chatwin', based on his opinion that the English author's travelogue, *In Patagonia*, which brought its author immediate fame, and which, according to the blurb on my edition, "reinvented travel writing", is a calumnious and dishonest assault on the sensibilities of Patagonians. Members of the Welsh community, in particular, were hostile to Chatwin's account, which they deemed snide and patronising.

I can fully appreciate why Bruce Chatwin made himself so unpopular with the Welsh in Patagonia. In many ways, he was precisely the kind of Englishman they had come to South America to escape from. In his Introduction to the 2005 reprint of *In Patagonia*, the admirably impartial Nicholas Shakespeare, also Chatwin's biographer, admits to the unwelcome incongruence of the arrival among these "private and religious farmers" of "a young man with a socking great forehead and blue staring eyes who bowled into their village wearing green Bermuda shorts and announced himself in a ringing public-school accent as Bruce Chatwin." The locals' reaction to his appearance reminded me of Xan Fielding's similar aversion when the freeloading Chatwin descended on his Spanish home with an unassailable sense of entitlement, convinced of his own irresistibility. Arriving promptly at lunchtime each day, he drove the otherwise restrained Fielding to distraction: "I can't stand it. Either we've got to go or Bruce has to come at a different time," he complained to his wife, Magouche, who in turn claimed that Bruce regarded himself "as a sort of present to mankind." "He felt he was welcome everywhere," Chatwin's wife Elizabeth recalled: "He couldn't imagine not being welcome."

And yet the liberties Chatwin took with those he wrote about in Patagonia have never been forgotten by them, and for good reason. As Shakespeare writes: "whereas V.S. Naipaul insulted the important, powerful people when he wrote about Argentina ... Bruce upset the little people, those who could not answer back." Particular offence was taken by individuals such as Edmundo Williams who, Chatwin implies, "because he was single ... was other things too." Edmundo's life was changed by his depiction in the book, and not in a good way. "He had received this stranger politely. He knew nothing about appearing in a book and suddenly, two years later, other strangers start coming to his door asking personal questions he does not want to answer." And it goes on: described by one of Shakespeare's informants as like "the captain of the First XI", and by another as "very narcissistic", Chatwin appeared on Nita Starling's doorstep requesting that she wash his clothes. She refused. When he received hospitality during his Patagonian jaunt, which was often, he didn't always offer thanks, disappearing at dawn without so much as a goodbye.

The alleged motive for his journey to Patagonia lay in Chatwin's boyhood fascination with a scrap of reddish fur, belonging to a giant sloth or mylodon, wrapped in tissue paper, inside a pill box, amidst an assortment of other curios from distant lands in the dining room of his grandmother Isobel's house. The piece of skin was a gift from Isobel's cousin Charles Milward, who, according to family legend, had run away to sea and was shipwrecked on the coast of Patagonia. The skin became a fetish for the boy Chatwin, "an object without real value" as he himself described it, "but desirable in great measure, which can thus inflame and satisfy a lover's illicit fantasy." "Never have I wanted anything as I wanted that piece of skin," Chatwin later claimed. He was an avid collector throughout his life and had been trained at Sothebys, where he worked for several years before setting out on his travels. W.G. Sebald, in a short essay titled 'The Mystery of the Red-Brown Skin' asserts that a longing for that piece of skin was the metaphor that sent Chatwin on his journey, where "he really did believe he found a tuft of sloth hair in the same cave." Chatwin's wife, Elizabeth, said that he did bring "something of the kind" back from the journey, and Sebald wonders whether the quest for the Mylodon skin and Chatwin's subsequent "mania for gathering and collecting" – and his need to invest the fragments he found with meaning – was an expression of some deeply felt need, "reminding us of what we, as living beings, cannot reach." Equating this insistence on the endowment of meaning onto objects with "the deepest of the many layers of the writing process," Sebald speculates that this is what lies behind the universal appeal of Chatwin's work. But there is more to this "lover's illicit fantasy", as Sebald pointedly observes: "Chatwin saw his journeys to the ends of the earth as expeditions in search of a lost boy, and thought he might have found him, as if in a mirror, in Gaiman, when he met the shy pianist Enrique Fernandez, who has since died of AIDS (like Chatwin himself) at the age of forty."

Jon Gower summarises the hurt still felt by some members of the Welsh community in Patagonia, decades after Chatwin's book was published:

> When Chatwin strayed away from the truth in his travelogues, real people, with real feelings, got hurt. As we know, he had upset people in the lower valley, and he didn't leave the Andean Welsh unscathed either. Clery Evans,

granddaughter of the legendary John Daniel Evans, still
bristles at the description of her father, Milton, as a drunken
clownish sot who would yell out, demanding, 'Gimme
another horse piss' every time he wanted another beer,
before 'draining the bottle'. Chatwin also redacts a story
Milton told him about sheep scab, with an off-colour punch-
line, but goes one step further when he suggests that Milton
tells the story over and over again. Little wonder his
daughter Clery is aggrieved, still hurting after all these
years. She thinks Chatwin's lack of Spanish led to a lack of
sophistication. Her view of him is splenetic, the views of a
cultivated, bookish woman who still feels the slight to her
loved one, and dismisses Chatwin like sweeping a fly off her
best china. 'Insignificant, a small insignificant man, dull and
charmless. He was interested in people only if they could
help him, or supply picturesque material. Or if they had
good bodies like the Bolivians.'

Chatwin's book has not stood the test of time, even of the few interceding decades. His prose is beguiling but stylised, on occasion lifted straight out of Hemingway: "A country boy stood by the bar. He was shaky on his feet but he kept his head up like a gaucho. He was a nice-looking boy with curly black hair and he really was very drunk." His account leaps from scene to scene in a way that suggests the minimalist's disdain for grand narratives, but fails to deliver either context or any cogent sense of continuity. As Paul Theroux, a friend of Chatwin's, asks: "How had he travelled from here to there? How had he met this or that person? Life was never so neat as Bruce made out." Besides, as Clery Evans mentions, he barely spoke or understood Spanish. How on earth did that work?

While Chatwin is entertaining at times – since the anecdote is his true metier and his constant fallback – there is an absence at the core of the work; too often the overriding impression is one of hollowness, specifically the hollowness of his claim that "I'm not interested in the traveller, I'm interested in what the traveller sees." There is no such thing as the impartial observer, and Chatwin's observations are so evidently prejudiced by his character and class that his stated determination to leave himself out of the story only makes his presence all the more evident. Chatwin's book is all about the traveller, even when it isn't. And there is something troubling about what is left out, the lacunae in Chatwin's account of his journey, as well as the fabrication or falsification of what he does see. But in the end it is not his inventions (or lies, as he himself called them) that many readers find offensive, so much as the indiscriminate way in which he inserts them, affecting the very people he has come, uninvited, to live amongst, as a sort of posh parasite. Where a more honest or accomplished writer might have forged this kind of decorative nonfiction or semi-fictionalised memoir with integrity – or at least without causing offence to its subjects – Chatwin invents in order to suit his own purposes, nefariously contradicting his own claim not to be interested in the traveller. He certainly did not heed Chekhov's advice to writers that when editing, you should look out for the parts where you lied. And I suspect he would have exasperated even his idol, Ernest Hemingway, whose short stories he carried in his rucksack, sending the old wino's famous bullshit detector into a frenzy of flashing lights.

★   ★   ★

On our second day in Puerto Madryn we climb into a minibus and head for Puerto Pirámides, to go whale-watching. The drive north allows us to take a look at the blasted interior, endless scrub falling away into the distance under an enormous sky. We pass a herd of guanaco, or a single family, as our guide for the day, César, explains: "one alpha male and many females." The males of the species fight for dominance, he tells us, by biting the genitals of their competitors. César's English is rather special, never more so than when explaining the sex life of the Southern Right Whale, and his spoken language contains rich examples of mispronunciation and creative translation. For example: "You remember when you were very chilled the Moby Dick?" (trans: 'do you remember, from childhood, the story of Moby Dick?'), and: "The whales is the boat of the chwain" (trans: 'whales have a lot of fleas', *chwain* being Welsh for a flea), and on arrival at the maritime museum in Puerto Pirámides: "In different rooms we have escalator of the worlds" (possible translation: 'as we progress through the museum, we are exposed to different geological and historical eras').

I enjoy César's surreal explanations, and he is an entertaining and charming guide, but eventually I eschew the group tour and wander off on my own to examine the skeleton of a whale. Afterwards, donning orange life jackets, we take to sea in a small vessel, and come up close to living specimens. The boat dips and bobs in the water, and as we approach the whales, one of them turns to dive, its mighty tail crashing into the water at our side with a loud thwack, causing our suddenly very small boat to lurch from side to side. Despite their size, at no point do we feel threatened by these enormous, benign mammals, and their interest in us – just another batch of tourists come to gawp – is minimal. I feel humbled by the experience, and shocked that for centuries these beautiful creatures should have been hunted down for their oil. The species is Ballena Franca or the Southern Right Whale, so called because it was deemed the 'correct' whale to hunt. The whales, inspiring in their majesty, fill me with an impending sense of loss, as though they were no longer real, but revenants from a world that has already disappeared.

The sky here is vast. The next day, it spreads like a giant mantle around us as we visit the Welsh-speaking community of Trelew. We join a class at the local school, and then do our stuff again, Mererid in Welsh and I in Spanish, at the Tertulia Literaria of the Asociación San David, coordinated by novelist and poet Carlos Dante Ferrari. The evening closes with poetry readings, and the following day we move on to Gaiman, a town with more than its fair share of quaint tea rooms. We eat a hearty lunch in the local pub, and are then whisked off to visit some chapels, and to take high tea in the town hall, where we are served scones with lashings of cream, Welsh cakes and jammy dodgers, followed by music from a four-piece male ensemble and poems by Mererid set to music and sung by a women's choir. In the evening, we are back in Puerto Madryn for a poetry reading in the Escuela Mutualista, coordinated by Ariel Williams, a poet and schoolteacher, who, I learn, caused a small scandal by refusing to award a chair when presiding at the Eisteddfod a couple of years ago. Such are the perils of close-knit communities. Ariel's poetry, however, written in sparse, laconic Spanish is a real find, and I immediately recruit him for my anthology.

Throughout our stay in Puerto Madryn, as well as on the trips to Puerto Pirámides, to Gaiman and Trelew, I take to photographing the dogs of Patagonia. These are generally large, laid-back strays, with no clear ties of affiliation; rather, as I glean from Anselmo Evans, the barman in the waterfront café at Puerto Madryn, they are adopted into a community and fed – if they are lucky – by more than one individual or family, so that they develop a routine by which they drop by on their selected people in the course of a week, without wearing out the compassion, or the scraps, of any single household.

> Even though you walk barefoot on the rough wharves
> of your own thought, you will have to be profoundly distracted
> not to receive in vain the friendship of the kingdom,
> not to go roaming with the possum.

Jorge Aulicino, 'A somewhat difficult syntax'.

Patagonia (Argentina & Chile), September 2013

Early on Sunday, after four nights in Puerto Madryn, we begin our overland crossing of the the boundless Patagonian hinterland towards the town of Trevelin and the Andes. When I recall that landscape I think of the Welsh word 'paith' (prairie), perhaps because, for me, its monosyllabic exhalation, ending in a voiceless fricative, echoes the English words 'death' and 'wraith' (though rhyming with neither). We travel in two vehicles: the first is driven by Hans Schulz, an Argentine of German stock, who has taken charge of this leg of the adventure. Hans, an anthropologist by training, has worked as a schoolteacher and a journalist, and is a well known figure in the Andean town of Bariloche, where he takes tourists, mostly North American, on excursions into the mountains and the adjoining prairie. A big-hearted, ursine figure with a booming, infectious laugh, Hans is also a thoughtful, engaging companion with a deep knowledge of the indigenous peoples of the region. I join Hans in his van, along with Jorge and Tiffany. The other car is an SUV belonging to the Chilean poet Verónica Zondek, who has driven from her home in Valdivia, near the Pacific shore, accompanied by the Argentine poet Jorge Aulicino, Auli to his friends (amongst whom I count myself). In their car also travel Mererid, Karen and Nia.

The first puncture occurs about two hours out, *donde Cristo perdió el mechero* (where Christ lost the cigarette lighter), as one of my preferred Spanish adages has it, to express the 'back of beyond'. There is very little traffic on this road, but eventually, after failing to remove the punctured tyre, we flag down a truck and ask the driver for a lift to Las Plumas, the next (and only) settlement on our route before Trevelin, where we have arranged to meet the other group for a pit stop. There we might borrow a mechanical tool to loosen the bolts on the wheel, as it is too stiff to change, and Hans has bent the crosshatch trying to force the issue. So Hans and Jorge stay with the van, while Tiffany and I head off in the truck on our mission. Its driver, who introduces himself as Rodolfo, and who resembles a younger and slimmer Sylvester Stallone, owns a cattle ranch off the road between Las Plumas and Trevelin. He speaks some English and tells us that although he has been to Europe once, he does not enjoy travelling because he has everything he wants in Patagonia. I believe him; he is a man who is evidently not only satisfied with what he has, but truly inhabits his native landscape. His family came to Patagonia in 1916 from Piedmont – 'by accident', he adds, without explaining further. He farms, like his brothers, but he leaves the day-to-day running of the ranch and its many thousands of cattle to a manager. He likes the solitude of the landscape here, likes what he calls the sense of *nada*, of nothing. This 'nada' reminds me of Paul Theroux's summary of the prairie: "The landscape had a gaunt expression, but I could not deny that it had readable features and that I existed in it ... I thought: Nowhere is a place."

Las Plumas is a strange little wild west settlement in the middle of the steppe. To give some sense of scale, it is capital of the Mártires department of Chubut province. Mártires has a land area of 15,445 square kilometres – three-quarters the size of Wales – but the population is only 977, giving a density of 0.1 people per square kilometre. Rodolfo drops Tiffany and me off at the settlement's filling station and garage, but before leaving, he invites us to visit his ranch once the puncture has been fixed. You are welcome to stay the night, he adds. How do we find it? I ask. Oh, it's easy, he says: it's about an hour's drive, on the right. You can't miss it. I peer down the road into the famous *nada* of the prairie. Perhaps he is right, and we won't be able to miss it. There haven't been any buildings in evidence along the road thus far, fifty kilometres from the place where we had the puncture. On the western horizon, the clear blue sky is fringed by a dense accumulation of cumulus.

Next door to the garage sits a tin-shack canteen where the other group is waiting to rendezvous with us – and has been waiting for quite a while. I explain the situation to Verónica and Auli, who head off to the garage, borrow the necessary tool, and drive back up the road towards our two stranded companions. Eventually, an hour and a half later, both vehicles reappear, the borrowed tool is returned to the mechanic, money is offered and refused and, having filled both cars with fuel, we are ready to move on.

After Las Plumas, the landscape changes: there are rugged hills and bizarre rock formations and spires and huge slabs of sandstone rising from the meseta, and clouds, on occasion vertical layerings of cloud like nothing I've seen before. All this remote splendour is intoxicating. The road spears its way through this lonely terrestrial magnificence. Nowhere is a place, I think. Tiffany, prone to exaggeration at times, declares that she could happily die here, which, I reflect, is not quite the same as saying it is a good place to die. Somewhere along the way, in the midst of this wilderness, we pass a track off to the right, and a dilapidated sign points towards a ranch, out of sight, that I guess must belong to Rodolfo.

Discounting the two hours at Las Plumas we have been driving for seven hours, most of it to the accompaniment of Hans's preferred Bob Dylan soundtrack, and the sun is beginning to sink, golden orange behind the slabs of timeless rock, as in the far distance the snow-covered mountains of the cordillera come into view. I am adrift in time and space, and it is as if all sense of self falls away and I am a particle spinning along this empty road alongside a mass of other, errant particles blown towards infinity, with no idea of what it is I am supposed to be, nor why I am a seeker of poets for translation into another language; nor do I even know what poetry is, other than through the living of it, of which this journey might be an example, so, since she is there, and I am curious, I ask Tiffany – who is a fine poet – what poetry is and she says: I don't know, but I know what poetry isn't; so I ask what it isn't, and she says: lazy language, cliché, sentiment, propaganda, theory written backwards. She elucidates: lazy thought lies behind lazy language, clichés of thought and emotion lie behind clichés of language and off-the-page sentimentality; propaganda has no place in poetry, she says, nor writing that is programmatic and which relies on a plan of execution even before the first word is written, and which expects the poem to carry out some kind of auto-critical function; that is not poetry, but a sort of writing by numbers and that is what I mean by theory written backwards. Poetry is … negative capability, she adds, after a pause, the freedom to dwell in a state of purposeful uncertainty. I am impressed by her lucidity and, as we continue to ply the ruined landscape, I jot down what she has said in my notebook.

Perhaps, I speculate, and not for the first time, as I digest those last words – 'to dwell in a state of purposeful uncertainty' – that is precisely the attitude one might hold as an ideal, in life, as in art.

Twenty kilometres outside Trevelin, shortly after nightfall, we suffer our second puncture. Parked at the roadside, the lights of Esquel and Trevelin visible in the distance, there is a tremendous, unholy silence around us, and I imagine an unspecified future, in which some vehicle passes this spot and its occupants catch a fleeting glance of us as we stand at the roadside, fragile ghosts suspended in an eternal present. To our great relief, Hans fixes the tyre with the bent crosshatch, and finally, five hours overdue, we arrive in Trevelin, have dinner at the designated restaurant, the manager greeting us courteously despite the meal having been prepared long before, the staff waiting for us, for all that we could observe, with exemplary patience, and we are then installed at the Casa de Piedra or Stone House, owned by a grumpy German, which, in defiance of its name, is done up in timber like a Tyrolean ski lodge.

After the crossing of the prairie – an experience that felt other-worldly at the time, and still does in memory – and our late evening arrival in Trevelin, the trip takes on a markedly different aspect. It feels to me as though the new geography, far from the Atlantic and the side of the Americas that faces – albeit at a great distance – the Old World, has given way to the much more radical idea of 'the West'; that insistent movement towards undiscovered places and the setting sun that so obsessed the adventurers of the nineteenth century, both here in the South as well as in North America. The pioneer spirit of those early settlers lives on in their descendants, here in the foothills of the Andes, in a way that differentiates them from their compatriots on the Atlantic seabord.

Besides being welcoming, Trevelin is pretty, and boasts a Welsh school and yet more tea rooms, including the splendid *Casa de Nain Maggie* (the name is a Spanish-Welsh hybrid meaning 'House of Grannie Maggie'). The following day, at a reception, local children perform a Welsh dance for us, and we return the gesture with a poetry reading. The table at which we read is draped with the flags of Argentina, Wales and Chile. To me, it feels strangely like a homecoming, although I have never been here before. I have always felt as though I might end up in a place like this, on the edge of nowhere. The great shadow of the Andes falls across the town, an invitation and a challenge. In the nineteenth century, Welsh pioneers, led by John Daniel Evans – Clery's grandfather – set out across the cordillera on horseback, and a breed of cowboys came into being whose descendants still farm the land. Evans and his comrades helped secure the territory for Argentina at a time when much of the land was disputed between that country and Chile. Thus the Welsh settlers truly became Argentines.

On a walk the next day, a horseman rides onto the road and

stops to pass the time of day. He is accompanied by four large dogs, who sniff at me respectfully but, like the horse, know exactly who is boss. He gives his name simply as Muñoz, and says that he looks after cattle belonging to a landowner from Bariloche. I ask to take his picture, to which he graciously accedes, one of his dogs posing with him.

We drive on to Bariloche, and stay at the sumptuous Llao Llao hotel, which reminds me of the Overlook, as depicted in Stanley Kubrick's film adaptation of the Stephen King novel, *The Shining*. The hotel's deco takes the Tyrolean chalet concept to a new level of grandeur, and Jorge explains to me that since 1939 this place has been a choice holiday destination for Argentine politicians and celebrities.

The walls of the corridors are lined with photographs of party-goers from the black and white era – just as in the bar of the Overlook Hotel, where Nicholson's Jack Torrance begins his maniacal meltdown. I pick up an old photograph album in one of the lounges, and find a picture of revellers, their faces heavy with eye-shadow, making thespian poses. Whereas the 1940s brought postwar austerity to most European gatherings, in Argentina people partied as though Scott Fitzgerald's Jazz Age had never ended.

We have been invited to stay for two nights, without charge, in exchange for performing at a 'cultural evening' for local residents, most of whom are of German, or else of middle-European Jewish descent. Hans, Jorge tells me, has achieved something of a miracle in helping bring these two historically estranged communities together. I am curious to learn how he has managed it.

Hans came from a German family with mixed affiliations. In 1936, his father was sent as a sixteen-year-old to attend a Hitler youth camp in the Fatherland, but returned to Argentina before World War Two broke out. After 1945, following their defeat, Bariloche became a popular destination for eminent Nazis, many of whom settled in the town and the surrounding area in uncomfortable proximity to its small community of Jews, who had come here to escape those same Nazis during the previous decade. Hans Schulz made it his business to bring into the open, and to own, the collective shame of many members of the German community, much of it brought to light by the arrest of the one time SS officer Erich Priebke, a close friend and associate of Hans' father. Priebke was held responsible for the murder of 355 Italian citizens near Rome on 24 March 1944, in the infamous Ardeantine massacre, and was extradited to Italy in 1996 after being outed by ABC news reporter Sam Donaldson. Fifty years earlier, in 1946, he had escaped from a British POW camp in northern Italy and in 1948 was spirited out of Italy via the 'ratline', an escape route organised by a pro-Nazi German bishop named Alois Hudal, with the blessing of Pope Pius XII. He went on to became a stalwart of the local community in Bariloche, first running a hotel and then a delicatessen selling smoked sausage and other German specialities. During much of Hans' childhood, while his father was president of the town's German-Argentinian Cultural Society, Priebke was vice-president. Priebke was also director of the Colegio Aleman, the German school in Bariloche, a school designed to inculcate traditional German values among its pupils.

Hans had also taught at the town's German School as a young man in the 1980s, but his contract was not renewed after he complained about the lack of instruction given to school pupils about the Holocaust, both at his school and elsewhere in Argentina. Seemingly, this lack has not been properly rectified. In August 2016, a report appeared in the Buenos Aires newspaper *Clarín* about a group of students from a German school in the capital who turned up at a fancy dress party in Bariloche, which was also attended by students from a Jewish school. The first group had swastikas painted on their chests and were sporting Hitler hairstyles and fake moustaches, calling members of the other group 'judios de mierda' ('dirty Jews'). The *Clarín* article reports that the Jewish students reacted violently and both groups of students were expelled from the venue. Apparently, if the pro-Hitler perpetrators had been over sixteen years of age, they would have been liable to up to three years in prison for brandishing Nazi insignia, which is against the law in Argentina. Instead, they were sent on an educational trip to the Holocaust Museum in Buenos Aires.

As I am compiling this account, six years after our visit to Bariloche, I receive news of Hans' sudden death, at the age of sixty-four. The news saddens me, and I wish that I had spent more time with him, got to know him better. He was a compassionate and generous man, a genuine free spirit.

★ ★ ★

We set out from the Llao Llao into the high cordillera, our convoy of poets taking the road into Chile as a snowstorm swirls about us. During the descent, on the Chilean side, the snow turns to sleet, and then to rain. The sodden landscape reminds me of north Wales. We arrive late at our hotel in Valdivia, delayed by both a long wait at the customs post and the weather, and are told we must leave straightaway for the first of our events, at which we speak about our trip across Patagonia – what it meant to us, which it is too early, for me at least, to ascertain – and then read our poems. Another event in a marquee the next day is advertised by a banner that reads *Olvidarse de Chatwin*, with our pictures attached, a rogues' gallery of travelling bards. Now that we are in Chile, the Chatwin theme feels a little redundant, and I am even starting to feel sorry for the man, especially since he met with such a miserable end, emaciated, raving, and terrified, an early casualty of AIDS.

I give my talk on the two Thomases, Dylan and R.S. – who have by now, in my sleep-deprived imaginings, transformed into Waldorf and Statler, that pair of cantankerous old men in *The Muppet Show*, heckling me from their theatre box in the afterlife – and Mererid takes part in a conversation with a Mapuche poet, Victor Cifuentes, about the poetry, and the struggle for survival of their respective languages, set, as both are, against the hegemony of English and Spanish. The Mapuche, whose territory spreads across the entire southern cone, mounted a significant armed resistance to the Spanish invaders at the time of the conquest, and again in the nineteenth century, when they defended themselves against the genocidal campaigns of both the Argentine and Chilean armies. Their culture and language remain under constant threat, despite recent attempts to renew an organised resistance, notably against the clothing company Benneton, who at the beginning of the new millennium bought 900,000 hectares (2.2 million acres) of land on the Argentine side, to rear sheep, which would provide wool for their famous sweaters. This turned Carlo Benneton, who had bought out the British-owned Argentine Southern Land Company, into the biggest landowner in the region. In Jon Gower's account, he cites Benneton as saying: "Patagonia gives me an amazing sense of freedom" – but that freedom, Gower warns, has a hollow ring to it, when one learns that his company went to court to prevent indigenous smallholders from scratching a living on the land he owns, the land that for 13,000 years has been the home of the Mapuche and their ancestors.

In the evening, back in my hotel room, I read about Admiral Lord Cochrane and Bernardo O'Higgins and all the British and Irish who, once the Napoleonic wars were over, found themselves unemployed in Europe and wound up fighting in the wars of independence across South America, and settled there, granted land and citizenship in one or other of the new republics; Colombia, Peru or Chile. It must indeed have seemed like a brave new world back then. With what fantasies of a fresh start did they begin their lives as South Americans? What stories and what other baggage did they bring with them from the Old World, and the realm of Mad King George, and what did they leave behind? Among the constant flow of migrants from the Old World to the New, they were among those, like the Welsh in Argentina, a generation later, who had been invited over by the fledgling republics, though it should be noted that from Cortés onward, up until the present day, no one consulted the indigenous peoples of the Americas about who should settle their land.

PART II

> Here they come
> the decapitated,
> the amputees,
> the torn into pieces,
> those with their coccyx split apart,
> those with their heads smashed in,
> the little ones crying
> inside dark walls
> of minerals and sand.
>
> María Rivera, 'The Dead'.

Teotihuacán, Mexico, April 2014

The ouroboros, whose earliest representation can be found in ancient Egypt, reflects the belief in time as a repeated cycle, or series of cycles, rather than as a linear progression. This understanding of the cosmos was predicated on beliefs concerning the annual flooding of the Nile and the daily passage of the sun. The first of these served as a marker of the year's beginning – of time flowing back on itself, in a loop – and the movement of the sun through the sky replicated this cycle, dipping into the underworld (the waters of Nun) at night, before reappearing in the sky as the next day dawned.

In Greek mythology this task was originally carried out by Helios, and later by Apollo, riding the chariot of the sun. Myths that involve the perpetual repetition of the same event, or series of events, appealed to the Greeks: Prometheus, tied to a cliff, whose liver was removed daily by a visiting eagle; Sisyphus, condemned forever to repeat his task of rolling a rock to the summit of a steep hill, and Ixion, who was tied to an eternally spinning wheel; all invoke a variety of eternal return.

The image of the serpent consuming its own tail – which was later adopted by the alchemists of Renaissance Europe — was also found in the New World. In Mesoamerican cultures, the figure of Quetzalcoatl, the feathered serpent god of wind and air, of dawn, of craft and knowledge, is sometimes depicted as an ouroboros. Its appearance supports the argument that the universe, or at least the human worlds it contains, are themselves subject to destruction and return, in a repeating cycle. And the following words, from the Venezuelan historian, Mariano Picón-Salas, came as a revelation when I first read them in his book *De la conquista a la independencia:*

> Firstly, and in direct contrast to the vital optimism of the Renaissance, of which the Conquistador was, after his fashion, an agent, the indigenous peoples conceived of history in terms of doom and catastrophe. No idea could be further removed from the indigenous mentality than the Western idea of progress. In Aztec theogony, in the terrible legend of the suns, the universe had already been destroyed four times, by tigers, by the winds, by rains of fire, and by water. Each destruction engendered a new race of humans who retained nothing from the previous race, and who were equally impotent before destiny.

No idea could be further removed from the indigenous mentality than the idea of progress. It is a realisation at once shocking and exhilarating to learn that a belief as deeply held as progress might not be universal; that it might, by contrast, be inconceivable. The legend of the suns utterly contradicts the European enlightened or humanistic worldview, whereby the map of human progress is one on which we bravely advance towards a determined destination, like Armstrong on the moon, making his small step which was also a giant step; that we are making inroads, that we are on our way to a better place. Picón-Salas' words, by contrast, stir a familiar suspicion that the idea of progress, in a strictly human sense, is a fallacy.

Walking up the steps to chapel every morning at my boarding school in the 1970s, confronted by the names of the dozens of boys who gave their lives – were sacrificed – in Two World Wars, I remember feeling that all this history, all this preoccupation with death and sacrifice, perpetuated by traditions rooted in patriotism and empire, was of little interest to me or others of my generation; but I also recognised that the whole enterprise of war, duty, and sacrifice represented something fundamental for the tribal culture into which we were being schooled. It suggested a willingness, in principle, for the individual to give his (and in those days it usually was his) own life for a Big Idea. The daily ascent to chapel, and the insistence, throughout our grooming, that if this was good enough for the Old Boys, it might be our fate too, reinforced the notion that the cycle was on repeat, generation after generation, and therefore I never was convinced that there was such a thing as progress, beyond the obvious scientific and medical discoveries that improved the quality of everyday life. There was, rather, a recurring timeline, which went round and round, in which wars would persist, people would continue to die pointlessly for causes which their descendants would cease to care about or else forget, and that ultimately humankind, and specifically men, resorted to behaving like wretched murderous brutes whenever the need, as they saw it, arose.

These thoughts about progress, and of eternal return, preoccupied me as I stood before the temple of the feathered serpent, Quetzalcoatl, in May 2014, on a visit to Teotihuacán, in Mexico.

The site of a vast ancient metropolis, Teotihuacán is little more than an hour's drive from Mexico City. The day I visited, a powerful wind was blowing across the altiplano, raising dust clouds that swirled above the plain and which stirred in me, as such winds always have, a sense of fugitive reality. This feeling of being at the mercy of the wind, and the suggestion of transience that it conveys, sharpened the elusive but palpable excitement I felt at entering the ruins of a vanished world.

I had taken a tourist coach trip and before reaching the site itself we made a scheduled stop at a service station and store, where we were invited to make use of the bathroom facilities, which, we were told, were limited on the site of the ruins. Across the yard from the shop, which sold the usual tourist paraphernalia – reproductions of Aztec masks, ceramic models of animals, real and mythical (dogs, jaguars, coyotes, winged serpents) – was a small enclosure, and behind the wire stood a pair of xoloitzcuintli, or xolos, the hairless dogs that are supposedly the most ancient domesticated breed of canine, dating back over three and half thousand years. Archaeologists have discovered ancient xolo bones at digs, and drawings of dogs that resemble xolos appear on cave walls in the area. The dog's name derives from two words in Nahuatl, the language of the Aztecs: Xolotl, the god of lightning and death, and Itzcuintli, meaning dog: the dog of Xolotl. Its role in Aztec mythology was to guide the souls of the dead through the underworld, Mictlan, and to this end xolos were buried alongside their owners. They were sacred pets, keeping evil spirits at bay; they were also believed to have special healing powers and because they generate heat are used to this day as makeshift hot water bottles. The xolo's hairlessness comes about due to a genetic mutation that is also the cause of its lack of premolars. This trait makes for easy identification on archaeological digs.

My first reaction to the xolos was one of revulsion. Their hairlessness seemed pitiful, as though the dogs, rather than being merely naked, had been flayed alive. It came as no surprise that these animals were also a valued food source for the ancient Mesoamericans who bred them. In the sixteenth century the Spanish invaders also developed an appetite for canine protein, and in the years following the Conquest they almost ate the xolo into extinction.

No one knows for certain who built and occupied Teotihuacán: the Totonac, Otomi and Nahua peoples have all been put forward. The site, which was established over two thousand years ago, covers an area of twenty square kilometres, of which only about a quarter has been excavated. In its day, it was the most populous city in the western hemisphere and contained thousands of residential buildings in addition to the pyramid-temples, which were comparable in size with the largest pyramids of Egypt. The city was sacked and burned in the middle of the sixth century and was abandoned by 700 CE, that is, eight hundred years before the Spanish Conquest.

The principal monuments, the Temples of the Sun and Moon, and the Temple of Quetzalcóatl, are joined by a causeway, known as the Avenue of the Dead. The pyramids must have possessed immense symbolic significance for their builders and the people who lived beside them; archaeologists maintain that this was a society dominated by a powerful priesthood and that the primary purpose of the pyramids was to sacrifice people and animals to the sun and to the ruling gods, among them Quetzalcoatl and the rain god Tlaloc, as well as the god of spring, Xipe Totec, and the Great Spider Goddess, associated with darkness and the underworld, and whose name – if she had one – is not known. In order to keep the sun moving across the sky, and avoid succumbing to perpetual darkness, it was necessary to sacrifice people; most especially to spill their blood, since this appeased the gods. Countless human captives were slaughtered here, and the removal of the victim's heart was a common practice, as was decapitation.

We do not know for sure what caused the city to fall, although theories abound. One of the most convincing of these suggests an internal upheaval: there is evidence of extensive burning in the palaces and temples occupied by the ruling classes, but no signs of external invasion. Did the people rise up against the priestly caste? And if so, what might have caused their revolt?

Accounts from around the world suggest that during the years 535-542 there occurred some sort of global climatic disaster. This may have been caused by either a comet or, more likely, a massive volcanic eruption, from which dust and ashes filled the sky. A drop in temperature, and reports of widespread crop failures, famine, drought and a "dry, dense fog" appear in accounts from as far afield as Ireland, the Middle East and Peru. "A failure of bread" was recorded in the Annals of Inisfallen for the years 536-42, and summer snowfalls were reported in China during the same period. Analysis of oak rings over those years indicate abnormally slow growth in Ireland, and similar results have been found in trees in California and Chile. The evidence for some cataclysmic event over this period is overwhelming, and among the most likely candidates for a volcanic eruption is Ilopango in nearby El Salvador. Ashes and debris would have created a thick veil in the sky, and with the sun obscured from sight, the people of Teotihuacán might well have questioned the efficacy of human sacrifice, on which their cosmology was based, with the result that they attacked and murdered their rulers.

Following the city's demise, its occupants vanished or dispersed, along with numerous other Mesoamerican cultures, before the ascendancy of the Aztecs around 1300. Nevertheless, evidence of Teotihuacano influence can be seen at sites in the Veracruz area, occupied by the Totonac people. And it was here, in 1519, that Hernán Cortés made his first inroads towards the Aztec capital, Tenochtitlán – modern day Mexico City – which he effectively destroyed two years later, with the aid of his Totonac allies.

In Teotihuacán, the gory practices of the city's original inhabitants have not deterred New Age cultists from contriving their own cosmology around the pyramids. The configuration of the buildings has been subject to much speculation, including claims that the main structures along the Avenue of the Dead formed a precise scale model of our entire solar system, despite there being no evidence that the planets Uranus, Neptune and Pluto were known to pre-Columbian societies (and they were not discovered by Western astronomers until 1787, 1846 and 1930 respectively).

While I was standing at the top of the Temple of the Sun, a blonde Caucasian woman, dressed in flowing robes and festooned with beads and bracelets, opened her arms to the sun and started chanting, in a garbled drone, verses which, no doubt, she believed were connecting her to some cosmic force or deity. At every Spring Equinox hundreds of such devotees will climb the 360 steps to the summit of this, the largest of the pyramids; they will stand, like her, with arms outstretched, face the rising sun and carry out homespun rituals, in the belief that at this precise moment, when the portals of mystic energy are thrown wide open, they occupy a unique place in the cosmos. As a bonus, these fans of the paranormal will get a fine view of the vast Walmart store built illegally, a short distance from the temples, in 2004. An investigation later proved that representatives of the giant US chain had bribed Mexican officials in order to go ahead with construction in a protected zone, but the monstrous supermarket remains, a constant reminder of corporate power and administrative corruption in the modern era, oblivious to the chanting of the sun-worshippers looking down on it. It seems, on reflection, a neat collocation of fantasies, the incantatory drone of the faithful drifting out across the altiplano towards the concrete and steel tabernacle of unfettered consumerism.

At the end of the Avenue of the Dead stands the Temple of Quetzalcoatl. Upon its carved wall, which was originally painted hematite red, is depicted the feathered serpent, one of the manifestations of the god. Several mass graves were discovered beside the temple in the 1980s, which, my guidebook informed me, contained the bones of around two hundred men, women and children. They had been sacrificed, hands tied behind their backs, dispelling any notion that such victims were volunteers. 'Mass graves', sadly, is one of those terms that has regained currency in Mexico over the past two decades, along with 'mass killings', as I had discovered two years before, in Guadalajara.

> Another flower but the same but withered: no two,
> no three: only an instant only a hummingbird
> man lasts here on earth.
>
> Luis Felipe Fabre, 'Xochicuicatl'.

Mexico City, April 2014

On returning to Mexico City from Teotihuacán, the wind does not let up. I'm not tired, in spite of hours spent walking in the heat of the day. In my small hotel in Condesa, where I have been resident for the past week, Luis, on duty at reception, offers me a mescal. He has a stash of the stuff, nicely packaged in small, shapely bottles. Mescal used to be regarded as the drink of the poor, but has made a comeback in recent years, usurping tequila as the beverage of choice among the fashionable classes. Mescal is edgy. The taste is chthonic, earthy and mineral. My visit to the Pyramids and the Temple of Quetzalcoatl has unsettled me, and I am quickened by the alchemy of wind and sun, which the mescal does nothing to dispel.

By now it is getting dark. I walk a few blocks from the hotel to the nearest taquería, El Califa, and eat quickly, as though fulfilling an obligation rather than enjoying a meal, then move on to a nearby bar, run by expatriate Argentines, where I take a seat outside. I bring out my tattered copy of Juan Rulfo's short stories, *El llano en llamas*. It is dark, but artificial light spills onto the pavement from the bar and it is just about bright enough to read by.

Juan Rulfo was writing in the wake of the Mexican revolution, which coincided with his own childhood in an orphanage in Jalisco. These were dangerous times, and the young Juan, looking out onto the street, often saw corpses hanging from wooden posts. As a child, he spent much of his time reading, because, he claimed, you couldn't go out for fear of getting shot. The stories in *El llano en llamas* lead the reader into a space of silence and mystery, where reality breaks down and we enter a sort of afterlife, if the afterlife that awaits us is joyless, drained of colour and populated only by the most wretched of the earth. But there are ghosts, of that we can be sure. Ghosts are the elusive subjects of Rulfo's dark and perplexing novel, *Pedro Páramo*, which, on its appearance in 1955 made a profound impression on the Spanish-speaking literary world, earning accolades from writers such as Jorge Luis Borges, Miguel Ángel Asturias and Gabriel García Márquez. The Chilean writer Jorge Edwards has described the novel as "dominated by a disturbing ambiguity: we cannot tell which characters are alive and which are dead, and speaking to us from the afterlife."

But it was in his short stories, published two years earlier, that Rulfo learned his craft. "The practice of writing the short story disciplined me," he once wrote, "and made me see the need to disappear and to leave my characters the freedom to talk at will ..."

Rulfo's stories are bleakly beautiful, pared down to essentials, although they take false turnings and lead to many dead ends. Without wishing to reinforce stereotypes, it must be conceded that the rhythms and lacunae of Rulfo's prose remind one of what Octavio Paz wrote about 'the Mexican' in his once influential, though now largely discredited study, *The Labyrinth of Solitude*: "his language is full of reticences, of metaphors and allusions, of unfinished phrases, while his silence is full of tints, folds, thunderheads, sudden rainbows, indecipherable threats ...". There are threats aplenty in Rulfo's stories, but they are unformed, vaguely defined, and usually at some distance from the place of narration – yet always getting closer. Events take place in a half-light, as characters stumble towards yet another failure, or death.

In the first story of Rulfo's collection, 'They have given us land', a group of four landless men trudge across an arid plain. They have been allocated land rights by the government in a feeble attempt at reform, but the ground beneath them is dry, stony, utterly unsuitable for planting anything that might grow. There had been more than twenty in their group when they set out, and they had horses and rifles, but now there were only four; their rifles and horses have been handed over to the government official who tells them that they do not need them, and that they should be grateful they have land at all; the landowners would certainly never have given them any. But in fact they have nothing, apart from a hen, which one of them keeps hidden inside his coat. "After walking for so many hours without coming across even the shadow of a tree, even the seed of a tree, nor the root of anything, we heard the barking of dogs." The men feel a glimmer of hope: a village must be near. But the smoke and the sound of the dogs have been carried on the wind; they are still far from anywhere, and the reader is left wondering whether the village was not some kind of hallucination.

A black cloud passes overhead and the men hope it will rain, but they are cheated:

> A drop of water falls, big, fat, making a hole in the ground and leaving a lump as if it were spittle. It drops alone. We wait for other drops to fall. It doesn't rain. Now if you look at the sky, you can see the storm cloud far away, running, in a hurry. The wind from the village nudges up to it, pushing it against the blue shadows of the mountains. And the drop that fell by mistake is devoured by the earth, which makes it disappear into its thirst.

The raindrop is a 'mistake', the men are tired, the sun is too hot. When they finally reach some huts, the man with the hen disappears and the others enter the village, but the story ends there, with no sense of closure. We do not learn what they do, only that the land they have been given is now 'up ahead'. But the land that is up ahead is the same as the land that lies behind them, parched and good for nothing. As Juan Villoro writes, in Rulfo's short stories "actions take place in a time that never stops recurring, a territory that shrinks or expands in the perception of the witnesses ... The narrative discontinuity does not lead to a story that must be 'put together' by the reader, but rather a plain on which everything has always happened. Few actions are recounted twice; however, circularity is forcefully implied: every instant is repetition." Following the logic of the ouroboros, what lies ahead mirrors what lies behind, in an endless cycle.

In another story, 'Don't you hear the dogs barking', a man carries his adult son on his back to try and find a doctor in the town of Tonaya. The younger man is wounded. It is night-time and the father cannot see where he is going. The reader likewise struggles to follow the direction of the narrative, confused by the lack of any explanation on the father's part. The sound of dogs barking raises the hope that they are approaching civilisation, and as the pair draw near to the town we learn through the older man's faltering monologue that his son is a thief and a murderer, and he is only carrying him out of respect for the boy's dead mother.

In these two stories, the barking of dogs indicates the existence, if not of hope, precisely, then of some form of life, of human dwellings at the very least. But perhaps that is a false reading, since the barking of dogs might also signify death: in Mesoamerican cultures, as we have seen, dogs, as guides to the underworld, were frequently buried with their people. And at the end of Malcolm Lowry's *Under the Volcano*, as if in bitter acknowledgment of this custom, a dead dog is thrown down the ravine after the body of the murdered Consul.

Juan Rulfo's biographer, Reina Roffé, presents Rulfo as a writer preoccupied by "the disillusionment that failed historical processes produce in the individual and collective consciousness." His characters, she claims, inhabit an existence where joy is unknown; they have been banished from paradise. "Nomads," she writes, "who, by necessity or desire (always unattainable), are 'elsewhere'; ontological or geographical exiles, whose dreams fade away with the onset of actual fact." Roffé's account seems to suggest that such a description was equally applicable to Rulfo himself. She describes a man "wholly dedicated to the pursuit of failure." Shy and reserved, in dread of public events where he might be obliged to speak of his writing, he was prone to bouts of destructive drinking, and on one occasion was found lying naked and comatose in the street, his clothes having been removed by beggars. Carmen Boullosa has even suggested that *Pedro Páramo* could "be profitably explored ... as a novel about the alcoholic experience; certainly it recounts the worst night of sweaty intoxication imaginable and also describes the mother of all hangovers." While Boullosa's summary might appear reductive, it is true that the desperate sense of absence at the heart of *Pedro Páramo* could be likened to the most abject cravings of the addictive experience, in a realm populated by hungry ghosts.

Rulfo left behind only around three hundred pages of writing, but those pages, according to García Márquez, are as important to us as the extant writings of Sophocles – quite a claim. He published his two books in early middle age but for the next thirty years did not publish anything, although he continued taking and occasionally publishing photographs, as he had done before embarking on his career as a writer. He destroyed the long awaited second novel, *La Cordillera*, a few years before dying at the age of sixty-eight, in 1986. Following his death, his widow, Clara Aparicio, sanctioned the publication of his notebooks and some fragments from the unfinished novel, although, as she confesses in her introduction to the notebooks, Rulfo would not have approved, and she felt she might be doing "something awful" in publishing them. The notebooks came out with the Mexican publisher Era in 1994, but are now out of print and practically unobtainable.

Juan Rulfo once explained his long literary silence in an interview: "Writing causes me to undergo tremendous anxiety. The empty white page is a terrible thing." We can recognise Rulfo's empty white page in the desolate plain that the four men traverse in 'They have given us land', with a single drop of rain falling from the leaden sky. While that raindrop might, in another context, be indicative of hope, it is hard to read it as such in the landscape created by Rulfo, where it is likened to a lump of spittle.

I close the book and can hear the wind, gentler now, rustling the leaves of the trees that line the street. An hour has gone by. I feel utterly infiltrated by these stories, as though I were not sitting outside a Mexico City bar, but out there on the windswept plain with Rulfo's refugees, wandering through an eternity of dust and nothingness, *nada*. The empty white page that Rulfo found so terrible reminds me of the map I have been mentally filling in during this trip to Mexico, the map of my own travels. It is there, on every page of my notebook, which lies open on the table beside *El llano en llamas*, and I am reminded of something I once read: "We are always mapping the invisible or the unattainable or the erasable, the future or the past ... and transmuting it into everything it is not ... *into the real.*" And I ask myself, or else I ask the wind that has accompanied me all the long day: *What am I doing here?*

I might reply that I am an eavesdropper on the lives and conversations of others, and that, perhaps, is what attunes me so closely to what I have just been reading. A story by Rulfo makes of you a bystander, an eavesdropper. Juan Villoro puts it this way: "The stories in *El llano en llamas* derive their power from what is revealed in an almost accidental way by means of dialogue or stream of consciousness ... The acoustics in Rulfo are those of the accidentally overheard."

This idea of arriving in a strange place and bearing silent witness to the lives of others brings to mind Alastair Reid's essay, 'On Being a Foreigner'. The personage which Reid designates as the 'foreigner' is distinct from the 'tourist', who is like a dilettante, dipping his toe into the waters of another culture, or the 'expatriate', for whom every other place is compared, constantly and unfavourably, against the ideal of the home country.

The foreigner, in contrast to the expatriate, doesn't really have a home country. His involvement, according to Reid, is with where he is, at any given time. "He has no other home. There is no secret landscape claiming him, no roots tugging at him. He is, if you like, properly lost, and so in a position to rediscover the world, from outside in." The foreigner retains, perhaps as a relic from some mysterious childhood epiphany, the idea "that there might be a place – and a self – instantly recognisable, into which they will be able to sink with a single, timeless, contented sigh. In the curious region between that illusion and the faint terror of being utterly nowhere and anonymous, foreigners live. From there, if they are lucky, they smuggle back occasional undaunted notes, like messages in a bottle, or glimmers from the other side of the mirror."

Sometimes I feel as though I have always been a foreigner, since the first journeys I took with my parents as a small child to places that were, in those days, considered exotic; crossing the Pyrenees on dirt roads in our battered Ford Zephyr; watching red fliers – propaganda against the regime – rise against the backdrop of the Acropolis in the warm wind of the Colonels' Greece; trips to places with names nowadays made familiar by package deal holidays. Alone in Mexico City – known as DF (Distrito Federal) to its residents at the time but since January 2016 rebranded, to conform with the modern fetish for extended acronyms, as CDMX (Ciudad de México) – I feel again the faint thrill of foreignness, and am at ease with it. But the question remains: what am I doing here? And since all travel reflects the traveller back to himself through a shifting lens, I reply, with Reid's words: *I am recording glimmers from the other side of the mirror.*

★ ★ ★

I made my way back to the hotel on Avenida Benjamin Franklin. Back then, it was safe to walk around residential areas of the city alone at night, but Mexican friends tell me that now, at the time of writing, this is no longer the case. The conflict that was wreaking havoc in a number of Mexican states over the time I was in the country has now extended to the capital. A friend spoke to me recently of not wanting his eighteen-year old daughter to live in Mexico, and therefore plans for her to study in Europe. I hear stories of this kind all the time. Any Mexican parent who can afford to do so is likely to think in these terms.

To return to my question, what am I doing here? I could respond that I was carrying out my duties as Creative Wales Ambassador, the portentous title bestowed on me by the Arts Council of Wales for the year 2014, and in which role I had already spent most of the past week giving readings and lectures at different locations around the city. Much of this was facilitated by my friend Pedro Serrano, who had also been responsible for putting me in contact with many of the Mexican poets I aimed to include in my anthology, some of whom I knew already, and others that I would meet over the coming weeks, both here in the capital as well as on my travels in the east and north of the country (I had been advised against travelling west to the state of Guerrero, as originally planned, due to an upsurge in narco violence there). Pedro, an enchantingly unceremonious and absentminded type, and a distinguished poet himself, along with his friend, the philosopher-poet Carlos López Beltrán – one of the few people I know who combines a penetrating intellect with a true gentleness of soul – were the editors and translators of *La Generación del Cordero* (*The Generation of the Lamb*), a landmark anthology of contemporary British and Irish poetry in Spanish translation, published in 2000. These two friends were, in a sense, my guardian angels during the Mexico City phase of my travels.

The day after my arrival, I was whisked off to the National University of Mexico (UNAM) – an institution that boasts student numbers equal to the entire population of Cardiff – by Lucrecia Orensanz, with whom I had been in correspondence for a while, and who translated into Spanish the lecture I had prepared in honour of the Dylan Thomas Centenary, which of course no one knew or much cared about here in Mexico – and why would they? – and which in any case clashed with the Octavio Paz centenary, which itself had become a casualty of the media attention being lavished on Gabriel García Márquez who, though Colombian, was a longterm Mexican resident, and who, by dying the previous week, had selfishly taken the limelight away from Mexico's only Nobel laureate.

At UNAM I was due to give a reading and Q & A, as part of the 'Books and Roses' festivities celebrated on St George's Day, 23 April, which in much of the Spanish speaking world — though originating in Catalonia, whose patron saint is the eponymous Saint Jordi – is an occasion to gift your romantic partner a book or a rose. On the bus across town to University City, Lucrecia told me something about herself. Her father, who was a marine biologist, left Argentina after the military coup in 1976, the family settling in Baja California. Lucrecia said that although she had been in Mexico since the age of five, and spoke Spanish like a Mexican, there was an identifiable something about her, a 'foreigner' quality that Mexicans noticed and which consequently made her feel like one. Usually she shut this down by saying she was brought up in Baja and that was what explained her 'difference'. But if ever anyone got wind of the fact that she was, by birth, an Argentinian (even though she didn't feel like one) then her outsider identity became that much more apparent, and people reacted correspondingly: "Ah, so that's what it is!" People are always seeking neat explanations to justify their prejudices, she said, and Mexicans, in particular, are keenly aware of their Mexicanness, or *mexicanidad*.

The notion of 'core identity' is one that interests me, and I wanted to know more. What were the precise distinguishing features of mexicanidad? I wondered. Lucrecia answered that she had spent her lifetime pondering this very question, but was no closer to an answer than anyone else she knew, though she did say that for Mexicans, 'face' is of supreme importance, and extreme politeness often translates as the saving of face. Mexicans would always accept an invitation, she told me, even if they had no intention of turning up. This seemed to fit with another paradox: Mexicans were among the politest people on earth, and yet their country was torn apart by violent crime, a contradiction addressed, at least in part, by the English philosopher R.G. Collingwood, who wrote: "The most beautiful manners I have met with are in countries where men carry knives". But the question of mexicanidad also persisted in more subtle ways. I was talking only the evening before with Pedro's wife, Alejandra, who had referred to the profoundly layered and complex nature of Mexican society. "As an outsider, you might spend a lifetime trying to integrate," she said, "but you would never truly succeed." I recalled the anthropological concept of 'density', of some cultures being harder for the outsider to penetrate than others; cultures that are intrinsically resistant to outsider integration, less porous. But perhaps for the foreigner, as Alastair Reid used the term, the porousness or otherwise of a place is an irrelevance. Reid's foreigner never intends to integrate. Perhaps, at heart, foreigners know that home is a state of mind rather than a place or a people.

Lucrecia deposits me at UNAM, and hands me over to the novelist and journalist Jorge F. Hernández, a true professional, who had also hosted my main event at the Book Fair in

Guadalajara a couple of years before, and claims to have shed fifty kilograms in the interim. There is certainly a lot less of him than the last time we met, though fifty kilos seems a preposterous amount of oneself to lose. I am also introduced to Ana Franco, a poet and editor on the magazine *Periódico de Poesía*. Ana acts as a general guide and counsellor in helping me find my way around the city that first week. Over the next few days, I give a reading at the Cultural Centre of Condesa, deliver my Dylan Thomas lecture to a small but resilient audience at the *Círculo de Traductores* (Translators' Circle), where I have a rambling conversation with Pedro about translation before a bemused and supremely patient audience. I also enjoy informative and fruitful meetings and delicious meals with Ana, Pedro and Carlos, Luis Felipe Fabre, and other writers in Condesa and Coyoacán. I discover that Mexican food in Mexico is so much better than its ersatz manifestations elsewhere.

One morning, alone in the city centre, I visit the derelict remains of the Templo Mayor, the Aztec temple at the heart of the city of Tenochtitlán, destroyed by Cortés in 1521. Much of this area was entirely buried for centuries. In the course of their erasure of the Aztec civilisation, the conquerors built a church over a part of the precinct formerly occupied by the temple, which was later replaced by the vast Gothic cathedral that stands there now; the adjoining areas were used for housing and civic buildings.

Inside the Museo del Templo Mayor, I come face to face with a Tzompantli, or wall of skulls, constructed on a scaffold of poles, through which human heads were hung. These artefacts are associated with the cultures of Mesoamerica from around 600 AD up until the time of the Spanish Conquest. In Luis Felipe Fabre's poem 'Xochicuicatl', the poet mimics the physical structure of the Tzompantli both through sonic repetition and by contriving to build a small 'wall of skulls' in the second stanza:

> One skull next to another skull next to another skull
>   on top of
> another skull next to another skull next to another
>   skull
>   on top of
> another skull next to another skull: tzompantli-verse.

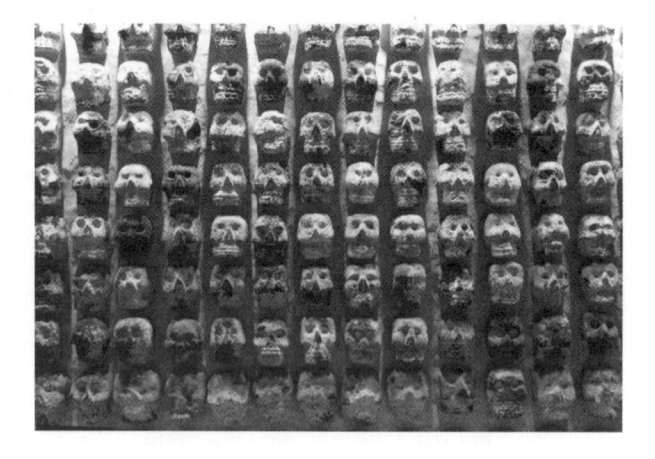

The skulls, lined up like bricks in a wall, present a spectacle that is unspeakably terrible. Although I knew about such things, I had no idea that the impact of standing before one would be so distressing. The Tzompantli has currency in today's Mexico also: victims of narco-violence are frequently decapitated, their heads exposed in public places.

In the next room, I am confronted by a statue of Mictlantecuhtli, the Aztec god of the underworld and of death. The English description below the statue, complete with misprint, reads:

> Mictlāntēcuhtli is conceived by the Aztecs as a half-gaunt being in a position of attack with claws and curly hair … The liver hangs out from his thorax because according to Aztec beliefs this organ was closely related to Mictlān or the underworld.

As someone who has received a liver transplant, such imagery resonates quite vividly.

Claudio Lomnitz, in his exhuastive study, *Death and the Idea of Mexico*, explores how Mexico came to have death as its national icon, a question which was also addressed by Octavio Paz in *The Labyrinth of Solitude*. Further to the idea of a 'national icon', as Lomnitz would have it, we can witness how – through the proliferation of skulls, including icing sugar and chocolate treats for the children that adorn the festivities for The Day of the Dead – the image of the skull remains as integral an item of Mexican iconicity as it has ever been. Masks are also a feature of the Day of the Dead celebrations, of course, a tradition which has seeped through into North American and European festivities and mingled with other traditions, such as the Irish Samhain, into the globally celebrated Halloween. I am intrigued, like so many visitors to Mexico before me, by the local fascination with skulls and masks, but discussion of the topic is now such a ubiquitous feature of travellers' accounts that it has become something of a cliché.

Tourist guides will tell you that Mexicans like to display images of skulls at Day of the Dead festivities in order to trivialise death, to make it commonplace, to deny it real significance by flaunting it through macabre displays, even to the extent of eating chocolate skulls and skeletons. But this seems rather a simplistic explanation. A mask conceals, but to wear death on the outside conceals nothing: it only reveals what we wear on the inside, what we carry inside us – our own eventual death. Javier Marías writes somewhere that we are "dead men on leave", and that one cannot conceal what can never be erased. So, it might be argued, this ubiquitous Mexican symbol of the mask of death, the grinning skull, is a way of anticipating our status as fragile ghosts, a way perhaps of trying to con or cheat or temporarily delay Death into thinking we are already dead, so that Death cannot choose us, he needn't waste his time with us. But even that only constitutes a double bluff, and Death would surely not be fooled by that.

> In the mirror of midday
> the night's end was taking shape,
> beatific, inscrutable.
>
> Pedro Serrano, 'Dark Ages'.

Mexico City, May 2014

Frida Kahlo once said that her life had been defined for her by two disasters: being involved in a horrendous traffic accident at the age of eighteen, and meeting Diego Rivera. Ironically, considering Rivera's immense status in Mexico as one of *los tres grandes* – the three great muralists of the post-revolutionary era (the others were David Alfaro Siqueiros and José Clemente Orozco) – Frida has since been raised to a higher position than Diego in the hierarchy of world fame, especially since being adopted as a feminist icon, a collocation that is regularly employed in reference to her. The litany of torments that she endured at the hands of men and her own damaged body over the course of a lifetime may have contributed to this status, yet Frida does not come across as a victim; she was an exceptionally resolute woman who made her choices and stuck with them in spite of the many misfortunes that befell her.

I took a bus from Condesa to Coyoacán and walked up the hill to San Angél, where Frida lived and worked – in separate buildings, connected by a footbridge – with and without Diego Rivera. In her house I watched a short film about her life, then crossed the elevated walkway to Diego's studio, a monument to his earthy, sensual energy, where a number of his large, papier-mâché models were on display, as well as a series of phographs of the artist at work.

I was struck in passing by the resemblance Diego bore to Dylan Thomas, about whose life and work I was, at the time, somewhat reluctantly occupied.

The physical similarity between the two can only be glanced from certain perspectives, but for me at least, it is noteworthy. Apart from the classic 1940s bohemian style, there is something very particular about both men's dimpled double chins, fleshy lips and shifty eyes, a soft pudginess of face and body. Such is their fame and familiarity in their respective homelands that both Diego and Dylan are often identified by their first names only.

I returned down the hill to Coyoacán, in search of food. I had been told that the market stalls offered good value, but had just recovered from a bout of gastroenteritis and diarrhoea (the famous Montezuma's revenge) which had left me bedridden for a couple of days, and I needed to exercise some caution with regard to what I ate. The long walk, and an unexpected attack of loneliness, as well as my inability to choose between the many places to eat in the marketplace in Coyoacán, where I wandered uselessly for half an hour, conspired to lead me to a nasty, strip-lit pizzeria, where I consumed something doughy and bland, before pressing on with a visit to Frida's blue house, originally her parental home, where she eventually settled.

Leon Trotsky, briefly her lover, was a neighbour, until he received an ice-pick through the skull, wielded by Ramón Mercader, an emissary of Soviet dictator Joseph Stalin. Mercader spent twenty years in a Mexican jail for his crime, but was awarded the Order of Lenin *in absentia* by Stalin, and was later named a Hero of the Soviet Union. He lived out the remainder of his days in Castro's Cuba. Allegedly his last words were: "I hear it always. I hear the scream. I know he's waiting for me on the other side."

It had clouded over and there was a queue outside the blue house when I arrived, and the straggle of beggars and street people selling cheap wooden toys added to a general sense of misery. Inside I joined the mass of people crowding the rooms, phones in hand, but I certainly didn't feel like taking photos of the paintings, all of which can be found in reproduction. This didn't deter a very large gringo with an iPad, who barged his way to the prime spot in each room, oblivious to the presence of others, holding his device before him like a weapon. I did however photograph a poster of the inter-uterine development of the human child, as this seemed pertinent to Frida's own story: she had always wanted children, but suffered numerous miscarriages.

I was moved practically to tears by visiting Frida's home, not so much by seeing her instantly recognisable paintings, but by the objects she kept around her, especially the extraordinary collection of Mexican votive miniatures and the clothes she designed, including the painful-looking contraptions she was forced to wear as a result of her deforming accident.

Stepping outside the crowded house and standing in the small garden to smoke a cigarette, I reflected on the phenomenon that was Frida Kahlo, and the curious, almost fanatical adulation she attracts in some quarters, which seemed disproportionate, as though exemplifying the way that our mediated culture exaggerates and contorts the realities of individual lives and achievements. I tried to understand my irrational, enraged response to the man with the tablet leaping ahead of me into each room, and a black cloud still hovered above me, here in the garden, a cloud holding all the injustices of the world and letting fall a thousand miseries amid the sorry remnants of Frida's life, come to ground beneath the Mexico City drizzle.

Several years later, as I write this, I try to reach inside my own unaccountable sadness that afternoon, but cannot find anything to pin it down, or recover its underlying cause. It was just one of those days that crop up unannounced and which fill the solitary traveller with a seeping, insidious gloom, reminding you that even in the world's most populous city, you can feel utterly demoralised and alone. My mood that day brings to mind Patrick Leigh Fermor's uncharacteristically bleak interlude one third of the way through *The Broken Road*, when he suffers, in his words "one of the rare attacks of gloom and doubt that now and then tempered the zest and excitement of my travels," which, after a long rumination on the possible sources of his dejection, give way to "a more general and far more disturbing problem, one which only assailed me at moments of depression and low resistance: what on earth was I up to?" As I have mentioned before, this existential question with regard to my wanderings in Mexico and elsewhere in Latin America cropped up occasionally and made me distrust everything that I had taken for granted when I set out, even to doubt the validity of the whole enterprise; the hubris of attempting to map the poetry of an entire continent, and these misgivings were accompanied by a fear that my own lack of intellectual, organisational and linguistic resources would never do justice to the task I had set myself.

On leaving the blue house, I walked straight into a heavy downpour, but the rain suited my mood. I carried on aimlessly through Coyoacán, soaked to the skin, and visited a church where there was a Christ on the cross, with a head of real human hair, bleeding profusely and realistically from the wound in his side. But this contemplation of suffering, following on from my visit to Frida Kahlo's house, only raised the question of how little Mexico is doing for its women. The number of femicides (defined as "the killing of females by males because they are female") first drew widespread attention during the 1990s in Ciudad Juarez, and the numbers have continued to rise across Mexico to this day, standing out as one of the horrors of recent history. Recent reports claim that approximately ten women are murdered every day in Mexico, though the number of these declared to be the result of *violencia de género* (gender violence) is disputed.

On another day, I am taken by the poet Pura López Colomé, a charming, erudite woman, who speaks perfect English – and happens to be Seamus Heaney's Spanish translator – to visit an exhibition organised by the *Movimiento por la paz con justicia y dignidad* (The movement for peace with justice and dignity), whose motto is 'estamos a la madre' – a distinctively Mexican expression that translates roughly as 'we have had it up to here'. This group was set up by the poet, writer and activist Javier Sicilia, following the torture and murder of his teenage son, Juan Francisco, along with six others, by narco gang assassins in March 2011.

Since his son's death, Sicilia has, with great integrity, developed an organisation that calls for a withdrawal of the military presence from the streets, the legalisation of drugs, and an end to political corruption. He has led demonstrations and marches across all of Mexico and much of the United States. In 2011, he was named Person of the Year by *Time* magazine. His influence in starting up a popular, non-aligned movement directly confronting the perpetrators of violent crime and political corruption in Mexico represents an act of immense personal courage. His organisation has found followers in every walk of life, precisely because so many people have been affected by the drug wars, whether as victims themselves, or else having lost family members or friends to the violence. Furthermore, unlike the many self-defence groups that have sprouted up across the country in opposition to the terror perpetrated by drug gangs – which simply promote a never-ending cycle of violence met by more violence – Sicilia's movement is based on entirely peaceful means of protest.

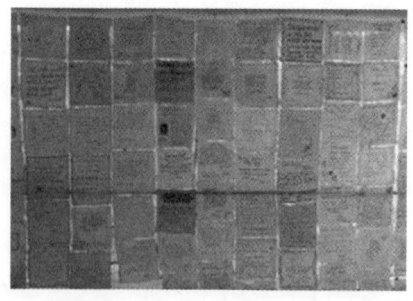

Among the displays at the exhibition, the most moving are rows of handwritten letters, designed to resemble the structure of a Tzompantli, or wall of skulls. Having recently seen such a construction in the nearby national museum, the image of the original is fresh in my memory; the hanging memorials of letters, addressed to the missing by their loved ones, serve as a reminder of all the disappeared, who in Mexico are too many to be counted. It seems to me, as I read these despairing messages, that the cycle of violence, destruction and waste were part of some terrible continuum from which there could be no escape.

With Pura, I also visit Sanborns coffee house, the site of a famous photograph from the revolutionary wars of the early twentieth century. The gentlemen in the picture below are Mexican revolutionary soldiers, snapped having breakfast at the celebrated and once exclusive café on the 12th of May, 1914, when Zapata brought his army to town for a meeting with Pancho Villa. Generals Feliciano Polanco Araujo and Teodoro Rodriguez, are caught enjoying a cup of hot chocolate.

At first sight, I had not imagined that they might be officers of such elevated rank, but appearances can be deceptive, especially in wartime. The men's inscrutable expressions are mesmerising, even at a distance of one hundred years. The cluster of soldiers behind the generals are enjoying the occasion; perhaps the unfamiliar ceremony of the photographic session amuses them. But how must these men have appeared to the waitresses serving them, accustomed as they were to a more genteel clientele? In the second photo, the waitress in the foreground, standing straight-backed and po-faced as she proffers a cup and saucer to General Rodriguez – who, however, pays her no attention, his own eyes, like those of his compadre, Araujo, being fixed on the camera that captures his image – is subject in turn to the concerned gaze of her colleague, further down the counter. One can only imagine her terror and confusion in a world suddenly turned upside down.

After taking leave of Pura outside Sanborns, I decide to return to my hotel in Condesa by foot, a distance of around six kilometres from the Zócalo. Half way, I stop off for a drink at a bar and, the moment I enter, memories of places I have always known surge through me. It smells of old wood, polish, and the vaguest trace of bleach, but is pulsating with an obscure energy, and apart from a pair of workmen in overalls seated at the bar, is empty. I have never been here but I know this place, recognise it as the original or prototypical bar, the bar of all of history's lost causes, and I feel that familiar elation on stepping inside, with the bright midday sun illuminating a shower of dust motes, a joy that only a drinker can feel in anticipation of the first shot of the day, borne along by the siren call of a deeper drinking. I order a beer and know right away that I could very easily stay in this place for a long time, with its odours – now overlaying the others – of tequila, abandoned dreams, and death.

I am caught momentarily between the predictable imminence of oblivion and the knowledge that this is the very last thing that I want. The reprobate character I think of as Gaston, first conjured by my teenage self in a field near Reading, but now, like me, in his fifties and tracking my every footstep across Latin America, is with me here in Mexico City – has in fact accompanied me into this very bar – and he, I know, wants to get to the bottom of things, specifically to the bottom of a glass of tequila or mescal. Although Gaston is, in a sense, a figment of my imagination, a spectral figure like a cardboard cut-out against the dust-specked rays of sunshine inside the bar, I can sense him taking physical shape, can actually see him. And by the look of him, he has gone downhill since his appearance at the Reading Festival all those years ago as a naïve and personable seventeen-year-old in a patterned Indian shirt and colourfully patched jeans. Panic takes hold; I knock back my beer and hurry on my way.

For a few days, during my stay in Mexico City, my camera has developed a mysterious ailment, as I perceive it, and the pictures I take turn out cloudy and obscure in patches. Rather than trying to find a practical remedy, I begin to suspect that this blurring of the image is a consequence of the inner turmoil and confusion that has beset me since visiting the ruins at Teotihuacán, and which has somehow managed to leave a mark on the world I photograph. This kind of magical thinking, by which my own unsettled state of mind might somehow affect the images being captured on camera, derives from a long-held animistic belief in the inherent qualities possessed by certain, nominally inanimate objects. It is only on returning to my hotel that I realise the solution: I take a clean cloth and wipe the lens. How ridiculous I have been, conjuring a mystical explanation to account for something as simple as a smudge on the lens of my camera! But then, as I gently rub the lens clean, it occurs to me that the clouding of the captured image is in some way cognate with the terror of the white page expressed by Juan Rulfo, and my not unrelated desire to drink myself into oblivion; and I wonder if my initial misreading of the blurred images is not, in fact, without significance, and that I am being reminded – by providence, by the universe – to clean my own lens, and to watch my step in my journey across Mexico, and to take care how I represent the things I witness.

> This building doesn't satisfy anyone,
> it is in its time of crisis,
> to knock it down you'd have
> to knock it down right now,
> later it's going to be difficult.
>
> Fabio Morábito, 'Time of Crisis'.

Xalapa – Coatapec - Veracruz, May 2014

Leaving behind the clamour of the metropolis, I catch a bus and cross the wide Mexican altiplano. Behind the tinted windows are strewn the blackened remains of trees and cactus, upon which perch large, dark birds. Half asleep on the silent bus, which ploughs like an ocean liner across the prairie, I think about the birds outside, peering into passing vehicles from their watch-posts. I fall asleep and dream that the birds standing aloft the cacti are truly enormous, and that they have a name that no one can pronounce. Even the locals are confused because they cannot utter, or even remember the name of these birds, which means, in their language, 'those whose croak inspires terror.' It is not known, the people in my dream tell me, whence the name originated, nor have any of the birds been heard to croak; they all remain implacably silent. If one of the birds were to call out, it would signal the end of the current universe, the death of the sun, and the whole terrible process of regeneration would begin once more, following the previous cycles of destruction by (i) tigers, (ii) the winds, (iii) rains of fire, and (iv) water. The inhabitants of the plain, when they die, are roasted in a clay pit and eaten by their relatives and friends. Their livers and other inner organs are consumed by their closest kin. Their feet are cut off and left out for the birds whose name no one can remember, as it is believed that this will prevent them from making their dreadful sounds. Mictlantecuhtli, Lord of the Dead (he of the protruding liver) is in there somewhere, hovering in the debris of my dream.

When I am fully awake, or at least in a state resembling wakefulness, I wonder: did I actually see those birds, or did I hallucinate them? It is so hard to distinguish at times between the things we see and the things we remember and the things we think we remember and the things we never saw but read about, and the things we wish we had seen and so retrospectively invent, and the things we will never see but have experienced vicariously in a story told by someone else, a friend or stranger. And then a mist falls upon the plain and the next time I look there is a forest, barely visible through the thick cloak of fog, and the windows of the bus have steamed up with the change in temperature. But the birds, I know, are gone.

We arrive at Xalapa in heavy rain, I hail a taxi from the bus station and find that the route across town is cordoned off for a Mayday demonstration. The taxi driver curses impressively, finds a way around, and drops me off at my hotel, a modest establishment with rooms at ground floor level that overlook an inner courtyard.

I am hungry and set off up the street, turn into Callejón Diamante, and enter La Sopa canteen. An older man with a white moustache, white shirt and white cowboy hat is playing the harp. I clock the harpist clocking me, which gives me pause for thought: why do some people act as if they recognise you, when they could not possibly recognise you? Or is the pretence of recognition a ploy they use in order to get into conversation later? Has this guy mistaken me for someone else? Do I have a double? My mind is adrift with the kind of chaotic speculation that often comes over me when I am in a new place, and on other random occasions.

I head towards the rear of the cantina, sit at a corner table, my back to the wall, and order: chickpea soup, pork in salsa verde with pasta, and a beer. The soup arrives, along with tortillas wrapped in a cloth. I take in my surroundings. The cantina has a pleasant, floral ambience, as though it were located in a small city park, complete with bandstand. The musicians take a break, and the cowboy harpist makes his way down to the washroom. When he passes my table he nods and says "Buenas tardes," in familiar fashion, confirming my sense of mistaken identity. But this is not so strange, I reflect; a friendly old fellow in a Stetson who plays the harp, saying hello. He reminds me of the wise cowboy in *The Big Lebowski*, played by the actor Sam Elliot. I finish the chickpea soup and await the arrival of the main course. The harpist comes out of the men's room, stops by my table, greets me again, and then says, in Spanish: "Around here they call me the Ambassador," and reaches out his hand for shaking.

Now this I do find odd; first, as his introduction suggests that the cowboy does not in fact know me, and that either I was mistaken in forming the impression that he thought he did, or indeed, that he mistook me for someone I was not; and secondly – and more significantly – I was under the impression that *I* was the ambassador, or at the very least a variation on the theme of ambassador. I am about to say something to this effect, and then realise I have been spending too long inside my own head: this happens when one is travelling alone. One begins to make assumptions that other people are privy to what one might be thinking, and this is absurd. I do not have a monopoly on the role of ambassador. I am not even a proper ambassador. Perhaps 'The Ambassador' is the harpist's stage name. Or perhaps, I reflect, he is a retired drug baron nicknamed 'The Ambassador' for his talent in negotiating his associates' passage to the afterlife, who has since mended his ways and taken up playing the harp in a Xalapa cantina, where no one knows of his sinister past and his reputation for dealing out summary justice. Nonsense, I reply to myself, there is no such thing as a retired drug baron, only dead ones; in fact there are no such things as 'drug barons', just narco bosses. He is simply a nice old man who plays the harp. "Don't be fooled," the voice retorts, inside my head – and now I detect the salacious tones of Gaston, mouthed in an exaggerated French accent: "he has contacts; consider those birds perched on the cacti, back on the plain."

I try to ignore this rather worrying intrusion – as well as the confusion offset by contending with two conversations at once – and I stand, to be polite, shake the man's hand with firm sincerity, and I smile back at him.

"Mucho gusto," I say. He seems on the verge of saying something in return, his gaze lingering on me, but changes his mind, perhaps realising that I am not someone he especially needs to know, and moves on, back to his harp.

When I leave the cantina it is still raining. On the way, several pick-up trucks pass by, carrying soldiers dressed in black waterproofs. I retire to my room and read another story by Juan Rulfo, have an early night.

The next morning, immediately after breakfast, I set off for the Museum of Anthropology, a half hour's walk under light but persistent drizzle. It is still early, and the place is almost empty. Beautifully laid out, the museum is spacious, bright, and populated with large and imposing stone carvings from the Olmec era (2,500-500 BCE). I am impressed by the simplicity and solidity of these forms which strike me as carrying an intangible, spiritual quality that is, however, quite beyond my ability to decipher. I find them deeply moving, but realise that I cannot possibly 'see' these works for what they are, in the spirit in which they were created, and that this, rather than being frustrating, provokes a feeling of wonder at their richness of expression in and of itself, and I am left without comprehension, as though understanding were itself irrelevant, and the beauty of these implacable, sombre faces, lay precisely in their inaccessibility, their removal from all interpretation. One smaller piece, in particular, engages my attention.

In 'Dualidad', as it has been named, the face is half-covered by a dense, featureless carapace, as though the subject were in a crisis of self-disclosure, and was being violently silenced against its will. The half-face that is revealed remains impassive, unaware that this terrible erasure is being visited on it. It speaks to a duality which I feel very keenly at present, a striving to rid oneself of another, past identity. It unsettles me in the way that only an uncannily familiar object can, as though reminding me of something or someone I am trying to forget, and to which, however, I am permanently conjoined. I am entranced.

I spend a couple of hours wandering through the halls, becoming saturated with Olmec images of human figures, including several which depict men, or androgynous beings, alongside their totem animals, and a smaller array of jaguars and serpents.

On leaving the museum, I decide, on a whim, to visit a neighbouring town, Coatepec (the accent is on *at*): it fulfils at least one of the criteria I employ when deciding whether or not to visit a place: I like its sound, which carries the resonance of something at once remote and reassuring. I flag down a taxi driven by a man with stupendously fleshy earlobes, which remind me of small whoopee cushions or rolled dough or molded plasticine; this in turn leads me to speculate whether the ears continue to grow throughout a person's lifetime, as I read somewhere. Once we get going, and he decides I am a harmless foreigner, the taxi driver chats openly about corruption in Mexican politics. He tells me things are getting worse, that the governor is corrupt, that the police are corrupt, that everything in the State of Veracruz, as he puts it, has gone to shit. We drive out of Xalapa in the rain. The traffic moves very slowly. It has been raining all morning and all last night, and throughout the previous evening, and as far as I know it has never not been raining in Xalapa.

Just outside town there is a roadblock. The young patrolman, barely out of his teens, fluff on his upper lip, carries an automatic rifle and wears black body armour, leg armour, the works. He inspects the taxista's ID and looks at me intently for several seconds as though the act of staring could itself squeeze from me a confession of guilt. I am unsure whether the best response to this is to look back at him, or cast my eyes down in submission to the interrogatory gaze, so end up doing both. He looks at me for an unnecessarily long time, as the rain clatters down on the roof of our car, before waving us through with an impatient gesture.

We arrive in Coatepec and immediately get stuck in another traffic jam. Nothing moves for fifteen minutes. The taxi driver asks directions of a fellow taxista whom we are stranded alongside, but the traffic doesn't budge. I spot a restaurant, pay the driver, and get out. It is mid-afternoon by now, and I need to eat. The restaurant has a covered inner patio with a garden area, and tables around it, out of the rain. In the garden there are roses and other flowers. The members of a large family group are finishing their meal and spend at least twenty minutes taking photos of each other in every possible combination, so that no one has not been photographed with everybody else. They have commandeered the only waiter in order to help them in this task. Every time I think they are about to leave and release the waiter, who could then come and take my order, they reconvene for a new set of photos. One of the men, a Mexican, has very little hair but a long grey ponytail, which always strikes me as a terrible style choice. One of the women – I suspect she is

Ponytail's sister – is with a tall gringo. Perhaps they have just got married, but in a registry office rather than church, and this is the celebratory meal. He has long hair also, but not arranged in a ponytail. He speaks Spanish well, with a norteamericano accent. When the waiter is eventually released I order tortilla soup and start leafing through a magazine I bought at the anthropology museum. My Mexican cell phone makes a noise to announce that I have received a message, which reads, in Spanish: "Adults who sleep too little or too much in middle age are at risk of suffering memory loss, according to a recent study." I look at the message in consternation. Too little or too much? So, you're fucked either way. Having suffered from insomnia for much of my adult life, I am an avid consumer of any information that purports to throw light on my infirmity. Such information is almost always unhelpful. But now, it would seem, there are casualties of both too little and too much sleep. Who sends this stuff? The screen says to connect with 2225 to find out more. Then another message: "Japanese fans of Godzilla were very upset with the new film's trailer to find that Godzilla is very big and fat: read more! 3788." Then a link. How do you switch this crap off?

Coatepec is full of attractive buildings with courtyards. I head down to the Posada de Coatepec, a hotel in the colonial style, and go in for a coffee. A slim man of around fifty with fine features, a neat little moustache, not quite a pencil moustache, and dressed in polo gear, greets me in friendly fashion, and I greet him back, once again under the impression that I have been mistaken for someone I am not. A blonde woman, also in white jodhpurs, follows the man. There must have been a polo match. How strange, I think: I had not associated the game of polo with the Mexican upper classes. The hotel offers a nice shady patio, but we don't need shade, we just need to be out of the rain. I sit on the covered terrace and start writing in my notebook. Before long, the man who was in riding gear but has now changed into khaki slacks, pale blue shirt and black sleeveless jacket, comes and sits on the terrace also, nodding at me as though we were by now old buddies. Immediately three waiters attend to him, bowing and scraping; one of them is even rubbing his hands together in anticipatory glee at the opportunity to serve this evidently Very Important Person. The man takes off his sleeveless jacket, his gilet, rather, and immediately the second waiter scurries away, returning with what appears to be a hat-stand for very short people but which is, I realise a moment later, a coat-stand. Clearly the Very Important Person cannot do anything as vulgar as sling his coat over the back of a chair. Another waiter opens a can of Diet Coke at a safe distance, and only then brings it to the table, along with a glass brimming with ice. He is bent almost double, as if to ensure that no part of his body looms offensively above the person of the celebrity guest. It is one of the most extraordinary displays of deference I have ever witnessed. Then all three waiters – the one who brought the coat-stand, the one with the Coke, and the one who was rubbing his hands, who appears to be a kind of *maître d'* – vanish inside like happily whipped dogs. Left alone, the man makes a phone call in a loud voice. He is barking instructions to some underling. He is clearly someone who is used to being obeyed, like an old school caudillo. When he has finished his call, he looks around and gets up, heading towards the restaurant, where his company – family and friends, I guess – are seated. He takes his drink with him, but within seconds one of the waiters appears out of nowhere, grabs the coat-stand, and follows him in with it.

I have to go. I have arranged to meet a poet, José Luis Rivas, back in Xalapa, in order to discuss poetry matters. Rivas has translated T.S. Eliot and Derek Walcott into Spanish, and is a well-known name in Mexican literary circles. I take the bus this time.

As I walk down the street from the bus station towards my hotel, a pick-up truck packed with soldiers passes by. A machine gunner is perched on the back, and he swivels the weapon to train it on me as the truck continues on its way. I am just a visitor to this town, but I have now been the subject of interest to the security forces a couple of times, and am beginning to feel a little paranoid. What would it feel like having this happen every day? How long before you cracked?

The rain has eased. I stop for a drink at a cafe and sit outside. A little girl approaches my table and tries to sell me a rose. I buy one, give her ten pesos, and tell her to try and remember not to ask me again. Barely has she disappeared when a stooped, toothless old fellow comes along, one of that breed of beggar who has become oblivious to rejection and insult. He stops by my table and implores in abject fashion until I relent and give him ten pesos also. I move down the street and sit outside a bar called Cubanías, and am again approached by the little rose girl, whom I remind of our agreement; she smiles coyly and backs away. I think about solitary travel, and of the hundreds of hours in which one engages in interior monologue, and the occasionally insightful moments when everything appears to make sense, or when you think you should remember something specific – the crow alighting on that tree there, the little beggar girl's way of pushing her short hair behind her ear, the distant sound of a police siren – just in case that moment later makes sense to you, slots into a sequence of memories, and you realise why you remembered it, that it has a unique place in the order of the universe, the patterning of the ineffable, even though it doesn't matter, none of this matters, as long as you have faith in the persistence of the murmur, and can be at ease with the perpetual babble of those background voices, of people sitting around about you, along with your own internal accomplices, whose voices come on like ambient music, and which you can tune into at will. At times the two sources – the voices of the exterior world and the interior – join together in a stream of juxtaposed sound, and that is the persistence of the murmur ...

In addition to this pervasive background murmur, memory is a constant interloper, relaying information in its haphazard way, though as I get older it is less a case of 'I remember' and more as though memory were seeking me out, as if some autonomous force of memory were collaborating with my efforts, infiltrating my ability to make sense of things, rather than 'I' making sense of the things I remember. In which case, does memory belong somewhere 'out there' in the world – like consciousness, according to the panpsychists – and I merely tap into it? At the same time, I am all too aware that while memories are often unreliable, it is only through the act of re-constructing them that we make sense of our lives. "Life is not what one lived," claimed Gabriel García Márquez, "but what one remembers and how one remembers it in order to recount it."

But even that is not an entirely satisfactory explanation, as it leaves a constant and consistent 'I' at the centre of the remembering. How to describe one's memories in a way that avoids saying 'I remember', 'I recall' – in language that always places agency with the one doing the remembering? Are all memories stored in the brain, or are they instead triggered in the brain, as I have suggested, from their place elsewhere, 'out there'? How about 'I stumble across a memory, or 'I pick up on a memory', or 'a memory finds me'. Maybe not these words exactly but something to suggest that agency is not always mine?

The poet I am due to meet, José Luis, turns up two hours late in our designated restaurant, by which time I am several drinks down. We shake hands. He apologises for his tardiness; he was delayed returning from Mexico City. I don't feel like eating again, but José Luis orders pasta. He has a familiar, musty odour about him, not entirely unpleasant, which I try, and fail, to place. He gestures towards the empty glasses on the table and says, with a smile: "I see you've discovered *palo y piedra*." What's this, I wonder? I am drinking beer with a tequila chaser. He explains that 'palo y piedra' (stick and stone) is a term used for this combination of beverages. I can understand why. While waiting for him I have been entertained by the mariachi band who are playing the restaurant, delivering the usual mix of melodious sorrow and remorse, which, together with the alcohol, and my meditations on memory and consciousness, have gradually rendered me less and less inclined to speech. I certainly don't wish to talk about poetry, or plans for my anthology, which have ostensibly brought us together. Fortunately, José Luis talks almost exclusively about corruption in the state of Veracruz, the big news story of the moment. He tells me about the shopkeeper he knows who had to close down because he couldn't pay the protection money that kept going up and up. These people are everywhere, he says, the ones who put about the suffering, and who are the bane of the earth. And their victims, they are everywhere too: the poor people who endure this continuous indignity and oppression, the ones who suffer. In Mexico they pay up or they sell up or they get killed.

I recall – the memory is triggered in me – that in Sicily, in 1983, during the winter that I spent living in an abandoned farmhouse outside the small town of Scoglitti, I used to visit a sea-front restaurant nearly every day. I had become friendly with the proprietor, and one day I dropped by for lunch and these two guys came in; short, thick-set thugs, who spoke for a while with Luca, the owner. After they had left, over coffee, Luca told me that this had been going on for a while and at first he had tried to ignore it in the hope that it would go away, *they* would go away, but they did not go away, they kept coming back, and although he would not pay them – he would, he said, never pay them – he knew that one day he would just cave in and sell up, which is what they wanted, so the new owners, who would buy the place at a cut price, would be their people, would tow the line and not make a fuss; they would pay up and be 'grateful' for the protection. I do not tell José Luis this story, of course, because he does not need to hear it. In this part of Mexico, such protection is everyday reality. I have a final tequila, and a coffee, with José Luis. As I bid goodnight to him, I recognise what his odour is: he smells, improbably, of the vestry at St Edmund's church in Crickhowell, where I attended Sunday school as a child, and which I revisited a few years back, at my mother's funeral.

Three months after I have left Mexico, in September, La Sopa, the restaurant where I had eaten the day before and had met the man who chose to be known as The Ambassador, closed down. Its owner, Pepe Ochoa, was quoted in a news article as saying that he could not keep paying the extortion money demanded of him by crooks: "We are sorry to disappoint our customers," said Ochoa, in an interview posted on the *Plumas libres* website, "but like other places in Xalapa we couldn't keep on working simply to pay the extortion money demanded by these criminals." The article goes on to claim that it is "an open secret that hundreds of businesses of all kinds are suffering extortion in spite of the promises offered by the authorities to guarantee their safety." The 'authorities' in this instance refers to the State government, and in particular the Governor of Veracruz, Javier Duarte. The scandal surrounding Duarte finally blew up in 2016, after presiding over an administration whose violence and greed outraged the public, and two years later, in September 2018, Duarte was convicted of embezzling millions in state money (with which he bought artworks and luxury homes) and sentenced to nine years' imprisonment. Although police seized properties and cash equivalent to $120 million, he did not have to pay damages.

During the six years of Duarte's administration (2010-16), Veracruz became one of Mexico's most dangerous states. I learned about all of this later, in May 2017, when the writer Juan Villoro visited my home in Cardiff. Juan told me that while Duarte was governor, hundreds of people disappeared, bodies were found buried in a series of clandestine mass graves, and seventeen journalists were murdered, with five more 'gone missing'. Meanwhile, in an attempt to clean up his image, Duarte was actively supporting the Hay Festival in Xalapa, which had been held annually since 2011. In February 2015, Juan helped compile a public letter of protest, signed by three hundred supporters, including Elena Poniatowska, Noam Chomsky and Salman Rushdie. The upshot was that the festival's directors were compelled to abandon their Xalapa event, and this succeeded in bringing the abuses of the Veracruz government to the attention of a global audience.

It would now seem, however, that most of Duarte's associates in power have been exonerated. In December 2018, his chief of police, Arturo Bermúdez, suspected of 'disappearing' at least fifteen people, walked free, and four more of the governor's close associates have also been released. It is not unlikely that Duarte will follow them.

The following day I walk to the bus station and wait for the midday service to Veracruz. The driver ascends, closing the door behind him and carefully sifts through some papers, before attaching them to a clipboard, which he places in the plastic rack to the side of his seat, and releases the electronic door, to allow us passengers on. He is clean shaven with an owlish face, enhanced by round spectacles, his head topped by a tight covering of black curls, and he wears a curiously disengaged expression, a man carrying out a task to which he has long since become oblivious. And yet there is something shifty and spectral about him, as though he were not quite there, and I begin to wonder about those mysterious, ill-defined and ghostly beings who drift unnoticed amid the human horde, visitors from the ranks of the dead perhaps, or else some other place unknown to the living.

I recall an episode from one of the *Don Juan* books by Carlos Castaneda, a writer largely unknown to readers under the age of fifty, but one who exerted an extraordinary influence over an entire generation of youthful mystics and would-be shamans in the 1970s. In one of the books, Don Juan, a Yaqui sorcerer from northern Mexico, explains to Castaneda that some people are not people at all, but what he calls 'person impersonators.' Castaneda asks his teacher, Don Juan – not unreasonably – whether the driver of the bus on which they are travelling could be a 'person impersonator'. I cannot remember Don Juan's answer, but am considering the same question now, as we sally forth from the city.

Sitting five rows back in the half-empty bus, looking out at the lush green landscape that brightens our descent towards the coast, I wonder at all the millions of copies of books Carlos Castaneda sold before he was unveiled as a fraud and, more extraordinary still, even after the revelations emerged that he had fabricated his anthropological fieldwork from the confines of his study, thick with the smoke of the joints he routinely consumed, and that he was a fantasist and a charlatan – as well as an abusive and narcissistic bully – people continued to buy his books because they wanted to believe in something, because they wanted to believe he had an answer to questions that they could not find answers to themselves.

We pass a roadside billboard with a massive poster of the finely featured, discreetly moustachioed man whom the waiters fussed over in the Posada of Coatepec: he is a candidate in the forthcoming elections. The whole performance on the patio now makes sense, the fawning and running around after him and the ridiculous carry-on with the coat-stand. I make a mental note to write down his name but am sleepy, and by the time we arrive in Veracruz I have forgotten it. I wonder later whether he, too, was one of those spectral forms identified by Don Juan; whether he too, was a person impersonator, and had brought an entire cast of underlings with him from whichever realm he had emerged.

I haven't booked anywhere in Veracruz so take a chance on the Grand Hotel Diligencias on the Zócalo. It's expensive, and has seen better times, but I'm only staying one night, so I take it. Back in Mexico City, Pedro Serrano had told me this was the place to be, if you can tolerate the noise from the plaza. I book in, drop off my bag in my sixth-floor room, and set out towards the port, where I take a boat trip around the bay, and admire the statue of The Immigrant, a Spanish Civil War refugee standing with his battered suitcase on the harbour front.

Some boys are diving for coins, and I watch them for a while, astonished by the amount of time they spend underwater. I'm thirsty, and enter a convenience store, looking for something to take back with me to the hotel. I spend ages deliberating. Am I actually thirsty, or is that a euphemism for wanting alcohol? I consider buying tequila, but do not want a full bottle, which is all they have. If I buy a whole bottle I will drink it, no doubt about that. On the bottom shelf, behind the counter, there is a row of unlabelled plastic bottles, always intriguing. I enquire of the shop assistant what they contain, which turns out to be cane liquor: You don't want that, *caballero*, he tells me, with a sigh. Or, at least, that's what I hear. A dim sense of déjà vu floods over me, as I notice someone nudging me, his elbow in my ribs and, to my consternation, see that Gaston has materialised at my side. He stands a couple of inches shorter than me, has curly, greying brown hair, and is scruffily dressed in jeans, tee shirt and torn bomber jacket. He has a scar running diagonally across his left cheek, and around his neck a leather cord from which hangs a pendant – a silver ouroboros. I resist the temptation to touch it. The pendant horrifies me; it feels like an appropriation, or a theft.

"Cane liquor. That sounds exactly what is required, *manito*!', he says, in an obscene, breathy whisper."

"... ?"

"Why don't me and you go back to your grand hotel, and talk about old times, hein? We can settle down with a nice lovely tall glass of Mexican cachaça, and later hit the town, make a night of it, n'est-ce pas?"

I move to cuff him on the side of the head, but realise, of course, that he isn't there. I have merely conjured him from the darkness of my incertitude. I am on edge. I head back to the hotel with a modest haul of high carb treats: potato crisps, a pack of chocolate biscuits, a couple of cans of beer and some mineral water. I need to stay sober tonight.

Later, leaning over the balcony of my hotel room, I watch as the Zócalo slowly stirs into life. It is hot and the air is dense, the sky thick with clouds that have shown no sign of either breaking up or unloading themselves all day, either on the drive down from Xalapa, or here in Veracruz. A *son* band has started up six floors below, and a couple begin dancing, moving with slow steps, and are gradually joined by other couples until the mass of dancers resembles a slowly-stirring, multi-hued beast circling a corner of the enormous plaza.

I turn around sharply, certain that someone has entered the room behind me. Of course, there is no one there. The door is locked. But my nerves are not what they might be, and I feel strangely threatened, here in this big hotel, in the noisy, humid city, especially after the relative quiet of the green coffee-growing uplands of Xalapa and Coatepec, places that, despite the heavy police presence, felt less overwhelming. Once I have inspected the room and the corridor outside, and found nothing, and nobody, I return to the balcony, as a fresh tsunami of noise sweeps up from the square.

As night falls, I venture downstairs and sit outside the bar attached to my hotel, where, however, the noise is no less shattering. There are now several bands playing in the plaza, which, to use a common analogy, is the size of three football pitches. Nearby is a group of bikers from – according to the inscriptions on their leathers – San Luis de Potosí, who have parked their machines in the southwest corner of the square and planted massive speakers alongside them, from which blasts heavy metal at a volume which smothers most of the other sources of sound, the throbbing bass lines reverberating with an echo in the hollow of my gut. Just as in other countries, the bikers are predominantly middle-aged men, wearing inscribed black tee shirts that barely cover their bulging bellies. They rev the engines of their Harleys, sending out a deafening challenge to the mariachi band playing closest to their patch. There are, however, at least four other mariachi bands sounding off just now, and a larger band for the dancers further down the square. To add to the cacophony, hundreds of birds, occupying the many trees around the plaza, maintain a shrill and maniacal chirruping, flitting frantically from perch to perch en masse, dislodging a rival group from a neighbouring tree, which fly off, squawking in complaint, to find another haven. Police sirens and an unremitting blasting of horns from the bumper-to-bumper traffic add to the great commotion. A fresh contingent of mariachi trumpeters arrives to my right, offering a more immediate assault to the eardrums.

This is, quite simply, the noisiest place I have ever been, its orchestral volume rendering the second noisiest place – the Plaza del Castillo in Pamplona on the opening night of the San Fermín fiesta – into sedate chamber music by comparison. But here, unlike Pamplona, there is no particular fiesta to celebrate, it's just a normal Saturday night in Veracruz. I was told to expect a lot of noise, but nothing could have prepared me for this aural onslaught. It is beyond the tolerable limits of sound; a dense, geological layering of noise upon noise, a sonic assault of massive dimensions.

Outside in the street, a big red Ford truck pulls up, and five fat men pile out. At the table in front of me, a smartly dressed man with European features is writing in an A4 pad. What is he writing? Amid all this blaring, toxic racket, could there be a second scribe, my double, doing exactly as I am doing? Could he, at this very moment, be describing how there is this person seated behind him, a cover version of himself? I conjure with the possibility that he is a spy, inspired no doubt by the short story I was reading on the bus journey down from Xalapa. In 'The Wanderer', by Luisa Valenzuela, the female protagonist seems to enter into or be entered by – effectively the same thing – the novel she is reading, a theme that also appears in Julio Cortázar's story 'The Continuity of Parks', in which the realities of the reader and the story being read interweave, tilting into one another to create a mesh in which the actual reader, the fictional reader, and the story itself become indistinguishable. I feel as though the man at the next table, writing in his notebook, is somehow vitally connected to my own experience of the evening, just as the protagonist of Valenzuela's story is infiltrated by a stranger on her flight from Heathrow, who interrupts her reading, and whom she likens to a spy: "The spy reads as we read, undercover, searching in every page for his own reflection and his reflection is there but it doesn't satisfy him. On the contrary, it enrages him."

Could it be that the man at the table in front of me, the putative spy, is writing an account that mirrors my own? That he is spying on me just as I am spying on him? More worrying still, if I allow him to enter my account, might his story become my own? But perhaps this is all a delusion, and writing belongs to no one. "Writing," according to Maurice Blanchot, "is to pass from the first to the third person, so that what happens to me happens to no one, is anonymous insofar as it concerns me, repeats itself in an infinite dispersal."

Could it be that there is always another, doing exactly what you are doing, thinking your thoughts, writing your story, singing your song? You can resist him or you can be him, but you cannot make him go away for good. He will always be back, like the cat in that old episode of Sesame Street, impervious to expulsion or drowning or kidnap or being fired from the mouth of a cannon; however you might contrive to rid yourself of that cat, you will always fail and he will always return.

Most of the tables are filled with Mexican holiday-makers or weekenders, and to my right sits a small, slight gringo who bears more than a passing resemblance to Stan Laurel, and wears a forlorn moustache and camouflage cargo shorts and a tee shirt with an inscription that I can't quite make out without standing in front of him and peering, which I have no intention of doing. He is talking to his much larger Mexican friend, in English. The Mexican begins every other sentence with the words "one day", regardless of the construction that follows, and he terminates many of his utterances, incongruously, with the Spanish words *esto y esto y esto* ('and so on'). One day I crossed the ocean and came to Veracruz and sat on the terrace of a bar listening to a man at the next table talk to his friend or accomplice or partner in crime ... *one day I this one day I that ... y esto y esto y esto.*

My double gets up to leave. He reaches down and from the floor picks up a hard yellow hat, of the kind worn on construction sites. This was not in the script. It dawns on me that, like the driver of Castaneda's bus, he is a person impersonator, posing as a surveyor or building site manager, and in this capacity was busy filing a report. A report on the building under construction or on the weather, or on me. I am not sure I entirely trust his departure. He will not be away for long.

The Mexican who is sitting with Stan Laurel is doing most of the talking, while Stan, who may or may not be listening, nods his head sagely. The other man is becoming animated and his big round face is wet with perspiration. He says, or I think I hear him say, "one day you will see where went the elephant." Next, he says: "one day you want fuck with me or you want talk up the history of conscious memory" – but that surely cannot be right, I must be mishearing. And then he says, especially loudly, and I hear this for real: "One day she will say I work every day every day every day. Shit! Some days I don't give passion. *Shit!*"

The bikers amble by in a large group, all wearing those inscribed leather waistcoats (or 'vests' as they say in the States) and blue jeans. In the square itself I can see jugglers and clowns and drag artists and con artists and little stalls selling cigars and wooden toys and junk of every possible description.

A very young woman, with a haunted look and delicate features, carrying a child in a sling on her back, comes by selling knick-knacks made from woven thread. The pair to my right, who, I realise now, are quite drunk, each give her a twenty peso note (about one US dollar), the gringo pointing insistently to the child as he hands his offering to the mother, as if to say 'the money is for her, and it's because of her, your child, that I am bestowing such munificence on you.' Alcohol-driven largesse. The woman in the group at the table directly in front of me hisses loudly to catch the waiter's attention. He ignores her. She tries calling "Joven!" (Young Man!) instead, which works, and he half-turns, careful not to dislodge any of the bottles and glasses he carries with acrobatic skill on a tray held high above his head.

The shiny black wooden surface of my table reflects the revolving overhead fan above me, turning the table-top into a spiralling vortex, inviting me in. I stare for a long time into this swirling mirage.

It strikes me – with the gratification that accompanies a rare insight – that I don't truly know anything, and probably never will, excepting perhaps the smallest details of a single life, things which can barely be summarised, let alone communicated. But at least, in the fragments that are granted me, I have the salvation of continuity, and can enjoy the exquisite tension of the unfinished journey.

Stan Laurel and his friend leave. When I get up to pay, I notice that Stan has left his small backpack leaning against the wall beside his table. I tell the waiter, so he can keep it behind the bar until the poor fellow realises he has left it somewhere.

Later, I take a turn around the plaza. An old man with no shoes, extremely drunk, takes a slim bottle of cane liquor from his back pocket, swigs the remaining dregs and slings the bottle away with an angry gesture. He then begins one of those hallucinatory boxing matches that some drunks get into, taking swings with his fists, to the left, to the right, and he staggers on, fighting his imaginary enemy.

It is past 3.00 a.m. by now. One of the last performances of the night is underway: a tight-rope walker, who has planted his rope between a tree and a lamp-post. He is pretending to be drunk, supping from a cane liquor bottle identical to the one the man with no shoes just threw away, quite possibly the same empty bottle, picked up from the street. The man with no shoes abruptly stops shadow boxing and stares in confusion at the tight-rope walker for a few seconds, before letting loose a string of profanities, and stumbles on his way across the square.

In the breakfast room the next morning I see the little gringo, who no longer looks like Stan Laurel, and ask after his rucksack. He has it, but didn't know it was me who handed it in. He is grateful, but his display of gratitude is only an excuse to make a few derogatory remarks about the dishonesty of Mexicans. I'm not interested in listening to him, and walk away while he is still talking.

> How, unless you drink as I do, can you hope to understand the beauty of an old woman from Tarasco who plays dominoes at seven o'clock in the morning?
>
> Malcolm Lowry, *Under the Volcano*.

Cuernavaca, May 2014

Caminar en esta zona no le recomiendo: es muy peligroso, said the security guard on the graveyard shift at my hotel in Cuernavaca, as I set out for a midnight stroll. "I don't recommend walking in this area: it's very dangerous." I am staying at the Hacienda Cortés, a sugar mill built in 1530 by the conquistador, Hernán Cortés, for the son he had with his mistress, La Malinche, and worked by the family – or rather, their slaves – until it fell into disuse and was, much, much later, reinvented as a hotel. Guests are housed in small bungalows, each with its own tiny patio garden.

Earlier there was a storm, rocking the trees outside my room, which shed leaves like thin leathery hands and a quantity of other solid matter, along with a downpour of such intensity that I put off heading downtown, settling instead for the more local comforts of the hotel restaurant.

On the latest leg of my Mexican journey, I have just spent a day and a night in Mexico City, returning to the capital from Veracruz to attend a tertulia, a literary discussion group organised by the poet Fabio Morábito and friends. Afterwards I visited the barrio of Mixcoac, passing Octavio Paz's family home en route, before returning to the more familiar territory of Condesa, and dinner at Luigi's with Pedro and Carlos.

The night before, I broke the journey from Veracruz by stopping off at the town of Puebla, where I had made vague plans to meet up with yet another poet. There, I witnessed an incident, insignificant in itself, that I could not shake off. As I was walking into town, an Indian woman – 'Indian' is not considered to be an offensive term in Mexico and Central America – utterly bedraggled, with long grey hair and dressed in rags, came running past me, chasing after a huge SUV, crying out, at volume and in some distress "Don Roberto, Don Roberto ..." She carried on at pace up the street calling out *Don Robé ... Don Robé* ... for an entire block, and I followed her until I could see the vehicle turning at the next set of lights. When I got to the junction, she had stopped, and was resting, hands on knees, her crevassed face fallen into a state of resigned torment. She seemed elderly, although poverty and stress and struggle probably added twenty years to her features. I asked her if she needed help, but she seemed not to see me. I asked again, are you all right? And she stared at me as if I were mad, as though the question – *¿estás bien?* – were so idiotic as to defy rational consideration. I cannot imagine what her story was, or what she felt she was owed by the object of her chase, the cruel, oblivious Don Roberto. Quite possibly, of course, she was delusional, and there was no Don Roberto in the car that had driven away, only a random stranger, but the quality of her distress convinced me that some terrible injustice had been committed against her. The scenario was timeless, and her gasping of the honorific 'Don', as her spindly legs carried her in desperate pursuit somehow epitomised the gulf between want and privilege, his status and her subjugation. The image stayed with me as I rode the bus to Mexico City the following day, the massive form of Popocatépetl to my left caught fuzzily on my phone camera above the misty woodlands and broad meadows that gather around its base.

The journey impressed on me the extraordinary diversity of the landscape; that within a few hours one can pass from the coast, across prairie, forest and the high sierra. The only constant is the truly awful music being played full volume wherever you go.

Back on the bus to Cuernavaca, the perennial Mexican bus, we pass through the sprawling shanty outskirts of southern Mexico City and into the mist again. Daily travel awakens in the traveller a sense of permanent dislocation, which is of course what the word means, displacement, an absence of *locus*. I am drawn to Cuernavaca, not only for its alleged splendour, lying as it does, under the volcano – "plumed with emerald snow and drenched with brilliance" – and the setting for Malcolm Lowry's famous novel, but also because my friend, Peter, who died destitute on the streets of Athens thirty years ago, came here sometime in the 1970s in search of Lowry's ghost, and to drink mescal.

I plan to read *Under the Volcano* in its proper setting, and I take my copy along with me to the dining room. Within an hour or so I am just as astonished – more so perhaps, because better able to acknowledge the scope of the achievement – by Lowry's novel as I was the first time I read it, half a lifetime ago. I digest Michael Schmidt's Introduction along with the chicken consommé, intrigued to discover that Schmidt grew up in the same streets that backdrop the story, and so I proceed to consume the first few chapters with my steak, *nopales* and avocado, washed down with a bottle of Chilean red, and I linger over dessert (fig tartlet and pistachio ice cream), then order coffee and a tequila. I have not eaten so much in months, and certainly not since my arrival in Mexico. By eleven, I have been reading for over three hours, having forgotten enough of the story for it to read like new.

In Lowry's novel, we accompany the ex-Consul, Geoffrey Firmin, as he lives out the last day of his life – which also happens to be the Day of the Dead, November 2nd, 1938 – in Cuernavaca, which Lowry calls by its Nahuatl name, Quauhnahuac. Much of the novel is recounted in a stream of consciousness, describing the lurid visions of a man in the throes of alcoholic meltdown. The novel also narrates the events of the day in the external or material world, in which Geoffrey's estranged wife, Yvonne, returns to him after a separation of several months. Others present – for at least a part of the Consul's final day – are his half-brother Hugh, who has been intimately involved with Yvonne in the past, and is still attracted to her, the film director Laruelle (another of Yvonne's ex-lovers), and a cast of minor characters who inhabit the actual town, as well as the infernal multitudes that populate Geoffrey Firmin's increasingly haunted imagination, as the story unfolds with steadily measured suspense – but with all the digressions of a mind in the throes of disintegration – towards its hallucinatory and terrifying climax. This duality, between the inner and the outer, between the spectacular writhing of Firmin's tortured soul and the quotidian events that need to be negotiated if he is to have a function as a human being – an 'animal with ideas' – lies at the heart of the novel, which serves as a tortuous, self-loathing self-portrait of its creator. ('Function' – not at all incidentally – is a word that is uttered with sinister insistence in the closing chapter by the police officer who will kill the Consul).

The novel has attained mythic stature for readers, its fans including numerous writers from Mexico and elsewhere in Latin America, as well as from the English-speaking world, since its publication in 1947, after a strenuous, decade-long gestation.

Despite filmic potential – as a classical tragedy set against a dramatic landscape – it has only made it to the cinema once, in one of John Huston's last ventures, and although Albert Finney's Consul is superb, the film fails to convince in its portrayal of the other lead characters, Yvonne and Hugh, perhaps for the very reasons that the novel fails: they are really not that interesting. Essentially, Lowry was concerned with a single character: the Consul, Geoffrey Firmin.

★ ★ ★

Foiled in my plans for a late night constitutional by the watchman's warning – I tend to err on the side of caution these days – I return to my room. Despite being a long-term insomniac, I am optimistically convinced that from time to time I will 'catch up' on all the sleep I have missed, but that rarely happens, and I suspect I will remain in a state of lack for the rest of my days. Instead, I read, drifting in and out of consciouness, a rhythm that especially suits the reading of this book.

At one point, quite early in the novel, the Consul insists, with typical grandiosity, that he is involved in a 'great battle', although he is, at that moment, doing nothing more than discussing whether to go on a visit to the bullfight in a neighbouring town or to stay at home with Yvonne. That notion of 'the battle', the sense of carrying a massive burden, of suffering this great responsibility to 'come through' in a struggle for survival, is drawn upon by the Consul when he resists the opportunity of going home, of calling off the trip, of simply spending some time with poor, exhausted Yvonne. Laruelle, his friend, reminds him: "you've got her back ... you've got this chance," to which the Consul replies, with magnificent self-importance, "You are interfering with my great battle" – and again, rhetorically: "You deny the greatness of my battle?" At the end of this passage the Consul continues speaking, taking Laruelle's part in the conversation as well as his own: "even the suffering you do is largely unnecessary. Actually spurious." But Laruelle isn't there anymore. The Consul is talking to himself. For much of the book, if he is not talking to himself, he is addressing one of his inner demons or "familiars", which amounts to the same thing.

Lowry's own "great battle" with alcohol has been well documented, and not least through critical analysis of his masterpiece. He was never able to replicate the success of his singular, most powerful novel, and the reason is clear: he was too drunk, too much of the time. One of the best studies of Lowry and his writing is by the American writer and rock musician, David Ryan. In his intimate, exacting essay, Ryan says that Lowry, like most addicts, never developed a healthy self-identity, remaining wrapped in a state of infantile narcissism. Drawing on Lacanian theory, he claims that Lowry's behaviour as an adult, his mammoth drinking binges and voluntary disappearances, suggested an inability to distinguish between himself and the world around him, resulting in chaos with every misconceived utterance and histrionic gesture. That would certainly be true of his Consul, Geoffrey Firmin. And the 'mirror' theme is supported in a couple of anecdotes recorded by those who knew Lowry.

Another of Lowry's biographers, Douglas Day, provides an anecdote from an old friend of the author, James Stern, who "recalled how fascinated he [Lowry] was with mirrors", and recounts one episode at a party when Lowry disappeared, and Stern found him in the bathroom, in front of the mirror, snorting blood from his nose, which he caught in his hands and "thrust up to the ceiling, so that the whole place was red and white", all the while staring at himself in the mirror and laughing. Lowry's French translator, Clarisse Francillon, remembered "his habit of slyly watching for audience reaction whenever he was behaving outrageously."

How to tally this narcissism with the self-hatred that accompained it? Here was a person disgusted by himself, torn apart by self-loathing, a beneficiary and a victim of the toxic British class system. Much has been made of the five months he spent, after leaving his exclusive private school, as an ordinary seaman on a merchant ship, out of which experience he wrote his first novel, *Ultramarine*. We are reminded, in the biographies, of how Lowry was dropped off on the quay at Liverpool docks in his father's chaffeur-driven Rolls, and then attempted to muck in with his ship-mates. Could there have been a more abject induction into working-class life for a posh and self-conscious eighteen-year old? And then the silent treatment, which Lowry received from his shipmates throughout the long months of his Big Adventure. "I hate those bloody toffs who come to sea for experience ... done a good lad out of a job," he overheard one deckhand exclaim, and "Jesus, Cock ... we've got a bastard duke on board or something." And the gloomy admonition from one of them: "we should be working for you, but look, you're working for us!"

Then straight off to Cambridge, where this ugly egg became a strutting, pipe-smoking duckling, a bibulous, garrulous bundle of mischief, the fellow you dread turning up at your party, the man who, years later, in British Columbia, paid a drunken visit to his neighbour, a carpenter who had a child with learning difficulties. Lowry stared at the afflicted child, turned to the carpenter and asked: "What kind of man are you if this is the sort of kid you produce?" Hardly surprising that the man punched him full in the face and then pushed him out of the cabin and onto the rocks that lined the shore, from which place Lowry staggered, bleeding and crying, back to his shack, calling out to Margerie, his long-suffering wife, for help.

Among the many photographs of the writer posing, glass or bottle in hand, one shows him holding a mirror, reflecting his own image as he is being photographed; and this inevitably leads to the question: why do so many of the photos of Lowry – including those on the dust jackets of books about him – show the writer shirtless, dressed only in bathing shorts, staring at the camera in a manner at once glazed and pompous, trying to make an impression with his meagre moustache and his chest pushed out like a bantam cock, as in a series of photos of Lowry at Burrard Inlet? Why so many photos of a half-naked Lowry, with bared torso and abundant chest hair?

The picture on the back cover of the Penguin Modern Classics edition of *Under the Volcano*, on the other hand, displays the author in tweed jacket and tie. The gaze, we might surmise, is intended to be piercing, but our attention is distracted by the sparse filaments of the faint moustache, the suggestion of vulnerability in the chin and the full cheeks, a vaguely satyric pointedness to the ears; what the portrait suggests to me is that the sitter knows that he is meant to be there, but is unfortunately elsewhere, unobtainable, or more likely nowhere, waiting for this to be over with so he can go get another gin. More gin, buckets-full if at all possible, rivers-full, oceans-full of gin. This fantasy, which I am attributing to Lowry, in fact originates in the Consul's delirious outburst in Chapter Ten when he attempts to recall an earlier life in Granada, Spain:

> How many bottles since then? In how many glasses, how many bottles had he hidden himself, since then alone? Suddenly he saw them, the bottles of aguardiente, of anís, of jerez, of Highland Queen, the glasses, a babel of glasses – towering, like the smoke from the train that day – built to the sky, then falling, the glasses toppling and crashing, falling downhill ... bottles of Calvados dropped and broken, or bursting into smithereens, tossed into garbage heaps, flung into the sea, the Mediterranean, the Caspian, the Caribbean ... the bottles, the bottles, the beautiful bottles of tequila, and the gourds, gourds, gourds, the millions of gourds of beautiful mescal ... How indeed could he hope to find himself to begin again when, somewhere, perhaps, in one of those lost or broken bottles, in one of those glasses, lay, for ever, the solitary clue to his identity?

Oh, that beautiful tequila and beautiful mescal! The simplicity of the descriptor reminds me of Ernest Hemingway's choice of adjectives when writing to his friend Archie MacLeish in June 1957. Having been restricted by his doctor to a single glass of wine per day with his evening meal, Hemingway looks forward, with euphoric anticipation, to "a nice good lovely glass of Marques de Riscal". This is an impossible utterance in the mouth of anyone except a besotted devotee, but as expressed by a writer who avowed a parsimonious approach to adjectives, the collocation of 'nice', 'good' and 'lovely' must be regarded with deep suspicion.

Malcolm Lowry's grotesque diminution, his descent into the wretched, querulous, abusive and occasionally violent individual, who choked to death on his own vomit in a rented house in Hove, England – a place epitomising parochial English decorum – represents a pathetic shadow death compared to the Consul's fictional passing, flung down a Mexican ravine after his drunken debacle in the El Faro bar, and followed by a dead dog that someone hurls down after him.

* * *

It always seemed to me that what literature and alcohol had in common was that both allowed, momentarily, the ability to watch the world from a place of enhanced perception, to provide the illusion that you were really engaging with the stuff of life at a heightened level. Lowry summarises this clairvoyant state perfectly in *Under the Volcano*, when the Consul attempts to explain to his wife, Yvonne, why he is the way he is:

> But if you look at that sunlight there, ah, then perhaps you'll get the answer, see, look at the way it falls through the window: what beauty can compare to that of a cantina in the early morning? ... for not even the gates of heaven, opening wide to receive me, could fill me with such celestial complicated and hopeless joy as the iron screen that rolls up with a crash, as the unpadlocked jostling jalousies which admit those whose souls tremble with the drinks they carry unsteadily to their lips. All mystery, all hope, all disappointment, yes, all disaster, is here, beyond those swinging doors.

And a little further on: "how, unless you drink as I do, can you hope to understand the beauty of an old woman from Tarasco who plays dominoes at seven o'clock in the morning?"

We might compare this passage with Ronnie Duncan's account of a visit to Crete with the Scottish poet W.S. Graham, in which Graham expresses an idea that would be familiar to Lowry's Consul. Duncan is trying to get Graham to come out for a walk, to visit a museum, rather than continuing to drink himself into oblivion – as he has done every day of the trip thus far – on the balcony of his hotel room:

> So I held on like a terrier and eventually he gestured around the balcony – at the sea, mountains, beach and the tumble of houses on either side – and said that his task was to turn all these into words. 'It is all', he said, 'better than I could ever have hoped' – reminding me that he'd said this on arrival. And then it came to me that there was really nothing

else he wanted or needed: this one experience of a Cretan setting, supplemented by visits to some all-Cretan tavernas, was all he could encompass or wished to encompass.

Lowry and his early morning cantinas, just as Graham and his Cretan tavernas; both of them are evoking a sense of epiphany. Compare "not even the gates of heaven, opening wide to receive me, could fill me with such celestial complicated and hopeless joy" with "all he [Graham] could encompass or wished to encompass." And again, consider this eulogy to Lowry, written by his close friend Earle Birney, and cited in Schmidt's Introduction: "... his whole life was a slow drowning in great lonely seas of alcohol and guilt. It was all one sea, and all his own. He sank in it a thousand times and struggled back up to reveal the creatures that swam around him under his glowing reefs and in his black abysses." Both Lowry and Graham shared the conviction that alcohol might open the gates of perception. How extraordinary that so much can be invested in an alcohol-enhanced vision of this kind, in which you are – or else believe you are – seeing more sharply, engaging more profoundly, empathising more absolutely, feeling more deeply; in other words, it might be said, replicating the aims of great literature.

How well I recognise this joyous, delusional state. During the most intense periods of my own drinking career this was all I wished for: to watch it all, to bathe in it, to sink into the sun-dappled splendour of the world. Perhaps – eventually – to turn it into words. I started serious early morning drinking while living in Xania, Crete, in my early twenties. It had always been taboo, I guess – recalling the story from my schooldays of the boy whose mother slept with a bottle of Scotch at her bedside – but once I started round-the-clock drinking, the chips were in; even I understood what it signified. And for my friend Peter, who lived in a tin shack next door, but who had once lived in Cuernavaca, intoxicated absorption in the beauty of the moment was his creative mission, although he had long since lost the impetus that originally drove him – to turn it into paintings – and now the drinking was simply an everyday necessity, and he had stopped painting, working instead as a comedic or parodic waiter at the once notorious *To Diporto* fish restaurant in Odos Skridlov, the street of leather, until he was too dissolute even for that place, whereupon I inherited the job. How pervasive was this myth among the artists I grew up amongst, the ones I read and admired, the ones whose pictures I watched being made in the Slade School of Art when I was an undergraduate in London and where I spent more of my time than among my fellow-students at the LSE; how prevalent this belief or conviction that drink and drugs would somehow help us experience life more deeply. Those raki mornings with Peter, when the morning sun flooded the ramshackle square in the Splanzia quarter, where we lived, with its pots of red geraniums and the sheets hanging out over the railings of the brothel next door, the sounds of the town waking, the glorious sense of detachment too – to be a part of it and yet apart from it – these are the things I felt in regard to both my Cretan and, much later, my Mexican sojourns, until a final, disastrous visit to Guadalajara put an end to this bright and beguiling fiction ...

I am so comfortable in my whitewashed room that I don't want to sleep, and I read almost until dawn, completing the first half of the book, before drifting into fitful slumber. I wake at nine, anxious and utterly worn out, the fan above my head whirring insistently with a regular click at each revolution. Outside there is absurdly loud birdsong, and the sun is struggling to break through thick rainclouds. I drink a coffee, smoke a cigarette, and order a taxi into town, where I have arranged to meet up again with Pura López Cólome, a resident of Cuernavaca, who will be my guide for the day, and we will visit Cortés' palace to see the Diego Rivera murals, and walk the streets that furnish Lowry's novel. But already I am less concerned with the reality of Cuernavaca than I am with the one conjured by Lowry in his parallel city of Quauhnahuac. The actual place has been spoiled for me by its fictional double.

> The devil instilled in me a black acoustic fury:
> why write poems
> if everything that wounds has an empy touch,
> a tomb's usury?
>
> Julián Herbert, 'Dark'.

Saltillo - Mexico City, May 2014

As the plane surged upward, Mexico City receded beneath us, its yellow lights flickering in the enormity of space. I was on an early flight to Saltillo, in the north of the country, capital of the state of Coahuila, and the hub of Mexico's automobile industry. The city also boasted a thriving literary culture, and I was visiting as a guest of Julián Herbert, whose work I admired, and whose poetry I wished to include in my anthology. Julián is the author of a brilliant and sometimes gruelling memoir, *Canción de tumba* (published in English as *Tomb Song*), which describes the author's long vigil at the bedside of his dying mother, a woman who made her living as a prostitute and lived under a variety of aliases, and it reflects upon a turbulent childhood and adolescence with his four siblings, each the offspring of a different father: "I spent my childhood traveling from city to city, whorehouse to whorehouse, following the itinerancy imposed on the family by my mother's profession." Encouraged, perhaps, by this childhood initiation into the art of hustling, Julián's extraordinary gifts steered him into a curious upward mobility, and at the age of twenty-two he was appointed to a university post, teaching Spanish Renaissance poetry, a usurper in the ranks of the middle classes. "My precocity", he claimed later, "spoiled the experience for me a little, because while I enjoyed the luxury of giving classes to some wonderful individuals ... I was also confronted by a monstrous administrative system, a miserable salary, the conformism and ignorance of some of my colleagues, and the lack of passion of not a few of the students. At the age of thirty

I'd had enough, so I gave up my lectureship at an age when many are just setting out. I don't regret it." And yet, always present, as he puts it in *Tomb Song*, "in some dark corner of my consciousness is the weariness of having battled for the past thirty years with the sociopathic streak left by my childhood." Not surprisingly, given his background, Julián had a longstanding familiarity with substance abuse, and is the author of a short story collection titled simply *Cocaine: A user's manual*.

I had booked into a budget hotel on the edge of town, and had not yet unpacked when I was visited by woman who announced herself as Mercedes Fuentes, journalist and poet, and who told me that my accommodation arrangements were unacceptable, that I must collect my bags and allow her drive me to the Herbert family home – Julián, his wife Mónica, and four-year-old Leo – in a smart, gated community, where I was invited to stay in the house next door, belonging to Mónica's mother, away in Mexico City. Having deposited my bags for a second time, I was then driven by Mercedes to a downtown café, where I met four or five local writers, was served tacos, and made to feel at home. Julián turned up, a genial, compact force of nature, and I was presented with a beautifully designed pamphlet of my poems, in Spanish and English, produced by the State of Coahuila Arts Foundation, to celebrate my visit. I was humbled by the care that had been put into its preparation.

On the first evening I attended a gig by Julián's band, Madrastras (Stepmothers) in a packed, sweaty dancehall. Their music was pretty good, a collage of rock, jazz, and *son*. However, halfway through the second set, to my horror, I was called onstage to speak poetry, standing there, a middle-aged white man in petrified limbo, declaiming against the ominous thrum of what was now my backing band, the music pulsing forward in splenetic bursts of sax and quietly screeching guitar, an experience that took me back, briefly, and not in a good way, to my apprenticeship as a ranting bard in London's punk rock heyday. The following night I had another, less traumatising event with Julián at the wonderfully named Cerdo de Babel (Pig of Babel) bar, which again was packed, though I was under no illusion that this might be due to my presence, rather than Julián's.

Saltillo provided the most hospitable welcome I had yet received on my Latin American travels, an ugly, lovely town, as Dylan Thomas said of Swansea, though there was little else that Saltillo had in common with that coastal city, other than a high level of alcohol consumption, a factor that no doubt enhanced my appreciation of the place. Julián and I stayed on at the Pig of Babel long into the night and returned home in the small hours. Saltillo, in the course of only two days, had become my favourite place in Mexico, possibly the world, and the Pig of Babel my favourite bar. Such was Julián's own enthusiasm for the place that he once published a curious and entertaining essay in its honour, claiming, without exaggeration, that "all my friends who don't live here are jealous of The Pig; they want to take it home with them when they leave."

On Sunday the temperature had soared to 38 degrees by midday and my hosts put on an asado, or barbecue, and many of the people who attended our event at the Pig of Babel turned up for lunch. There was a great deal of meat, beer and tequila. Coahuila is a desert state, and the hot, dry breeze was a reminder that just outside town the prairie began, and stretched all the way to the United States border and beyond, a vast territory in which people and drugs were trafficked, dreams were shattered, and lives lost. I stayed up with Julián again, talking long into the night, the warm wind like a balm to the parched soul, and I think we recognised something in each other, no doubt the very aspects of ourselves that we did not talk about.

Overnight the temperature dropped by twenty-five degrees and Monday morning brought a discernible chill and a fine rain, but it brightened up just as swiftly by midday. After recording a radio interview with Mercedes, the three of us walked around the historic centre, and Julián pointed out an imposing building in the colonial style, which, he informed me, was once the Hotel Arizpe Sáinz, the favoured residence of Edward Hopper in Saltillo during his trips here in the 1940s. Attracted by the desert and the extraordinary light, Hopper made three visits, painting landscapes from the roof of the hotel. According to those who knew him during this period, Hopper developed a love-hate relationship with the city, admiring the architecture, but not the climate or certain aspects of the 'local character' – for which we might read a dislike of Mexicans. He found life in the city noisy and congested; he complained about the walls and towers and electric signs that obstructed the views. Nor could he find the right sort of blue-green oil paint for the mountains, settling in the end for watercolours to paint his landscapes. Having become disillusioned with Saltillo, Hopper abandoned the place, returning, however, for a final visit in 1951, although apparently not producing any new work.

At lunchtime on my last full day in Saltillo, I returned with Julián to the The Pig of Babel, ostensibly for something to eat, and we sat downstairs in the main bar, and began one of those long rambling conversations in which you might almost be speaking with yourself, the one person premeditating the other's remarks almost before he makes them and the stars above us on the false ceiling of the bar glittering down – though this memory might be as false as that ceiling – and the enticing aromas from the kitchen almost prompting us to ask for food; but in the end we forgot to eat, food always seeming to involve one step further than either of us could actually be bothered to take. We ate pistachios instead, and drank mescal.

Julián, like all Mexicans, was acutely sensitive to the mass violence that was taking place across the country on a daily basis. We talked about the latest abductions and kidnappings and disappearances, and the overriding sense of never feeling entirely safe, and the exacerbation of that fear where children were concerned, and we talked about the poem that Julián wrote, 'Dark', which I had translated for the anthology. In the poem –

which is dedicated to Javier Sicilia, whose teenage son, the reader will recall, was abducted, tortured and murdered in 2011 – the speaker tells of the anxiety of parenthood in a country famous for its disappearances. A long night passes in a state of anxious sleeplessness, the man's arm in the crack between two beds pulled together (but not tightly enough for a chasm not to appear between them), fearful lest his young son should fall into the narrow void, fearful lest the unthinkable should happen and his child disappear into the terrible gaping vaults that open up beneath the ground with a kidnapping, a disappearance, an act of extortion; and what a striking metaphor that is for the nocturnal terror that besieges a parent when their child is in danger, or perceived to be threatened by violence in any way, and I thought back to the previous Saturday, when I had gone for lunch with Julián, Mónica and little Leo, and how safe it felt at the restaurant inside their gated community, and how fragile and precious that sense of security must be in a country like Mexico, compared with my own European homeland, which, whatever its faults and failures, does not, by and large, subject its citizens to an onslaught of government-endorsed and police-sanctioned violence and extortion and abduction and murder and beheadings and dismemberment, and the slaughter of children, and the rape of mothers in front of their children, and mass executions and bodies piled up in trucks like the three trucks that were left on the street in Guadalajara just before the Book Fair and which had been replicated in some form or other many times since then; and I tried to understand how terrifying life must be for the random victims of narco crime, and the parents of all the abducted and murdered children of the past twenty-five years, including, it must be added, the thousands of children separated from their parents by US immigration forces on the instructions of President Trump, an intervention which, in 2018 alone, according to the *New York Times*, split up the members of more than seven hundred families in a policy that has continued unabated, the Trump administration cynically exploiting the COVID-19 pandemic in 2020 to accelerate its programme of breaking up families and sending children to destinations where they would have no one to care for them, or from which they fled in the first place, because their lives were in danger. Over the course of my travels in Mexico and Colombia I encountered many stories of the most heartbreaking kind, and although I never set out to chronicle mind-numbing horrors of this kind for their own sake, and have no interest in leaving behind a litany of desperate sorrows, I have begun to understand that what happens to one abducted child in Mexico happens not only to that child but to all children, everywhere.

I recalled some lines from María Rivera's long poem 'The Dead':

> they are called four children,
> Petronia (2), Zacarías (3), Sabas (5), Glenda (6)
> and a widow (a girl) who fell in love at primary school,
> they are called wanting to dance at fiestas,
> they are called blushing of hot cheeks and sweaty hands,
> they are called boys,
> they are called wanting
> to build a house,
> laying bricks,
> giving food to my children,
> they are called two dollars for cleaning beans,
> houses, estates, offices,
> they are called
> crying of children on earth floors,
> the light flying over the birds,
> the flight of pigeons in the church,
> they are called
> kisses at the river's edge,
> they are called
> Gelder (17)
> Daniel (22)
> Filmar (17)
> Ismael (15)
> Agustín (20)
> José (16)
> Jacinta (21)
> Inés (28)

Francisco (53)
gagged in the scrubland,
hands tied
in the gardens of ranches,
vanished
in the gardens of 'safe' houses,
in some forgotten wilderness,
disintegrating mutely
and in secret,
they are called
secrets of hitmen,
secrets of slaughter,
secrets of policemen ...

When I was in Mexico City I had asked Pedro and Carlos if there was a single poem that most powerfully represented a response to the continuous, everyday onslaught of violence in Mexico, and they both agreed it should be Rivera's, which was inspired originally by the murder of seventy-two Central and South American migrants by narco gangs in San Fernando, Tamaulipas, in 2010. This event, the first of several of its kind (they continue to this day) occurred when the *Zetas* gang captured migrants on their way to the US border. An Ecuadorean man, one of the three survivors, who had been shot in the face and neck but, miraculously, did not die, told police that the massacre had taken place after the migrants were unable to pay the gang and refused to work for them. Rivera's poem relates in relentless and unremitting detail the shocking litany of violence perpetrated on the victims of criminal activity in San Fernando and elsewhere, including the sexual violence perpetrated on women. Her poem has brought María Rivera threats of rape and violent death, in person and over social media, sending her into hiding and causing her acute psychological distress. When, in 2016, I sent María my version of her poem, after exchanging notes on a couple of translation issues, she wrote to me of her profound satisfaction that the poem was going to appear in English. "Because it was written, in part," she said, "in order to speak of the 72 Central American migrants who tragically never made it to the USA and remain buried in Tamaulipas, it is a form of poetic justice to know that this poem has a migratory nature of its own." Receiving letters of this kind are validating as well as humbling, and makes the dissemination of such works more necessary than ever. It also confirms the importance of translation, as described by Kate Briggs in her masterful book *This Little Art:* "We need translations, urgently: it is through translations that we are able to reach the literatures written in the languages we don't or can't read, from the places where we don't or can't live, offering us the chance of understanding as well as the necessary and instructive experience of failing to understand them, of being confused and challenged by them."

Back in the Pig of Babel, I picked up the tab, and noted with vague surprise the improbable number of mescals Julián and I had consumed over the course of the afternoon. The peculiarity of drinking mescal, I discovered, and not for the first time, was that even though, while one remained seated, one felt swaddled and swathed by the alcohol, and the phenomenal world stayed at a safe distance – especially in the darkened drinking dens preferred by Mexicans – the moment one stepped outside, and into sunlight, everything took on a dizzying vibrancy. The world was suddenly imbued with pure, holy light, and one's vision amidst the glare, fuzzy if not actually impaired, turned as much in upon oneself as outward, and both worlds were equally radiant.

We began to amble homeward through the incandescent streets, and although everything seemed at first to be in its right place, everything was normal – the buildings were present and correct, the dogs wandered freely and without restraint, doing the things dogs do – it was as though the visible world were at a slight remove from itself and was being projected instead onto a shimmering screen. Colours were more intense and I was hearing voices, well, not exactly voices, but mutterings nonetheless, and I knew that this was not a good sign, indeed, I feared a visitation from one of the Consul's familiars, or worse, from Gaston. I suspected, however, that Julián's presence was keeping the troublesome Frenchman at bay.

We were silent as we walked. It was a warm evening. We passed a large placard high on a wall that stated: *Jesucristo es la salvación* and, as if that were a cue, Julián flagged down a taxi. After a few blocks he stopped the car, jumped out and headed into an OXXO convenience store, emerging a minute later with two bottles of tequila. He handed me one, saying something like 'to help you through the night', I forget his precise words. Dusk had fallen quite suddenly, and with the night my mood darkened. Back at the house, I left my bottle of tequila unopened in the kitchen and collapsed on the bed without bothering to remove my clothes.

I slept deeply, but towards dawn woke several times after dreams of falling. These falling dreams were a recurring feature of my childhood and continued into adulthood, worsening over time; my dreamscape over the first half of my life featured many falls into deep chasms, waking in panic, heart pounding, mid-fall – since I knew that if I hit the ground I would be dead. The dreams stopped when I gave up drinking, in my late thirties, but they had begun to return over the past year or two.

I managed to get back to sleep and when I woke again it was nearly midday. The world outside lay in dense fog and Mónica told me that all flights from the airport had been cancelled. I was due to travel back to Mexico City and needed to get to the airport to change my ticket. Mónica offered to drive me there, after picking up Leo from nursery, so I bade farewell to Julián, and received a bearish embrace. I felt a strong affection towards him, and wondered when we would meet again. At the airport I exchanged my plane ticket for another, to depart from neighbouring Monterrey. It was a two hour journey to Mexico's third largest city, and sitting on the coach it felt to me as though the entire sojourn in Saltillo had been a single drawn-out afternoon of intense white light, which I had spent stretched out on the rough sand beside a lake, with a prevailing sense that something which could not be named lurked just beneath the surface of the water.

I didn't see much of Monterrey. The plane left in the early evening, and as we approached the vast sprawl of Mexico City, far below us in the fading light, we passed through some turbulence; on the horizon a blood-red sun was descending over the mountains and a storm was brewing to the north-west. The sky crackled with jagged flashes of lightning. The pilot made an announcement in Spanish, apologising for the weather, and then the plane descended, juddering through the storm, and we eventually disembarked under a heavy downpour.

I found a taxi easily enough and we drove through the hammering rain. Visibility was so poor we overshot the small hotel on Avenida Benjamín Franklin that had become my Mexico City home. This happened all the time, not out of a desire to cheat the customer – besides, the price on trips from the airport is fixed beforehand – but because the layout of the streets in this area was complicated and no taxista could be expected to know his way around a metropolitan area of twenty-five million inhabitants. So, at my suggestion, the driver, who was one of those very correct and well turned-out Mexican gentlemen of late middle age, carried out an indiscreet U-turn at a major junction, and we were immediately pulled over by a pair of traffic cops, draped in rain capes, who had been lurking beneath nearby trees.

The driver was instructed to step out, and negotiations began. I could hear the young cop citing the precise name and number of the traffic regulation we had infringed, but I suspected this was an irrelevance. After some discussion the driver returned to the cab and reached inside the glove compartment for money. How much? I asked him. One hundred and fifty pesos, he replied. Here, I said, take a hundred. After all, I am at least partly responsible for this. He thanked me, stepped out, and I listened to the conversation through the open window of the cab. The police officer's spiel went: it's easier for both of us if you just cough up. In fact I'm doing you a favour, because the fine would cost you more if we went through the proper process. When the driver got back in the cab I asked him if he ever refused to pay a bribe and he shrugged and said that corruption was normal; this was how the law operates here. Most drivers pay the police rather than go through the rigmarole of following through with an infraction of a minor kind.

Back at the hotel, and hungry now, I borrowed an umbrella from reception and headed for my local restaurant, *El Califa*, where the waiter greeted me like the regular I had become. I ordered a bowl of chicken broth and a couple of tacos. At the table next to me two young people – he in a shiny suit, she laughing too enthusiastically at everything he said – shared a dessert, spooning ice cream into each others' faces.

A packet of sweets accompanied my bill, on a saucer. I opened it with difficulty and was confronted by some tiny things that resembled the hundreds and thousands that are used for cake topping. I had not met with these before, so I gave them a try. There was an explosion of sugar and chilli pepper inside my mouth, which was not at all agreeable. I dropped the remaining sweets in a bin and returned to my hotel. The rain had eased off while I was at the restaurant, but on the way back the sky cracked with thunder and the heavens opened once again.

★ ★ ★

Perhaps nowhere on earth is the contiguity of past and present more striking than in Mexico City. The next day, a Sunday, I take a walk through Condesa, past the Hippodrome and into Chapultepec park. It is a hot, sunny day, and I buy a couple of tacos and a beer from a street vendor and sit on a bench with my picnic. Before me stands a section of ancient, ornately decorated wall, seven metres high, one section split apart by a wide crack, no doubt as the result of one of the city's many earthquakes; behind the wall rise a pair of high towers, one newly completed, the other under construction, and from which emanates a constant hammering and pounding that echoes loudly across the hot afternoon, a deep thudding that resounds through the soles of the feet and up inside the hollow of my ribs, settling in the solar plexus. Through this crack in the ancient wall postmodernity surges skyward, loud and oblivious.

Wandering through the park, I find myself outside a shiny new building, which turns out to be an art gallery, the Museo de Arte Moderno, and to my great surprise and joy they are showing an exhibition of work by Leonora Carrington and Remedios Varo. It is the first time I have encountered Varo's work other than in reproduction, and I am immediately enthralled by her surreal landscapes, populated by strange and wonderful creatures; meanwhile, Leonora – like Dylan and Diego known to her admirers by her first name alone – is an artist whose work has interested me for many years. Born in 1917 to a wealthy family of Northern textile merchants, of English and Irish stock, Leonora was a wild, contrary child, and drove her parents to distraction with her eccentricities and her insistence that she was, by turn, a horse, a hyena, a bird or bat. Considered 'uneducable' and expelled from a series of Catholic boarding schools, she was packed off to Miss Penrose's school in Florence at fifteen, where she discovered the city's museums, and in particular the work of artists such as Uccello, Pisanello and Archimboldo. This galvanised her enthusiasm for painting, and despite intense family resistance – her father, Harold, maintained that most artists were either poor or homosexual, "which were more or less the same kind of crime" – she finally got her way. After a spell at finishing school in Paris, from which, needless to say, she was expelled, she was eventually granted permission to train as a painter, first at the Chelsea School of Art, and then at the newly-opened Ozenfant Academy, under its founder Amédée Ozenfant, but with little support, financial or otherwise, from her parents. This was not the life that had been planned for her: she was supposed to have been a society girl, and had been presented as a débutante to the king and queen of England, and she was courted by the sons of the aristocracy, none of whom provoked in her the slightest enthusiasm.

In London, Leonora met the German surrealist Max Ernst, twenty-six years her senior, and the couple became lovers, moving to Paris in 1937 before settling in the southern French town of Saint-Martin-d'Ardèche, where they lived out an Edenic, erotic interlude, working at their art and tending their vineyards, until the outbreak of World War Two drove them violently asunder. Ernst was arrested by the Gestapo – although he later escaped, and fled to the USA, where he married the heiress Peggy Guggenheim – and Leonora headed for Spain, where she suffered a mental breakdown and was committed, at her parents' instigation, to treatment in a psychiatric hospital, Villa Covadonga, an ordeal recorded in her short memoir, *Down Below*. While locked up in this institution, she remained under close and occasionally brutal supervision by the clinic's staff, as well as, incongruously, by her elderly nanny, who was dispatched by Leonora's parents to Spain, on a battleship, despite the difficulties presented by the war. Leonora, who had been diagnosed as psychotic, was treated with Cardiazol, an early form of convulsive electrotherapy, which provoked seizures and profound disorientation. Even after departing the institution (and her nanny), which she contrived with great difficulty, Leonora was pursued by her father's spies, with instructions to have her transported to South Africa, where Harold Carrington had arranged for his daughter's incarceration in another mental hospital. She evaded her pursuers and arrived in Lisbon, where she secretly married the Mexican poet and diplomat Renato Leduc, and escaped with him to New York.

In Manhattan, the surrealist set, encouraged by Peggy Guggenheim, had begun to achieve both success and notoriety. André Breton was there, as well as Luis Buñuel, Marcel Duchamp, and of course Max Ernst, who, despite his marriage to Peggy Guggenheim, continued to insist that Leonora was his very own *femme enfant* (a term employed by Breton to designate the innocence and irrationality of the feminine object of desire). Life in New York became insufferable to Leonora, and the clinging attentions and demands of Ernst eventually lost their appeal. Leonora was never happy with the role of muse foisted on their women by the male surrealists. It seems extraordinary that the supposedly enlightened males of the group should hold such traditional attitudes, and that artists of the calibre of Carrington and Lee Miller should have had to first graduate as glamorous appendages, or *femmes enfants*, to the group, before emerging from the shadow of their men.

Moving to Mexico City with Leduc, Leonora found it no easier to settle than she had in New York. She considered the lifestyle led by the group of artists clustered around Diego Rivera and Frida Kahlo as stifling as Peggy Guggenheim's set had been in New York. The aversion was mutual, Frida Kahlo referring to Leonora and her small circle as 'those European bitches.' According to her friend Elena Poniatowska's account, in *Leonora*, a lightly fictionalised biography, "Leonora stays well away from Frida Kahlo and her hair plaited with coloured ribbons. She is put off by her strident manner of speaking and the huddled chorus of women who follow her around singing her every praise. She concludes: 'I think that smoking is the only thing we have in common.'" She also drifted apart from Leduc, with whom she shared few interests, and who wanted her to perform the role of trophy wife, which interested her not at all, as she had made plain in her dealings with men hitherto.

But she did eventually settle, remarrying and bearing two sons to the Hungarian photographer, Emérico 'Chiki' Weisz, and remained in Mexico for the rest of her life, apart from a visit to England following the 1968 massacre of students in Tlatelolco – which had come close to home, both of Leonora's sons being active in the student resistance – and several extended sojourns in New York City. During all this time she produced paintings of a consistently vivid brilliance and mythic imagery, alchemical symbols, and of course animals, lots of strange animals. In the 1970s she also became a leading figure in the women's movement in Mexico. Her friendships with other women, first and foremost Remedios Varo, but also the photographer Kati Hora, the writer Elena Poniatowska and, in later years, Marina Warner, helped not only to establish the bedrock of her feminist vision, but also provided a deeper companionship than she ever seemed to achieve with men – other than with her own sons, Gabriel and Pablo.

Alongside her output of paintings, sculptures, set and costume designs, recipes and miscellaneous artefacts (including a beautiful set of tarot cards), Carrington wrote a series of strange and captivating short stories or fables, and a novel, *The Hearing Trumpet*, a small masterpiece that tackled the theme of environmental disaster long before global climate change became mainstream, and a prescient example of ecofeminism *avant la lettre*. As Lorna Scott Fox has pointed out, much of Carrington's written output corresponds closely with what Hélène Cixous has termed écriture féminine, "a fluid, uncategorical mode that affirms multiplicity and irresolution." We might go further with 'irresolution', as Carrington's work across diverse media suggests an openness to uncertainty and negative capability, and a keen observance of what the surrealists called 'hasard objectif' (objective chance), or what Jung – a far more important figure for Carrington than was Freud, by which she can be differentiated from the other surrealists – called synchronicity, or 'meaningful coincidence'. Wandering the rooms of the exhibition, I fall into a kind of trance, as though possessed by the spirit of Leonora, and all of her deeply personal obsessions: the duality of Celtic mythology and her lifelong interest in the Irish *aes sídhe* or 'fair folk' (*tylwyth teg* in Welsh); her use of dream symbology; her interweaving of themes from her study of alchemy, and her fascination with indigenous cosmology, as practised among the Maya of Chiapas.

★ ★ ★

On my last evening in Mexico City I join my friends Pedro and Carlos in a taquería to watch football: the Mexican Cup Final. The match is between León and Pachuca. The second of these cities is known as Pachuca la airosa (Pachuca the windy) and its football team has a curious history. It is the oldest club in Mexico, having been formed in 1901 by Cornishmen who arrived in the area to work in mines owned by one William Blamey, a merchant adventurer known to the Mexicans as El Manco (the one-armed man). The team was augmented by locals who took to the game, and eventually became one of the nation's leading clubs. The dish for which Pachuca cuisine is famed – harking back to those miners – is a variety of Cornish Pasty, known locally as *pastes*. This name is also used in reference to the people from that town, as well as its football team. On Thursday night, despite the howls of disapproval around me (we were drinking in a hotbed of León supporters), the *Pastes* won 3-2.

At the airport bar, before my flight homeward, a very *besoffen* German engages me in conversation, in erratic English. He is, I guess, in his late thirties and has a shaven head and small, red eyes. "Europe is finished," he tells me, thanks to the "dictatorship of Brussels." "We have many dictators in Europe," he says, "the last was Hitler, and before that we have the Swedish um, er ... what was his name ... Gustavus Adolphus, and the other was, er, er ...". He seems to be in physical pain, his face contorting as he attempts to remember the name of another European dictator. Napoleon? I suggest. "Ja, ja, Napoleon," he says with a sigh, relieved at being rescued from his struggle with history. "But now we have Brussels and all is finished." He stares at me dolefully, allowing the significance of this utterance to sink in, and then demands three tequilas from the barman, who fills a trio of shot glasses, his face utterly without expression – a vacancy that nonetheless conveys fastidious contempt.

The core of the German's argument, on which he continues to elaborate, is that Europe was much better off as a collection of independent nation states with their own laws and their own currencies. So, I ask, just to be certain: you are against the idea of a federal Europe? "Ja, ja," he says, nodding his shiny pate with extraordinary vigour. "Otherwise we will be always fighting the war against the dictatorship from Brussels."

I struggle to follow this logic, and want to point out to him that it was precisely because of the continual warmongering between these independent nation states – of which his own was perhaps the prime offender – that the idea of a European Union emerged, but I fear that his grasp of such a basic concept is imperilled by the dispatching in rapid succession of two of the three tequilas, and besides, I suspect, from his glazed expression, that he might, at this very moment, be dreaming of a Fourth Reich. What has he been doing in Mexico? I ask.

"I have been doing my work, which I do," he tells me, unhelpfully, and necks the third tequila. He explains that his flight to Geneva leaves at 9.00 pm and he likes to be the last one on board, "in order to make the others wait." This amuses him greatly and he guffaws into his empty shot glass, before setting off hurriedly towards Departures. I finish my drink and leave to catch my own flight to Paris, glancing at the departures board on the way. There is no 9.00 pm flight to Geneva.

> Yet I am sure of this —
> that somewhere in my body there is fiesta,
> with ribboned dogs, balloons, and children dancing
> in a lost village, that only I remember.
>
> Alastair Reid, 'The Tale The Hermit Told.'

Dumfries & Galloway, Scotland, July 2014

North of Preston, the landscape opened up, with a broad sweep of hills and a more generous allocation of green space. I began to draw slower breaths, releasing some of the tension that had been accumulating in my shoulders since joining the motorway near Tewkesbury, and which had stayed with me as I drove up the M6, in heavy traffic. Only now did the flow of vehicles begin to diminish and, as if to complement this leavening in the world of motorised things, the sun came out, a somewhat pale and arctic sun, to be sure, but no less welcome for that.

I was on my way to visit my friend, the Scottish poet Tom Pow. Tom had arranged for me to meet Alastair Reid, who lived in New York but spent part of every summer in the Galloway region of south-west Scotland, where he was born and raised. Tom had been urging me to meet with Alastair Reid for several years, and was keen to facilitate this meeting. I was familiar with much of Reid's work, not only the translations, but also his essays in the collection *Outside In*, in which I had been immersed for the past few days, and which included 'Notes on Being a Foreigner', a recurring source of reflection and analysis over the course of my travels. I felt the pleasant throb of expectation, happy to be spending time with someone I considered a mentor, even if we had never met, and whose own, promising career as a poet in the 1950s was later subsumed by his career as a translator and essayist. In his youth, Reid had been compared favourably to both Dylan Thomas and W.H. Auden, and was adopted by Robert Graves as a kind of protégé, and the two men remained close friends until Reid eloped with Margot Callas, Graves' muse of the moment, for which he was never forgiven. In Reid, it might be argued, the act of translation had replaced the need to write his own poetry, and I was curious to know how this had happened, partly because I could observe the same thing happening to myself. In the end, I never asked him, and perhaps that was because, at some level, I didn't care to know, or else because it was apparent from his answers to my questions that the topic was of no great importance to him, I cannot say for sure. What I did know was that Reid had met and befriended many of the Latin American writers of the day, including Mario Vargas Llosa, Gabriel García Márquez, Jorge Luis Borges, Pablo Neruda, José Emilio Pacheco, Enrique Lihn and Álvaro Mutis, some of whom he also translated.

Although I wasn't concerned by the fact — I was eighteen at the time — the first story I ever read by Borges, 'Tlön, Uqbar, Orbis Tertius', was in a translation by Alastair Reid. His name cropped up as the translator of other stories and poems by Borges, and later in the translations I read of Pablo Neruda. As well as introducing me, albeit unknowingly, to the work of Borges — a defining experience in my reading — this man had helped set me on the course that my life was currently taking, as a hunter and translator of Latin American poets on my journeys across Argentina, Mexico and Colombia. For this reason alone, I thought, as I closed in on Dumfries, there could not have been a better time to meet him.

At Tom's Victorian terraced home, we ate dinner, caught up with each other's lives, and watched the 2014 World Cup Final on television. Like most of the football-watching world outside Germany we were rooting for Argentina, but they and their talisman, Lionel Messi, disappointed, and the Germans emerged victorious, as they usually do in such contests.

The next morning, early sunshine promised a fine day as Tom and I set off in my car across the rolling Dumfries countryside towards our rendezvous. Alastair was staying in a converted farmbuilding that he rented each summer with his American film-maker wife, Leslie. She welcomed us warmly; the Reids and

Tom were old friends, and Tom had once stayed with them for a month in the Dominican Republic, before his own Latin American journey. Leslie led us into the kitchen, where first we had coffee and chatted for a while, following the typical Latin habit, preferred by Alastair, of observing social graces before getting down to business. After a while Alastair gestured to me and said, "Well, should we have our talk?" and we retired to a room overlooking the garden, which also served as his study, leaving Leslie and Tom to exchange news while Leslie prepared lunch.

At eighty-eight, Alastair was a little frayed around the edges, but alert and bright-eyed as a moorland bird. After a cautious start, conscious of the small recording device on the low table between us, we soon fell into fluent conversation.

I was still in the early stages of putting my anthology together, and we began by surveying the linguistic territory, especially the problem of the term 'Latin America'. Since I was not including poets from Portuguese, or indeed poets writing in the indigenous languages of the Americas, how was I to define or delimit the scope of my anthology, other than by the unwieldy term 'Spanish language American poetry?' Alastair made the point that there were many Latin American poets who don't like being called 'Spanish American' because they considered themselves 'American American', suggesting that for my anthology I might refer simply to 'Poets from Latin America' and locate them geographically and linguistically, as appropriate; and that is what I did.

I told Alastair that, following the course of my travels to date, I was best acquainted with poets from Argentina, Mexico and Colombia; I had yet to explore the Chilean poets in any great depth, and had read only selectively from elsewhere on the continent. He replied that he was puzzled by many aspects of Chilean poetry; the success of Raúl Zurita, for example, whose name he initially forgot, as opposed to Nicanor Parra, for whom he had a great deal of respect. Speaking of him in the past tense (he was in fact celebrating his one hundredth birthday that same month) Alastair seemed to think that Parra's so-called 'anti-poetry' started out as an 'anti-Neruda' poetry. Parra, he said, had a very definite intention to do anti-Neruda poems because Chile was so dominated by Neruda, and Parra resisted him. Parra was, Alastair said, healthy, mischievous and funny, which could not be said of his many imitators, in Chile and elsewhere. On the other hand, Alastair had a high regard for the poets of Colombia. He had recently been working, with Edith Grossman, on a collection of translations from Álvaro Mutis, and was pleased to learn that I was planning a book of poems by Darío Jaramillo, another Colombian poet he admired.

On the act of translation itself, Alastair was at once forthcoming and intriguingly elusive. He said that, for him, translation was a kind of bewitchment, but also an activity that necessitated a good deal of background excavation. He claimed, perhaps surprisingly, that translators were far more interested in mistranslation than in good translation, because mistranslation was so revealing. There was, he said, this curious linguistic no-man's-land that only translators know about, and from which emerges an astonishingly rich list of *untranslatables*, each item revealing something about the nature of language itself. That, he said, is why translation was not a business simply of transposing something into another language, it was about getting to the very edge of saying, where, if you look closely, you can see the curious unspoken depths that are being touched by one or two words.

Although the purpose of my visit was, at least in part, to gain advice on putting together my anthology, we had soon moved on to other themes, and it became apparent to me that Alastair was at his most fluent and relaxed when reminiscing about his friendship with Borges. His association with the Argentine writer, he told me, had its beginnings in a conversation with Mario Vargas Llosa in London, in 1964. Alastair had only recently started out as a translator, and Vargas Llosa, who was then a very young man, told him that if he was going to translate Latin American writers he would have to go there, to Latin America. "You can look up words in the dictionary," Mario had said, "but you've got to know what it smells like." It was at this point that the ghost of Borges entered the room, and seemed to hover between us for the rest of our conversation.

Alastair took Vargas Llosa's words literally, and bought a round-trip ticket from New York to Buenos Aires that allowed unlimited stops along the way, and that, he says, was how he got to know so many Latin American writers just as that explosion of new writing in Spanish, coined and marketed as *El Boom* by the Barcelona literary agent Carmen Balcells and publisher Carlos Barral, was underway. In New York he had met someone – "an extraordinary Argentine woman" – who asked him if he had read Borges. When Alastair replied that he hadn't read Borges or even heard of him, the woman told him that in that case she and Alastair "would have very little to talk about, and turned on her heel." Clearly unused to such treatment, Alastair decided to find out what he was missing, and since this extraordinary woman had known Borges well, she helped him to go and discover – as Vargas Llosa had suggested – what Latin America did smell like. By the time Alastair reached Buenos Aires, he was armed with an introduction to Borges, and went to visit him at the National Library in Recoleta.

On their first meeting at the library, Borges suggested they go out for a walk. As they set off down Calle Mexico, Borges, who was by now almost completely blind, gave Alastair instructions as they went along, asking him to note the names of the street signs and report back. Following Borges' detailed directions, they entered the Recoleta cemetery, and came to a stop before a statue. "Do you see a statue, a head?" Borges asked, and on receiving an affirmative, he told Alastair that the figure was his father's teacher at the university. There was something very bizarre about this first meeting, Alastair said, Borges holding onto his arm, showing him something that he couldn't see himself.

Alastair's words – "he was showing me something in Buenos Aires that he couldn't see" – reminded me of a passage in Edwin Williamson's biography of the writer, when Borges speaks of his realisation that he could no longer make out the words on the title pages or the spines on any of the 900,000 volumes he had in his care at the national library. The blind man maintaining a vast library of books he could not read, and the same man describing a statue he could not see: the two stories share an arresting poignancy.

Translating Borges was, according to Alastair, at times like re-translating something that had originally been written in English, and subsequently translated into Spanish. This, he explained, was due to Borges' long familiarity with the English language. His grandmother was English, and he was brought up bilingually, but learned to read in English first. The task of the translator, then, felt like rendering the story back into its original language, which Alastair described as a somewhat unsettling or daunting experience, and quite unlike translating other Spanish language writers. This merited a fuller explanation.

From an early age, Alastair said, Borges had learned to discriminate between the worlds represented by the two languages, Spanish and English. When he was a very small boy, his grandmother came to live with the family in Palermo, then a rural suburb of Buenos Aires, and he knew that he had to speak in a certain way with her, but with his mother, or with the domestic staff, he had to speak in another way; later he found out that the way in which he spoke with his grandmother was called English and the way he spoke with his mother and the maid was called Spanish.

Because of his father's immense respect for the English language – the household library was stacked with English books – the idea formed in him at an early age that 'literature' was in English, and so, Alastair continued, whenever Borges spoke English, which he liked to do, he did so very correctly, and with an extraordinary respect for the context. However, he would sometimes use expressions such as 'By Jove!' and Alastair would interrupt him, saying, "Borges, nobody says 'By Jove' any more." He may have spoken English with the utmost respect, but if ever they had conversations in Spanish, Alastair continued, when Bioy [Casares] or others were present, he was much wittier, much more malicious than he would ever have been in English. He was, Alastair said, well brought-up and extremely polite: he was gossipy in Spanish, but never in English, and that was his linguistic formation, if you like. But then, if he reverted to Spanish, he could be very bawdy and nasty and jocular.

As for translating him, Alastair went on, the models for his own poetry were in many cases from the English canon and so the process was relatively easy; this is what he meant by saying it was like translating something that was originally written in English and retranslating back from the Spanish. Alastair also found that the living, breathing presence of a writer – of hearing a writer, in this case Borges, speak his words – nearly always suggested fresh ways of rendering him. Although you can't say it's an imperative by any means, he added, it was nothing if not helpful to know your writers in person. This chimed with my own experience, since it was my practice to meet with as many of the poets I intended to translate as was feasible in the time I had available on my travels.

In the years that followed his first encounter with Borges, Alastair having returned to live in New York, where he was employed by the *New Yorker* magazine as a roving staff writer, the two men kept up a correspondence, and Borges was by now attracting a wide readership in the USA. Borges came often to the States, where he was invited to give lectures at various universities. He would frequently visit New York, with a travelling companion, and he would always get in touch with Alastair during these trips. One year, Borges was due to tour some colleges in New England, and the companion who was engaged to take him around fell ill, so Alastair was recruited to go instead. Consequently, they spent a lot of time together. Whenever they had to go to a literary gathering, and meet people, Borges would complain, with a sigh, at a loss why people spoke to him so respectfully about his work, when, really, it wasn't that important: "who was that man who talked to me about that awful story I wrote ... I'm so relieved you interrupted because I was very bored by the conversation." He would also ask, before an official function, in a resigned manner, whether there was anyone on the reception committee from Argentina, and if Alastair replied that no, there was no one from Argentina, Borges would say, "well that's a relief." When they were travelling, however, Borges would get onto one of his favourite subjects, Anglo-Saxon, let's say, or Robert Louis Stevenson, and they had, said Alastair, a far more amusing time.

Borges also came and stayed with Alastair in Scotland, and on one occasion Alastair's son, Jasper, was ill, and Borges went into his room and sat on his bed. There was a low murmur of voices coming from the bedroom, and afterwards Alastair asked Jasper what the two of them had been talking about and Jasper had responded, "Oh Papa, everything," because, Alastair said, Borges took this great pleasure in conversation, and he realised that for Borges, conversation was total experience, sensual experience, visual and literary, and that this interest extended to the language in which a subject was discussed, and they would occasionally be talking about some writer or other and Borges would say it was more appropriate to talk about this author's work in Spanish, and they would switch, and Alastair realised that Borges put a great deal of weight on what he was hearing because, being blind, it was his main source of lived reality, and so language was of primary importance to him, even though it was also deceptive and untrustworthy and fascinating, all at once, and consequently the paradox of blindness and language and perceived reality and listened-to reality were all part of a very complicated state of being.

Alastair spoke of what he termed Borges' 'impenetrable modesty', recounting an occasion when they gave a talk at the PEN club in New York, Borges having invited Alastair to come and help out. Borges always asked the audience to write their questions on pieces of paper, while whispering – here Alastair adopted a conspiratorial tone —"Don't bother about the questions, just look at them and see if any of them are interesting." In any case, Alastair knew which topics would get Borges going, and so preferred to make up the questions himself, and he, Borges, would say, while addressing the work of some poet or other, "I too have written a poem, at least I refer to it as a poem", or "I will read some lines from my feeble effort", and Alastair would correct him, saying he was not entitled to refer to his own poetry in that way, to speak of his own work in such derogatory terms as his "pobres versos," insisting that this was what critics were for, and it was not for him to cast such judgement, and would tell him, "sometimes, Borges, you use modesty like a club." In addition, Alastair said, Borges was continually apologising. This tendency to apologise, one might surmise, was intrinsically linked to his upbringing in what was deemed, at the turn of the last century, a correct and respectful use of English.

On one of Borges' visits to the States, he was accompanied by a young Argentine woman of Japanese heritage, Maria Kodama, whom he would later marry. Alastair painted a picture of Borges as being deeply in love with Maria, and she with him. He gave the impression that she brought Borges a good deal of happiness, which, after his earlier, disastrous marriage to Elsa Astete Millán, was almost certainly a good thing.

Alastair said that barely a day went by without him reading something by Borges. During our conversation, he frequently spoke of Borges in the present tense, despite the Argentine writer having died in 1986.

I was especially curious when Alastair began to speak about the term 'fiction' as a way of relating one's engagement with the world, as opposed to fiction as a literary genre. In all of his encounters with Borges, Alastair told me, he began to realise that this notion of a fiction was central to him: he referred to his own writing – essays, poems, stories or reviews – all as 'fictions'. He would say, "there's a fiction I wrote … there's a fiction about that." Indeed, Borges referred to everything that was put into words as a fiction, including service bills or listings in a telephone directory or the speeches of politicians. I was intrigued to learn that Borges referred to his essays as 'fictions', especially since 'fictions' (ficciones) was the title of the collection of short stories that first brought him international fame. I asked for clarification. Yes, Alastair insisted. "I too have written some fictions," he would say, referring to his essays.

In his own essay, 'Fictions', Alastair expands on the idea as follows:

> *A fiction is any construct of language – a story, an explanation, a plan, a theory, a dogma – that gives a certain shape to reality.*
>
> *Reality, that which is beyond language, functions by mainly indecipherable laws, which we do not understand, and over which we have limited control. To give some form to reality, we bring into being a variety of fictions.*

> *A fiction, it is understood, can never be true, since the nature of language is utterly different from the nature of reality.*

These ideas – especially the last of those listed above – are inspired variations of those he acquired from his conversations with Borges. Alastair's essay is in no sense Borges' work; Borges did not, he insisted, philosophise, considering philosophy simply another branch of the fantastical and the fictional – but it represents more or less the bones of Borges' thinking about language and literature. In Borges's universe there is no single truth, there are only multitudes of fictions, and we have to choose amongst them, to find those that fit us. It took him a long time, Alastair continued, to really encompass what Borges thought, and it boiled down to the idea that we have two realities: one is our perceived reality from early life onward, our learned experience, to which we keep adding as we learn and acquire new experiences throughout our life; and the other reality is the reality of language, which we use to make sense of our lived reality. The fictions that we conjure from language – whether in literature or in conversation – are very far from corresponding accurately to our lived reality, and yet they are the ones we believe in. So we are constantly facing the paradox of experiencing something, giving it linguistic form, and then betraying it. And always we have to re-make it … so human existence is essentially one of being a *ficcionero*, a maker of fictions. We are all ficcioneros, Alastair went on, continually making and re-making fictions, and failing. "There's an extraordinary poem," he said, "I'm sure you know it – 'The Other Tiger'? That's such an amazing poem, and the last stanza is extraordinary …" and Alastair recited from his own translation:

> I know all this; yet something
> drives me to this ancient, perverse adventure,
> foolish and vague, yet still I keep on looking
> throughout the evening for the other tiger,
> the other tiger, the one not in this poem.

I reflected on this notion that poetry can only ever approach – but can never quite capture – the ideal of the 'other tiger' it seeks to represent or evoke; that always there will remain a gulf between language and lived reality. Alastair, who had paused after speaking the last words of the poem, looked up again. "That's forever and ever and ever and ever," he said, looking at me. "It's a great corrective to poets, that one." And with this insight, Alastair had unwittingly gifted me the title of my anthology.

And on this topic – the ultimate evasiveness of the 'other tiger' – Alastair mentioned a poem of his own, 'The Tale the Hermit Told', in which the speaker attends a fiesta, and falls under the spell of the occasion. After a series of encounters, he is offered a glass of "golden wine" in which "the sun / was a small gold coin, the people looked like nuts. / The band were brass buttons, the towering mountains / the size of pebbles" ... On gulping down the wine, the speaker falls into a kind of otherworld, in which he lives "on bitter nuts and bark and grasses" and loses all sense of time. In the poem, he remains on this "barren mountainside. The years are nothing." Nevertheless, he believes that somewhere, in his body, "there is fiesta, / with ribboned dogs, balloons, children dancing / in a lost village, that only I remember."

The poem was written, Alastair told me, after taking LSD, "when you are exposed to these incredibly concise images of the natural world and you seem to be taking in the whole universe – but once you have seen, once you have glimpsed that, it becomes the fiction that stays with you, and a sensible reality remains always out of reach ... you could make your way towards the whole, but it was always going to evade you." I understood him to mean that on certain significant occasions, even though the essence – the other tiger – is lost, the moment provides a kind of template or imprint – a 'fiction' – which becomes fixed in time, and recurs indefinitely, as a memory.

Before we broke off for lunch, I wanted to ask Alastair about the essay that had so articulately represented his ideas on travel and identity, 'Notes on Being a Foreigner', and which had returned to me so vividly as I sat outside the bar in Condesa, in Mexico City, three months before. I told him how much I had enjoyed his essay, and how, when I had begun travelling on my own, in my late teens, I had begun to realise that I was more myself in other places than ever I was in the place where I grew up.

He nodded his head vigorously: "word for word, absolutely I felt that," he replied, and began reminiscing about his experiences in the Royal Navy as a postman in World War Two and immediately afterwards, when he was sent ashore to collect mail, often in countries where he spoke not a word of the local language; and it was then, he said, that he began to feel the thrill of being able to construct an entirely fictional identity, of being anyone he wished to be. Returning to the stark austerity of post-war Britain and rationing, he decided to go off and discover more fictions. He went to Spain, first to Barcelona, where he immersed himself in the Spanish language, prior to his move to Mallorca, where, he became a part of Robert Graves' inner circle, accompanying Graves on his US tour in 1957, before their epic falling out over Margot Callas. Of Alastair's relationship with Graves, James Campbell has written: "Reid was never forgiven. Graves wrote a poem about his rival, in which the phrase 'witty devil' is coupled in near-rhyme with 'oozing evil'. Reid never sought revenge for these and other spiteful acts. On the contrary, he wrote a judicious memoir, 'Remembering Robert Graves', for the *New Yorker*, in 1995, and later included in his selected prose, *Outside In*." Graves had, Alastair always recognised, given him so much, even – as Tom later reminded me – a way of being and of working.

'On Being a Foreigner', Alastair told me, is about suspending what you owe to your birth-right, and what you agree to obey, the rules that you abide by, especially in the early years of life. But, he went on, this suspension, or rejection of acquired information was something that happened over time, a process of gradual disbelieving. It still goes on, he said. Scotland was a place where everyone had secrets, and they hang on desperately to their secrets ("empty secrets", he called them). He had been shaking off this inheritance all his life, he said, and he still thought of it as an impediment to true awareness. By contrast, he was very content, very much at ease living in the Spanish language, because it didn't have those particular pitfalls, the linguistic entrapments that he had inherited with his mother tongue. Our native language pulls us back in, Alastair said, and he had been involved in the process of ridding himself of those entrapments all his life by bringing in other places, other languages, to replace the ones he was discarding.

For this reason, Alastair continued, it was very helpful for him to write 'On Being a Foreigner', since the essay was the first piece he'd written that contained that degree of self-examination, and it helped with self-definition, in a way that he hadn't approached before. He had read the piece again, not long ago, and still liked it. That's always a relief, isn't it? I said, and he laughed and had a small coughing fit.

Before I left, Alastair asked if I had any plans to visit New York, suggesting that we continue our conversation at his home there. I mentioned that I could make a detour on my way back from Colombia in the autumn. However, this never happened: two and a half months later, on 21st September, 2014, Alastair passed away.

PART III

> ... memory is fickle,
> at the customs post we lost
> something irretrievable.
>
> Catalina González Restrepo, 'Viaje'.

Bogotá, Colombia, September 2014

At Bogotá's El Dorado airport our plane makes an awkward touchdown; two long hops and a resounding bump, before finally landing. The city is on a plane high in the Andes, and because of strong winds pilots often struggle with the descent. Once on the ground, as *Lonely Planet* warns its readers, you might be advised to watch your breath: "Bogotá is at 2,640 meters ... Altitude adaptation takes time – the first day or two, take it easy." By taking it easy, I assume they mean one should walk more slowly than usual. I attempt a gentle stroll up to the shopping centre from my hotel. I need to buy a cheap phone, since I am going to be in Colombia for at least a month.

As I leave the hotel, a speeding courier crashes his cycle into the kerb and is propelled headfirst over his handlebars. He looks shaken, but when I offer him a hand, he says he's OK, and staggers to his feet. At the phone shop, a young man sporting a complicated haircut takes my passport and photocopies it. When he returns with my purchase order, I have a new name: Richard British Citizen. Since Spanish surnames are composed of two parts, the father's and the mother's names respectively, I guess it made sense to him that my father was called 'British' and my mother, 'Citizen'. Perhaps he thought 'Gwyn' was not sufficient. Walking back from the phone shop a wild-looking youth darts into the traffic without looking, causing a truck to brake and swerve across the road, narrowly missing a cyclist.

Not unnaturally, I am concerned that today might be a day for accidents or, at the very least, for near-misses. I proceed along the street, proud bearer of my new name, on the lookout for a third errant vehicle. The sky is cloudy and the air is thin. It rains for ten minutes, then stops. The sun is far, far away, behind the clouds, beyond the mountain peaks. I want to adjust to Bogotá, to try and like it a little more than I did on my visit last year. But Bogotá is not a loveable city.

Returning to the hotel I see a piece of graffiti on a nearby wall: *Donde están los otros?* Where are the others? Indeed, where are they? Have they crashed their bikes, or been run over by a truck? Or are they just late in arriving, because they have to walk so very slowly. Just as well we are not in La Paz, where the altitude is over four thousand metres. People there, I imagine, would walk really slowly, were it not for the fact that there is always a helpful street vendor to hand, selling coca leaves, which, I am assured, help with respiration. However, I am not suffering, and nor will I, from any of the advertised symptoms of altitude sickness, and nor do I require coca or any of its derivatives, at least not yet.

The festival I am due to attend, organised by the poet Federico Díaz-Granados, is titled *Las Líneas de su Mano,* which, depending on the context, might be translated as 'The lines of your, his, her, or one's hand'. I decide to ask Federico which of these collocations he intended, but in the end I never get around to it.

At almost every conference or literary festival of this type that I have attended over the past few years, a part of the activity has been given over to the celebration of some eminent writer, for their lifetime's achievement. Writers from the English-speaking world are often impressed or flattered by the respect afforded their peers in Latin America, as well as in other areas of the world, where to be a writer, or a teacher, counts for something. As well as the celebration of their life's work, a good deal of bowing and scraping goes on at these events in honour of eminent literary figures, who tend to be older, for obvious reasons, and male. This attitude of hallowed respect prevails, however decrepit, boring or lecherous the celebrity poet might be, as for example in Medellín two years before, when the Brazilian bard being honoured couldn't keep his tremulous octogenarian hands away from whichever of the younger female poets came within groping distance, a behaviour which was tolerated on account of his alleged greatness as well as his great age. It would seem that many of us are still attached to the archetype of the wise old man which, in many cases, turns out to be a misnomer. The fact of the matter is that many people simply get stupider as they get older; their prejudices atrophy, their most disagreeable traits come to the fore, and they are only interested in talking, or hearing, about themselves.

On the first night of *Las Líneas de la Mano*, a Mexican poet, who was celebrating his eighty-fifth birthday, was lauded in this way. During the sycophantic introductory remarks, made, in turn, by three of his acolytes, also guests at the conference, I was alarmed to learn that this venerable sage was responsible for one of "the three great works of misogyny" of the twentieth century. From their applause and hoots of mirth, his fans clearly thought that this was quite an accomplishment.

How on earth, I wondered, could it be considered acceptable to make a statement of that kind, especially in the context of a country like Mexico, where a new term, *femicide,* had been coined specifically for the murder of women, and where gender violence was of epidemic proportions? You do not need to have ploughed through the gruelling fourth section of Roberto Bolaño's *2666* – 'The Part about the Crimes' — to be aware of this, although it helps; simply reading the daily accounts of abductions, rapes and the murders of women will suffice. Or, again, these brave machos might try reading María Rivera's poem, 'The Dead', which, as we have seen, records in detail the crimes perpetrated against women in Mexico. How can it be acceptable for educated men to make jokes about misogyny, as they did at this event celebrating the old goat's birthday? By the same standards, would it be acceptable to joke that such and such a volume was one of the "great racist novels of the twentieth century"?

I had come across this group of Mexican poets before, and in Nicaragua had spent some time with one of them – quite an eminent figure in his way – and had considered placing a poem of his in my anthology, until, that evening in Bogotá, listening to the older Mexican read his work, I realised that the acolyte's poem was plagiarised, or at least, was heavily derivative of a poem by his *maestro*. So I let it go, and over the course of the conference, and in the weeks that followed, I forgot about the whole unsavoury event.

However, there was a sequel to this encounter, which I should mention, as it throws light on the strength of opinion surrounding literary matters in Latin America and the potential for actual violence that these opinions can provoke, especially when words are bandied about with ill intent. The so-called 'poetry wars' of the English-speaking world, which erupt from time to time, pale into insignificance when compared with the grave accusations made against the Colombian poet Juan Manuel Roca in March, 2018, by two of the Mexicans who championed the elderly poet that night in Bogotá. On what grounds, it is hard to say – perhaps it was due, in part, to the envy that Roca's success provoked in his less accomplished accusers – but in that month the two Mexican poets made the extraordinary allegation that Roca was an agent of the FARC, Colombia's guerrilla insurgents, as well – despite the apparent contradiction in the twin claims – as being a stooge of the Medellín Cartel. Such accusations, risible as they may have been, actually put Roca's life, and the lives of his family, in immediate danger. One does not make assertions of this kind in Colombia; nor, for that matter, in Mexico. Roca's own response was to shrug them off, stating merely that since he had never crossed paths with either the FARC or the Medellín Cartel, he had nothing to justify or defend. But the damage had already been done.

Although I mention this exchange only to indicate the fraught and at times explosive nature of enmities inside the Latin American literary world, wherein accusations can have potentially fatal consequences, there is a lesson to be learned from it, nonetheless: you should be mindful of what you say, because sometimes a careless remark will come back to bite you, and from then on the past won't leave you alone; advice I might have heeded myself, as I was shortly to discover, albeit on a less dramatic scale.

During my time in London, in my early twenties, I occasionally had walk-on roles as a poet – or what nowadays would be called a spoken word artist – with bands at insalubrious venues in the punk and immediate post-punk era. My most stellar performance took place alongside The Cure at a gig in Walthamstow. I don't have a clear memory of the circumstances and am unsure now whether the things that I remember are what actually took place, or whether some other ...misremembered version of events has overlaid them.

Because I foolishly mentioned it in an interview when I was short of ideas, 'The Cure gig' became an incident about which I was asked to give an account far more often than I would have liked, especially when interviewed by a fan of that band – which, incidentally, I am not. Indeed, I have never knowingly listened to more than a couple of songs by The Cure, and am unlikely to do so now. Nevertheless, this is precisely the way in which many fictions come about – through negligence on the part of the protagonist.

At my first event in Bogotá's Gimnasio Moderno – an elite private school, attended by the scions of the powerful and wealthy – I came onstage to the sound of 'Killing an Arab' pounding over the speakers, in front of over a hundred Colombian school students, who, I was certain, would have no idea who The Cure were, as well as a few weathered-looking individuals of my own generation, who probably would: the event was also open to members of the paying public.

I gave my reading and was then required to deliver a monologue and answer questions about various aspects of Being a Writer, a topic, of itself, in which I have very little interest. I had given this talk before, to unfortunate children in other parts of the world, as we have seen, and was in the process of delivering my usual spiel, telling them to read widely and voraciously, when it occurred to me that the whole Cure story might just as well be a lie. Had I, in fact, made this story up? Perhaps it would have been easier to claim that I had, and then I wouldn't need to recount what happened, when I couldn't actually remember much at all. However, during the extended Q & A, I was required to tell the story of what happened that night in 1980 when somebody introduced me to Robert Smith, and I ended doing my rant on stage (I hesitate to call it poetry) and was asked back by Mr Smith to do another set during the interval. These uniformed and well-behaved Colombian school kids, to whom I assumed I was talking of matters as remote as the Magna Carta, turned out to know as much about the British punk scene as I did. Punk is very big in Bogotá, as I was to discover, first hand, a few nights later; and here, in the illustrious Gimnasio Moderno, the audience posed an endless series of questions: Did I know the Sex Pistols personally? How about The Clash? Was I friends with Johnny Rotten? Johnny, I told them, makes commercials for a popular brand of butter these days (they seemed a little confused by this reply).

The Q & A was rapidly deteriorating into a sort of farce, and I suspected that I might have to make up answers to the onslaught of questions. I looked around helplessly, hoping against hope to identify a friendly face in the audience. I noticed my old pal Jorge a few rows back, grinning unashamedly at my distress. *Donde están los otros?* Where are the others? I wondered. I had a feeling this item of graffiti was going to pursue me for the duration of my Bogotá sojourn. The dark thought took root that these others had been disappeared, terminally.

But to my relief, everyone seemed to be enjoying themselves, and the older, one-time aficionados of punk, the ones of my own age, had almost as many questions as the youngsters. The more I reminisced about the London of that era, the more lucid I became: I recalled the 100 Club in Oxford Street, where I first saw the Sex Pistols; the Roxy in Covent Garden, which I visited most weeks, despite conspicuously failing to follow the dress code; bumping into John Lydon at his local in Camden town; my single encounter with Sid and Nancy at the bar of the Rainbow Theatre during an ill-fated Ramones concert when a group of enraged fans decided to uproot the seats in the stalls so that they could pogo themselves silly; all my half-remembered encounters with these jaded luminaries went down like gold dust among these unexpectedly well-informed Colombian fans, hungry for punk-era gossip. It was all very strange.

Back at the hotel, I flicked on the TV. The situation in Iraq was out of control, and there was footage of mass shootings in Baghdad, and I began to imagine how this question, 'where are the others?' could keep recurring in an infinite series of parallel Bogotás, to the soundtrack of The Cure playing their most famous song, with its horribly contentious but acutely contemporary title.

In an unexpected sequel to my trip down memory lane, Paula, the much younger Colombian girlfriend of Jules – a portly, flamboyantly moustachioed Gallic poet, who resembled Gustave Flaubert in his prime – invited me, along with some of the more adventurous members of our literary entourage, to an evening out on Bogotá's wild side. It was Saturday night, and we were headed, Paula said, for a club promisingly titled *Infierno* (Hell) where, she assured me, we could sample the delights of Bogotá's very own, thriving punk scene. The idea filled me with a kind of dread, but Paula was nothing if not persuasive; besides, I regarded such invitations as constituting research, and therefore ranking among my essential duties as Ambassador. I agreed to go along, against my better judgement.

When we arrived the place was still quiet, as 10 pm is early by Colombian standards, but Paula, who was hip and savvy, knew the manager and almost all the habitués of Hell; she did a whip-round among the delegation of international poets and procured a quantity of white powder (given where we were, this was almost inevitable) which was snaffled up in the toilets – a process that recurred at intervals throughout the evening – while the sounds of The Clash, The Damned, Sham 69, X Ray Spex, The Slits and others played deafeningly on the sound system inside the tiny club. This had the uncomfortable effect of casting me adrift in time, so that while a part of the present day me was here in Bogotá, I felt simultaneously possessed by an earlier incarnation of myself, for whom such places were once only too familiar. There was a sense of parody to all this, as if the past were mocking the present. However, I was just within my comfort zone; at least, until I ventured downstairs with Jules and we wandered by mistake into a comically elaborate pole-dancing show, from which I had to return – counter-intuitively – up the stairs to Hell, and in its pounding heart allowed the night to run its course, via a series of blurred visions and inane conversations, until dawn, which in turn dissolved into the cold Bogotá morning and a taxi ride back to the hotel, under leaden skies.

> Near the rocks, belly up, is God
> The fishermen in a line heave at the net
> And now he lies there, white eyes staring at the sky
> He looks like a terminally distracted swimmer
> He looks like a big fat fish with a very big tail
>
> Rómulo Bustos Aguirre, 'Marbella Scene'.

Cartagena, Colombia, September 2014

Cartagena de Indias sits in heavy, torpid heat. At the airport I take a taxi into town, having booked into a hostel in Getsemaní, which, Paula has advised me, is the hip place to stay. After a short drive through the largely deserted city, the driver drops me off in a narrow street just down from a church, La Santísima Trinidad, and its small adjoining plaza, around which loiters a group of local men, smoking weed, and a few travellers, humping backpacks. It is siesta time, and it takes an age for anyone to respond to the hostel doorbell, but when eventually a rather grouchy man opens up, disturbed from his afternoon nap, he waves his arm towards the interior of the building and at once shuffles back into his dark alcove, leaving me to find my way across the shadowy foyer towards a large desk. There is no one behind it so I sit on a sofa and wait, which I am happy to do, since the reception area is a cool, dark cave, an air-conditioned refuge from the broiling heat without. After a while, a woman appears, rubbing her eyes; she looks at my passport, checks me in, then leads me out onto the courtyard of what would once have been a spacious two-storied house, but which is now filled by a supernaturally blue swimming pool. She passes me the key to my room on the upper level, points to a door, and I ascend a staircase and proceed along a frail platform flanked by a wooden rail. Once inside, I am grateful for the air conditioning.

I try to sleep, if only for half an hour, but sleep evades me, so I read my pirated Spanish copy of *Love in the Time of Cholera* until, unable to concentrate, I venture outside again. On the street, the air is like hot, thick soup, but I wade through it on an ill-conceived shopping mission, in search of a battery for my camera. In the nearby Getsemaní market I approach one of the stalls selling phones and electrical accessories. A young woman comes over to serve me, breaks into a smile, retires to the back of the shop and returns with half a dozen tissues, gesturing towards my face. I thank her, self-consciously, realising – in my role of sweaty, beetroot-faced Beast to her svelte Afro-Caribbean Beauty – that I am simply another feckless tourist, foolish enough to venture out in the horribly humid heat of the tropical day.

Hot is the overriding theme of my visit thus far. On the first night I stay up writing, and after a couple of hours step onto the veranda outside my room to be wrapped at once in sweetly florid warmth. It is 3.30 in the morning and 32 degrees centigrade. The dense perfume of lush, climbing plant-life hangs on the air, and the world out there is silent apart from the barking of a lone insomniac dog. I stand on the terrace and smoke, until the lure of the air conditioning draws me back inside. I know I will not sleep, and pick up *Love in the Time of Cholera*. Having read Lowry in Cuernavaca, I feel inclined to read García Márquez in Cartagena; but I am apprehensive. I never fully appreciated *Love in the Time of Cholera* when it first appeared, back in the 1980s. I was still in thrall to the García Márquez of *One Hundred Years of Solitude*, and while acknowledging the meticulous skill of its composition, was confused that he had written what seemed like a nineteenth-century novel. Looking back now, I can see that my reaction revealed more about me than about the book itself. *One Hundred Years of Solitude* is a young person's novel, written in an explosion of creative energy over eighteen months and a million cigarettes, and *Love in the Time of Cholera* is a novel of maturity, or at the very least, of middle age. Its premise is the perennial fiction of eternal love, involving a trio of characters: the eighteen-year old Florentino Ariza falls for the schoolgirl Fermina Daza, and courts her throughout her adolescence, before eventually being ditched when, at the age of nineteen, Fermina marries the far more eligible and somewhat older Dr Juvenal Urbino. The doctor, returning from Paris, where he has worked with the leading physicians of the day, first meets Fermina during the time of cholera, when she is suspected of having the disease (it turns out to be only a mild intestinal infection).

Dr Juvenal Urbino, heir to one of the city's great dynasties, rises to even greater eminence for bringing the epidemic under control, imposing strict rules of cleanliness and quarantine for the infected. In the meantime, far from being defeated by the seemingly irreversible obstacle of Fermina's marriage, Florentino views it as a temporary setback, settles (but never settles down) and waits: he waits – as we are reminded on several occasions – 51 years, 9 months and 4 days, before proposing to Fermina at the funeral following Dr Urbino's death in a fall from a ladder while chasing an irksome parrot up a mango tree. Understandably, she tells him to get lost. This much – Urbino's death and Ariza's proposal – is covered in the long opening chapter, after which we flash back more than half a century to the time of cholera itself. But cholera, as Thomas Pynchon pointed out in his *New York Times* review of the book, has two meanings in Spanish:

> In their city, throughout a turbulent half-century, death has proliferated everywhere, both as *el colera*, the fatal disease that sweeps through in terrible intermittent epidemics, and as *la colera*, defined as choler or anger, which taken to its extreme becomes warfare. Victims of one, in this book, are more than once mistaken for victims of the other. War, 'always the same war', is presented here not as the continuation by other means of any politics that can possibly matter, but as a negative force, a plague, whose only meaning is death on a massive scale. Against this dark ground, lives, so precarious, are often more and less conscious projects of resistance, even of sworn opposition, to death.

In this novel, however, cholera – or disease in general – is also cognate with love. Perversely, in light of the novel's overarching themes of love and disease, by the end of the story it is only by concealing the more extreme and obsessive dimensions of his character, which have sustained him over half a century of longing, and offering her instead a more rational, refined and ascetic version of himself, does Florentino ultimately succeed in his goal of seducing Fermina. This is achieved through his daily letters to her, in which he dons the mask of rational 'Old World' wisdom and culture in preference to the raw, impassioned New World persona which Fermina rejected five decades before. Yet there is no suggestion in the novel that beneath this mask Florentino does not continue to harbour the same romanticised fantasy of Fermina that he always has. Their love is a third age re-enactment (or parody) of young love, but at the same time they both know they are play-acting at being their younger selves, and they both know they are not. The affair works because they are at ease with this ambivalence and can appreciate that it is perfectly suited to their narrative present; two characters living out the remainder of their lives in a sustained suspension of disbelief.

* * *

Being a port, and a Caribbean city, there is a more relaxed attitude here than among the dour highlanders of Bogotá. I ask directions of a passer-by and he offers to show me exactly where to purchase that elusive battery for my camera: he leads me down an alley, across a park, into a shopping mall, introduces me to the shop-keeper and then leaves, shaking my hand and wishing me well. However benign these first impressions, I am fully aware that the city has a dark and troubled history, and one of the reasons that drew me here was to research and read about its colonial past. I have also agreed to give a talk at the city's university, but that is not for another week. I have plenty of time to explore.

On my first evening, strolling in the old town, I come across a small garden occupied by pairs of men playing chess with formidable seriousness. Opposite them a strange little window is set into the side of an old palace. A plaque informs me it was at this spot that informers could report the misdeeds of their neighbours to the Inquisitors, for this was the Palace of the Inquisition.

The next day I return, in order to visit the museum that now occupies the Palace. It is a chamber of horrors, which are peculiarly expurgated to the visiting public through claims that the Inquisitors were nicer to people here than elsewhere, and that although their methods were not always pleasant, their ultimate intention was a good one: to help heretics make peace with God before meeting Him face to face. My guide book tells me that over eight hundred people were executed by the Inquisition in Cartagena between 1776 and 1821. I wonder if they shared the lofty concerns of their executioners. The museum information leaflet mitigates these crimes against the innocent by informing us that "only five" heretics were burnt to death and the "the Inquisition did not oppress the Indigenous population", a questionable assertion, to say the least.

The commonest accusations were concerned with heresy and, specifically, witchcraft. Any grudge against a neighbour – if your cow stopped giving milk, or your child became sick – might be twisted into an accusation of sorcery. A list of the thirty-three questions routinely asked in the interrogation of suspect witches hangs on the wall of the museum. Examples include such leading questions as: "What animals have you killed or put under a curse and why have you done it?" "On which children have you cast the spell of the evil eye, and why have you done it?" "Why does the devil strike you blows at night?" "How do you fly through the air at night?" Some of the instruments of torture used to extract confessions are also on display. They include the two devices called 'The Fork of Heresy', which prohibited all movement of the head but offered the victim the chance to murmur his or her confession; the second, an invention horribly named the 'Breast Piercer', was used on women "who had committed heresy, blasphemy, adultery, or other libidinous acts such as provoking abortions, practising erotic magic and other crimes."

As though to cleanse myself of these abominations, I wander down to the convent of the good priest San Pedro Claver. For almost forty years this man, a Jesuit from the Catalan village of Verdú, and a contemporary of Shakespeare and Cervantes, worked in Cartagena, defending, protecting and nursing newly arrived African slaves in the city. His munificence was legendary, at a time when people of colour were regarded as no more than beasts of burden by their dealers and owners. He is, in this depiction, the great white guardian, a placebo against all the terrors and ignominies of slavery. If only the truth were so simple.

The museum that honours him in the old convent reconstructs his modest cell, his living quarters, and houses an exhibition of the most terrible paintings imaginable – so terrible they are fascinating – celebrating his good deeds among the slave population, who are here depicted as almost imbecilic caricatures.

But at least there is a way out. Nearby, seemingly unrelated to anything around it, I find the sign on a nearby wall, 'Portal de las Animas': Portal of Souls. To where, I wondered, might these souls have fled?

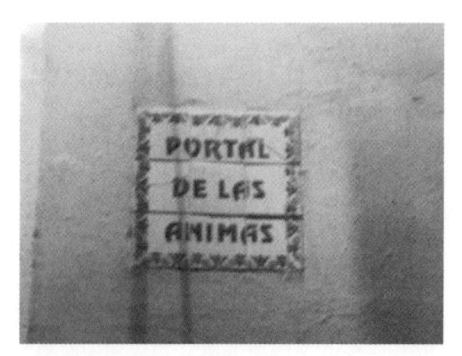

Sir Francis Drake captured Cartagena in 1586 – having raided it briefly two years earlier – and occupied it with his troops for two months, holding several important figures to ransom, including the captain who surrendered the marketplace, Alonso Bravo. Against the odds, the two men are said to have become friends, and Drake lowered the ransom, before departing from the city to continue his raids on settlements along the Spanish Main, among them Riohacha. This attack is referenced several times in García Márquez's *One Hundred Years of Solitude* and is ultimately the cause of the extinction of the Buendía family line, as Aueliano Buendía discovers, in a moment of retrospective illumination, that Sir Francis Drake had attacked Riohacha only so that he, Aureliano, and his aunt Amaranta Ursula "could seek each other through the most intricate labyrinths of blood until they would engender the mythological animal that was to bring the line to an end."

Cartagena was also the setting for one of the most humiliating defeats ever suffered by the British Empire, though until arriving in this city I had never heard of The Battle of Cartagena, and it was most certainly not on the syllabus at the school I attended, where, at the age of eleven, my schoolmates and I learned from Mr Bradshaw that the loss of the (North) American colonies was like playing rugby away from home, on a massive pitch, with an opposition that didn't play by the rules of the game, such were the sporting analogies by which we were taught world history back then. It was, we were assured, the only substantial defeat in the history of the British Empire – the only time 'we' failed in a colonial conflict. (In fact, the British suffered other humiliating defeats in South America alone, most notably in their two failed attempts to take Buenos Aires from the Spanish in 1806-7.)

The attack on Cartagena took place during The War of Jenkins' Ear, a conflict that arose out of Britain's contract to supply an unlimited number of slaves to the Spanish colonies, which had degenerated into a buccaneering free-for-all on the British side. The inciting incident – the arrest and ear-lopping of the eponymous Jenkins by a Spanish naval captain – provided an excuse for a greater strategy than mere vengeance. Ultimately the British wanted to gain control of all four major Spanish ports in the Caribbean: Portobelo, in present day Panama (which was captured by Admiral Edward Vernon in 1739); Havana, in Cuba;

Veracruz, in Mexico, and Cartagena itself, the jewel in the Spanish imperial crown. By its capture, the British hoped to seal off the main conduit for the transit of gold from Spain's colonies back to the mother country.

To this end, Admiral Vernon gathered together one of the largest fleets ever assembled – half as big again as the Spanish Armada of 1588 – comprising 186 ships, more than 2,500 artillery pieces, and over 27,000 men. The attack force included 10,000 regular soldiers and 3,600 recruits from the colony of Virginia, led by its Lieutenant Governor, Colonel William Gooch, and including in its number Lawrence Washington, older half-brother of the future President of the United States.

Vernon's fleet anchored in the Bay of Cartagena on 13th March, 1741. The Spanish defences during the siege were led by a one-legged, one-eyed, one-armed Basque by the name of Blas de Lezo y Olavarrieta, an admiral of the fleet and the prototype for all grizzled sea dogs of popular legend. His mislaying of body parts was initiated in the Battle of Malaga (1704) at the tender age of fifteen, during the War of the Austrian Succession, the leg being amputated *in situ*; the eye he lost two years later during the defence of Toulon, and his arm in the siege of Barcelona (1713). Blas de Lezo's physical state, as one contemporary Spanish account puts it, "was worse than lamentable" by the time he was entrusted with command of the fortress at Cartagena. He was, however – and despite his Pythonesque infirmities – a veteran of many sea battles, conqueror of the Ottoman forces at Oran and Mers-el-Kébir, and a renowned slayer of pirates, and he conducted the defence of Cartagena with exemplary skill and courage. The forces at his disposal amounted to only six ships of the line, 3,000 soldiers and a handful of local militia and native Indian archers.

After the British secured the nearby Fort Bocagrande, and the Virginians took the hill of La Popa, Admiral Vernon prematurely sent a message to Jamaica – the Caribbean headquarters for British operations – claiming that Cartagena had fallen; this, in turn was reported back to London, where there was much rejoicing; commemorative chinaware was fired, and medals struck, showing the humiliated Blas de Lezo kneeling before the victorious Vernon.

But this was all fake news. When the British attempted to storm the main fortress, Castillo San Felipe de Barajas, on the night of 19th April, Blas de Lezo led a devastating bayonet charge on the attackers, whose ladders were too short to scale the battlements, and who found themselves stranded in the deep trenches that the Spanish had dug below the ramparts. The British survivors of this carnage withdrew to the safety of their ships, and although the navy maintained a fierce bombardment of the city, Lezo had by then scuttled a half of his own ships, blocking the entrance to the harbour, and a frontal physical assault was now impossible. Less than two months after its start, with supplies running low and his troops decimated by an outbreak of yellow fever, Vernon was forced to raise the siege and return to Jamaica. The British had lost fifty ships and over nine thousand men, with a further 12,000 wounded or incapacitated by disease, against Spanish losses of under one thousand. Of the 3,600 Virginians, only 300 returned home.

In an abject act of revisionism, two months after my visit, the city mayor, Dionisio Vélez, welcomed the UK's Prince (now King) Charles to Cartagena by unveiling a plaque celebrating "the valour and suffering of those who died in combat while seeking to take the city and the fortress of San Felipe under the command of Admiral Edward Vernon." The ceremony was greeted with outrage by local residents, who claimed that it displayed an ignorance of history; the British invasion was an act of piracy, and the Prince's visit glorified colonial warfare. One angry citizen attacked the marble plaque with a hammer and it was removed shortly afterwards. It might be added that 'pirate' is a term commonly used in Spanish and Portuguese school history books to describe the English from Drake onwards – including that unfortunate naval captain, Robert Jenkins, the loss of whose ear famously instigated the war, and who, with a perfect sense of irony, later made his name by heroically defending his own and three ships under his command from attack by pirates. Meanwhile, a statue of the fearless Blas de Lezo, known locally as Capitán Cojo (Captain Pegleg), stands to this day below the Fortress of San Felipe de Barajas. I spent a leisurely evening walking the ramparts, and wondered at the folly of taking on such a man.

The next day, my thirst for historical knowledge temporarily sated, I sought out a beach, in order, as I imagined, to spend a few hours reading and writing in the shade of some leafy café, and to sample the local seafood. Las Playas de Boquilla, where I settled on going, is a strip of coast which once hosted fishing hamlets now uprooted and scattered to the winds to make way for luxury hotels. The village of La Boquilla itself is a little further down the coast and between it and the high-rise kingdom lie three kilometres of golden beach and a network of mangrove waterways. The day was overcast and humid, but I was determined to make the best of it, and as soon as my taxi arrived at the beach, I no longer had any choice in the matter: I was no longer a Foreigner, but a Tourist.

We were pursued by boys racing after the taxi, intent on selling me stuff – I have no idea what, as we didn't stop. We drove on down the beach, at speed. Asking the driver to drop me off after a kilometre or so, I stood on the strand, trying to decide what on earth to do next. The cafés were all closed, and the beach practically empty.

The Tourist (A) is perturbed by the amount of dissembling he has to indulge in when confronted by awkward situations. He defines awkward situations as those times when he cannot act freely, and is accommodating to someone else's agenda rather than following his own. This happens more often than he would like, even when he is alone.

A is accosted by B – a tall, wiry, knobbly-kneed Afro-Colombian – on the beach near La Boquilla. A is not looking for distractions, even though at some point he will be seeking out food. And there's the rub. The restaurant recommended in his guidebook – actually a palm thatch shack – is not yet open, and B, who is painfully persistent, has started his pitch by telling A he will provide him with a lunch of fresh seafood and rice.

I am a fisherman. Langoustine, crab, fresh fish. All fresh. I dive for lobster.

B has decided to speak in pidgin Spanish, perhaps because he thinks that A will understand him more easily. In this respect, B believes that tourists resemble children or domestic animals, and should be spoken to slowly and emphatically.

B tells A that he has a canoe and can take A for a ride through the mangrove swamps, the very same mangrove swamps, A recalls, that were used in the film adaptation of a story by García Márquez, but he forgets which.

I will take you in my canoe, says B, and you will look at the birds.

A knows from the guidebook – or thinks he might know, as the guidebook has already coughed up several inaccuracies – that these particular mangrove swamps are home, amongst other birds, to Wilson's plover, red-knot, gull-billed and large-billed terns; grey kingbird, lesser kiskadee, cattle tyrant, Wilson's phalarope, collared plover, semi-palmated sandpiper, solitary sandpiper, semi-palmated plover; black, least and brown-throated parakeet; Louisiana and little blue herons, reddish egret and ringed kingfisher.

Who, A wonders, was Wilson?

Although ornithology is not B's strength, he feels he should offer some examples of the birds to be seen hereabouts. Seagulls, he suggests, and falters. Storks.

He's making an effort, A thinks, but B doesn't know shit about birds, nor does he care for them much. After all, as a fisherman (if indeed he is a fisherman) they are his direct competitors. But B does know that other tourists come to see the birds, so why shouldn't this one.

A does not see any other tourists on the beach. He feels like the only tourist in Colombia. No, no, says B. Many tourists here.

Italy, Spain, Gringos. He points to a half-finished house back from the beach, next to a couple of new builds. This house people of Italy, that house people of Spain. That house, Gringos. B hawks, and gobs onto the sand.

At this point they are standing by a group of eight or nine dilapidated wooden canoes. Three of them are waterlogged, and half- submerged in the swamp. None of them looks seaworthy, or even waterproof. A is thinking: I've known this man for five minutes and he wants me to get into an antique wreck with him and paddle into the mangrove swamps, alone. A isn't overly concerned about the possible dangers of this. The guidebook states that local fishermen offer canoe trips through the mangroves and this man seems safe (though you can never tell) and besides, A is confident (perhaps foolishly) that he can look after himself in most situations. No; A's problem is that he knows, if he sets off in a canoe with B, that although he may enjoy the mangroves and the birds, he will be bored senseless having to make light conversation of the kind currently being sampled while B paddles them both, in a rotting canoe, across the swamp.

All of these canoes are mine, B says. All of them. You choose. You look at birds. I paddle. I give you good price.

A decides it is time to speak out.

B, he says, using the fisherman's name to assert his authority and intent. I do not want to get into a canoe with you. I do not want to get into a canoe with anyone, however agreeable the mangrove swamp. Nor do I wish to watch the birds, however gracious they may be. I just want to take a walk along the beach and later, when I return, I will eat the food that you have promised to cook in your restaurant.

B thinks about this, brightening.

But, he says, you cannot walk down there (nodding away from the thatched huts).

Why not?

It's dangerous.

How is it dangerous?

The water. Down that way the water is dangerous. And the rocks. This way (gesturing back towards the thatched huts) – this way is not dangerous.

A mulls things over. He decides not to pursue the argument about why the water might be safe in one direction, but not the other; he doesn't want to get into an argument about riptides.

B can scent victory. He points at a couple of canvas sunshades pitched near the shoreline. These small shelters dot the entire length of the beach.

You walk, you rest, you swim, says B. I make you food for two o'clock.

A looks at the sunshades. The sun is not shining. It is not yet ten thirty and it is still overcast, but hot. It is always hot; there are simply gradations in the heat and its stickiness. He could sit in a chair under the shade and read and write, which is what he intended to do by coming to the beach. He might swim in the warm surf. B will have won, but at least A will, most likely, be left alone, and he will not have to go looking for lunch. Besides, there doesn't appear to be any other restaurant on this strip of beach, at least not one that is open.

Which sunshade will you take? asks B.

Installed beneath the sunshade —one cannot be too careful, despite the dense coverage of cloud—A picks up his book. Almost immediately another man, C, approaches, wielding a cutlass in one hand and a green coconut in the other. A guesses C must be here with B's connivance, and he nods approval at the proffered coconut, so as to preclude another discussion. C lops the top off the coconut and inserts a straw. The coconut water is cool and delicious. The man asks for 4,000 pesos, which sounds rather a lot, but isn't, and A suspects he won't be disturbed by any other vendors if he stays where he is. The beach, after all, is practically empty. A seabird, quite likely one of Wilson's, with a large crescent beak, hovers directly in front of A, suspended high above the water, and then, in a sudden movement, it twists and dives, twists again in mid-dive, hits the water slick as an arrow and plunges beneath the waves, returning to the surface with a fish in its bill.

After an hour or more, A cannot tell how long, since he is reading and dozing, dozing and reading, a woman approaches. She has indigenous features, is of indeterminate age, slim build and melancholy aspect. She carries a plastic bucket. She tells A that she is going to massage his feet. A disputes this, but the woman already has one of them between her hands and is rubbing it gently. A really doesn't want his feet massaged like some lousy white colonial potentate, but nor does he wish to ruin the calm that has settled on him by beginning another pointless wrangle. The woman would not be offering to carry out this humiliating task unless she needed the money, so A relaxes and allows her to massage his feet and before long the two of them are talking. She has two sons, she says, one is nine, and a good boy; he likes to study and wants to do well. The other, who is thirteen, has fallen in with a bad lot and she fears that he will end up doing something stupid and ruining his life. She used to make a living giving massages at the luxury hotels down the beach, but now the hotels have a franchise with a company that brings in their own masseurs, and freelancers like her are not allowed to offer their services and they get chased away by security men if they even try to enter the hotels, which incidentally are built on the land where she grew up and used to live, until everyone was moved off the land so that the luxury hotels could be built. She is a good woman, and A feels for her. She is poor and wants her nine-year-old to do well, even if her thirteen-year-old is determined to ruin his life, and she wanders up and down the beach offering to massage the feet of strangers.

At two o'clock, B returns, and leads A to a table under the palm thatch, next to a shack at the top of the beach. On the table is a plate laden with seafood, fish and rice, just as promised. The pile of food is steaming and next to the plate sits a bottle of warm beer. A pays the man what he asks and eats his fill. Although it is delicious, he is forcing the food down. He cannot stop thinking about the woman who massaged his feet, and he is swamped by shame and remorse at the deep injustice of their respective roles; he a tourist on her native patch, the land already taken from her by a multinational hotel chain that offers holidays for tourists who never venture beyond the hotel compound; she, riven with worry at what might become of her thirteen-year-old, who, A is certain, already has his life story scripted for him. It involves petty crime, conscription into the ranks of some gang or cartel, prison and an early grave. He can only hope the nine-year-old makes good, but the odds must be stacked against him.

> Mompox does not exist. At times we dream of her, but she does not exist.
>
> Gabriel García Márquez, *The General in his Labyrinth.*

Mompox – Cartagena, September 2014

Stress-free travel is often a matter of balancing a desire for control with a willingness to abandon that control when it serves no purpose. If you find yourself in a place where schedules are treated casually and intentions declared on the spur of the moment, and you start fighting this attitude as though there were the least thing you could do to alter it, then you are in for a big disappointment. In other words, if you are always trying to be in control of the uncontrollable – especially in a country, like Colombia, that resists any kind of ulterior jurisdiction – you are doomed to misery and failure. Not that I am the most efficient seeker of travel information; I tend to get distracted at every stage. I don't like reading instructions or manuals, I don't like being told what to do, and I don't much enjoy being a tourist.

In Cartagena, I try to find the best way to travel to the old colonial town of Mompox, also known as Mompós (population 30,000). Santa Cruz de Mompox, to give it its full title, is located two hundred and fifty kilometres up the Magdalena river from Cartagena, and was founded in 1540 by Don Alonso de Heredia, whose elder brother Pedro settled Cartagena. It was also, significantly, the first city of the New Kingdom of Granada (which comprised much of modern day Colombia, almost all of Ecuador, northern Venezuela, Panama and Costa Rica) to declare independence from Spanish rule, on 6th August 1810. The town held a special place in the affections of the liberator, Simón Bolívar, to whom Gabriel García Márquez attributes the enigmatic accolade: "Mompox no existe. A veces soñamos con ella, pero no existe" (Mompox does not exist. At times we dream of her, but she does not exist). There is, I think, a special appeal in visiting a place that might not be there.

After some research, I come upon the Toto Express, which organises a truck service for four or five passengers. I speak with someone, possibly Toto himself, who asks me to be ready at 4.30 a.m. on Saturday morning. The vehicle takes an hour or so to collect passengers from Cartagena, and arrives in Mompox late morning. The price seems fair. I am sorted.

My companions on the trip are Washington, our driver, and three elderly Colombian ladies, Momposinas, as the inhabitants of Mompox are known, who are on their way home. These three señoras talk incessantly, and from their conversation I am able to catch a flavour of their lives, although I struggle with the inflections of their Caribbean accents. García Márquez, in *Love in the Time of Cholera*, refers enigmatically to Momposinas as having "indecipherable intentions", but these señoras were concerned mainly with everyday affairs, the prices in the market at Cartagena foremost among them. The oldest of them, riding shotgun, was also preoccupied with Washington's driving, although I thought he was rather good, considering the hazards of the journey and the tendency of other drivers to hurtle towards us on the wrong side of the road because of the mud-caked trenches and potholes. Although much of the route was covered, there were long stretches of dirt track to negotiate.

At one point, on a particularly poor stretch of road with a lot of oncoming traffic, we spent a long while stuck behind a lorry. A car passed us at speed, and Washington edged out carefully to see if it was safe for us to overtake, in turn.

"Such imprudence," says the señora in front, speaking with exaggerated formality. "And for what? Just to get ahead! I would rather be wise than imprudent, wait for an opportune moment to pass, and thus keep my life." This is met by a chorus of agreement from the two señoras in the back with me. Washington takes this as a personal criticism – although the woman's remarks seem to have been directed at the car that has just passed us – and he turns up the Ranchera music so loud the women cannot hear each other speak. The music is pretty dire but I don't complain, since Washington's feelings have been hurt once already, and to criticise the music might be a step too far. The señoras, in any case, are not complaining. Washington then takes what he claims is a shortcut and we encounter a gaudily decorated blue lorry, stuck fast in the deep vermillion mud, and completely blocking the narrow road. We do a three-point turn and take the long way around, crossing the River Magdalena by an ancient ferry, consisting of planks attached to three metal boats, and powered by an invisible motor. When we disembark on the other side, an obese man, bare-chested, folds of belly flab cascading over the waistband of his shorts, cigarette limp between his lips, pushes a wheelbarrow, laden with a cargo of jostling rabbits, onto the ferry. On the bank a pair of dogs are glued together by their hindquarters, determinedly facing away from each other but unable to separate or even to move. They appear bored and indignant. As we drive past, the dog facing our way catches my eye, and follows me with a hopelessly imploring gaze until we pass out of sight.

Having finished *Love in the Time of Cholera*, I am now reading another pirated and very badly printed Spanish edition of *Chronicle of a Death Foretold,* the movie version of which was filmed on location in Mompox. The settings for García Márquez's fictions tend to be a composite of places, real and imagined. Whatever the location, Gabo's literary vision is of a certain type of Caribbean town, locked into its past and possessed of a quiet fatalism: and yet, to compound the sense of paradox about their country, Colombians, according to one recent poll are the second happiest people on earth. Who on earth thinks up these surveys?

Mompox is a quintessentially Garcimarquesian place, in which the improbable – not to say the fantastic – seems to be woven into the fabric of everyday life, complete with plenty of colourful birds, iguanas and snakes. This might sound reductive, but stereotypes usually arise because they have a basis in some core reality, and Mompox immediately seduced me, no doubt in part because it fulfilled the expectations I had of it as a town that has already been dreamed in fiction. There was something both sensual and haunted about the place.

While still in Bogotá, a Google search had come up with phrase, "the very aristocratic and sorrowful city of Mompox". The Spanish colonial authorities built the Royal Mint here, supposedly out of reach of the English bucaneers (or pirates) who made frequent raids on Cartagena, from Drake onwards. It was a site of many confrontations during Colombia's serial civil wars following independence from Spain. More recently it was a no-go area, changing hands between FARC rebels and government forces over a period of years. Since Colombia's purge under President Álvaro Uribe, a few years back, it has been readied for the onslaught of tourism. But tourism, you might be warned, of a particular kind. It reminded me a little of the Greek islands in the 1970s, a tourism still in its fledgling, puppy-love stage, backpackers scouting the place before it became deluged by package-dealers. There is the same unawareness of 'service'; you often wait for whoever is behind the counter to finish what they are doing before they attend to you. This is done entirely without malice; it is simply the pace of life here, telling you what's what. There is a lot of smiling and a lot of mutual incomprehension. My question about the non-existence of internet in my hotel, which I had been assured was available in every room, was answered by a shrug, and when pressed, the explanation: well, you know, it comes and goes. Foreigners are still a novelty, and therefore quite amusing. My hotel, housed in an old colonial building near the centre, is decorated with the kind of bad hippy art that I thought had faded away with the flower power era.

On the first evening, I take a wander around the cemetery – often a good place to start – and amongst the ornate crypts and gothic family tombs, am delighted to come upon the grave of one Juan de Dios Wooggle Boivié. It goes into the catalogue of great names, and although I tried to research the name's owner online, I found nothing. However, I posted an account of my visit to Mompox on my alias, Ricardo Blanco's, blog, and four years later, in July 2018, received a message, stating simply "es la tumba de mi abuelo": it's the grave of my grandfather.

A small army of cats laze in the patio by the cemetery wall: they are not the feral, flea-bitten specimens one might expect in such a place, but appear healthy, with glossy coats and a haughty tolerance of my being there, on their patch. The cause of their wellbeing makes her entrance as I am seated on the patio wall, smoking a cigarette, in the form of an ethereal young woman, armed with a large packet of dried cat food, which she empties, not onto the ground, but into individual feeding bowls. The cats, extraordinarily, wait until the bowls are laid out in a line before diving in. The young woman turns and smiles at me beatifically.

From this dreamlike vision, I am brought down to earth with a starkly contrasting image. Walking back through the town, I pass a *residencia* for the elderly, and there, in a gesture of human frailty up against the unrelenting clamour of the world, is a man, clutching the bars that encase the open window, staring with a sort of intense vacancy down the street – as though all life were out there, on the other side of the bars, unreachable.

Saturday evening in Mompox. As I emerge into the street outside my hotel, I bump into Washington. He is taking a stroll with his brother-in-law, whom he introduces as Eduardo. Eduardo is a slim, muscular man who regards the world at large with a disagreeable expression, somewhere between disdain and ridicule. Washington invites me to come for a bite to eat with Eduardo and other members of his family. We sit out in the Plaza next to the church of Santo Domingo. Eduardo is a police sergeant, and he finds it entertaining that the family is seated around a table with a foreigner, occasionally leaning over in an attempt to speak a phrase or two of pidgin English. I have no idea why he does this, since I speak reasonably fluent Spanish. But there is a certain type of individual who finds foreigners intrinsically funny (perhaps to deflect from the fact that he finds them threatening) and Eduardo appears to be one of these.

We eat several plates of meat and potatoes – a variety of potato with a thick fibrous taste, which Washington tells me is called a *papa yucca*. It is accompanied by Aguila Light, a low-alcohol beer. Although Colombians enjoy drinking, perhaps, like the Russians, they do not consider beer to be a real drink, and Aguila Light conforms to this belief: to get drunk on it would demand extreme resolve. The conversation proceeds briskly: I am a guest, but no great ceremony is extended towards me, for which I am relieved. The family is accommodating and voluble. Along with Eduardo and Washington's spouses, there is a sister or cousin, Eugenia, the most articulate and educated member of the family – to the extent that the men defer to her opinions on certain topics – and four or five children, aged between seven and fourteen. I'm not sure who the children belong to, nor am I introduced to them. Children, it would seem, are just children.

Eduardo asks me what I am doing in Colombia. I reply that I am a university professor, and I am here to learn about the poets of Colombia; not, perhaps, the wisest admission to make to a cop. Washington, to whom I explained the purpose of my trip during the ride from Cartagena, adds that I am a poet also, and an "ambassador from my country." In my desire to be accurate, I provided more information than was strictly necessary during the five-hour drive from the coastal city, and the mangled version that Washington now produces sounds far more grandiose than anything I intended. You'll do well here then, *poeta*, says Eduardo, wielding the term like an insult, and gesturing around the square – with all these layabouts, addicts and *putas*. Poets every one of them, he says, and he laughs, but without any sense that he is making a joke. He asks me where I am from. Wales, I tell him. Never heard of it, he says, suspiciously. Is that a country? Yes, I say, it's a country. Does it have a government? Well, it has a government, I explain, but is not a sovereign state. If it is not a sovereign state, he replies immediately, gobbling up the phrase (estado soberano) and spitting it back at me, it cannot be a country. And therefore, cannot have ambassadors.

I begin to explain – and even as I do so I feel weary – that Wales is a country, of sorts; we have our own language and culture.

But my brother-in-law – he prods Washington with a vindictive finger – tells me you are an *Ambassador*. How can that be? Only *sovereign states* – he has adopted the phrase and will not let it go – have Ambassadors. 'Ambassador' is an honorific title, I begin to justify, wishing we had not got into this: I was awarded the role of 'creative ambassador' to come to Latin America and hunt for poets. *Creative Ambassador!* What was I thinking? And I actually use the verb *cazar*, to hunt, to add an element of ironic self-mockery to what I am saying. But irony is lost on police sergeants around the world. If my account sounds ludicrous to me, sitting in this dusty Colombian square, how must it sound to this leery small-town policeman? Eduardo regards me in silence for a moment, absorbing the information in much the same way, I imagine, with which he must listen to the alibis of local felons on a daily basis. You are, he pronounces, at length and with finality, the Ambassador of Nowhere. His face, which has been a rigid mask of sustained incredulity during the interrogation, suddenly crumples, and he roars with laughter, slaps me on the back, and orders more piss-weak beer.

The favourite tipple of Eduardo and Washington – indeed of Colombians in general – is aguardiente, an aniseed-based firewater. When, after supper, the children are taken home and Washington, Eduardo, Eugenia and myself retire to the *discoteca*, a rundown and forlorn establishment, Eduardo orders a bottle of the stuff, which we put away within the first hour. As soon as it is finished, another appears, and I begin to feel the onset of pre-emptive regret. Eduardo asks me if I have children, and I tell him I have two daughters. What age are they? he asks, and I tell him twenty-three and twenty-two. At what age do people get married in your country? asks Eduardo. That depends, I reply, but often not until they are in their late twenties or thirties. If they get married at all. Here, he says, girls get married at eighteen and in church. It's the way things have always been, he adds. It is pretty clear he accepts the conservative dictates of church and state without question. I remind myself that this is a country that has spent the last fifty years devastated by civil conflict, and Mompox itself was, until only a few years ago, occupied by the FARC. What might have happened to Eduardo during that time? How deep the rifts must run, and how certain the beliefs.

The conversation begins to falter. I fear our differences on political matters do not make for easy banter. I chat instead with Eugenia, who is not drinking aguardiente, but sticking with the low-alcohol beer. It transpires she is a schoolteacher, and she begins to talk to me about the difficulty of getting kids to attend school after the age of twelve, since most of them need to work, such is the poverty of rural Colombia. As well, she adds, glancing over at Eduardo with a cynical nod, as the ridiculous expectation to get married at the earliest opportunity, and the power of the church ... she drifts off, clearly not wishing to say more in present company. The volume of the music in the discoteca makes conversation difficult, and besides, my head is not really in this place, or any other identifiable location. Instead, I simply nod along to the melody of her Caribbean Spanish and watch the handful of dancers, all of them middle-aged and half-drunk, as they circle aimlessly around the dance floor. I cannot help comparing this scenario with my preconceptions about the way Colombians *should* dance: the wild rhythms of *salsa, cumbia,* or the local *porro,* youthful bodies bounding with intent, now morphed into this moribund chug around the dance floor to the lachrymose accompaniment of some Latin crooner.

At the end of the evening Eduardo, magnanimous in his cups, refuses to let me walk home – although we are only three blocks from my hotel – and he hails a tuk-tuk. There is room for two passengers, but the four of us pile in. When we get to my hotel Eduardo leaps from the mototaxi and hammers on the thick wooden door with its iron knocker, invoking all the authority of his station. I reckon, through a fog of aguardiente, that this will not make me the most popular of the hotel's residents the next morning, but there is little I can do about him. He is, after all, the law here in Mompox.

Late the next the morning, I go to the plaza for a coffee, just as the church of Santo Domingo is discharging its worshippers from Sunday Mass. Churches in Colombia are packed and religious paraphernalia is everywhere. Washington, I noticed on the way from Cartagena, crosses himself every time he passes a church, and at random other moments while driving. Secondly, and not surprisingly given the country's recent past, there is a deep and widespread hostility to both drugs and drug users. In a certain sense, the drug trade and those associated with it are seen by the Catholic right as responsible for all the woes that Colombia has suffered.

As I sit outside the cafe, I am approached by a young dreadlocked type who taps me for spare change. I give him a few pesos – the equivalent of around twenty pence – and he goes off happy. Two drunks sitting nearby, sharing a bottle of aguardiente, tell me off, explaining that the boy will spend it on *la droga*. They are incensed and one of them waves the bottle around in his rage as he explains to me the gravity of my error, oblivious to any inconsistency between his attitude to drugs and his own benighted state. It goes like this everywhere that the legal drug of alcohol fuels its consumers with moral indignation about other addictive substances. But in Colombia, of course, the rationale runs deeper than elsewhere.

I try to arrange a boat trip up the Magdalena. The banks are thick with wildlife – especially birds. I know very little about birds, as I have already confessed, but it seems a shame to be on the famous river and not take the opportunity to explore a little. A would-be entrepreneur, Lazaro, offers to find a boat for me. Lazaro is incredibly thin, languorous but edgy, and blinks a lot, reminding me of a lizard. Unfortunately, he doesn't have a mobile phone, and Lazaro the lizard has to borrow mine (Richard British Citizen) to speak to his contacts. This seems like a poor start, but I give him the benefit of the doubt. He tells me to meet him at three that afternoon in the Plaza de la Concepción. He finds me having lunch at the nearby Comedor Costeño, a cheap and friendly restaurant on the riverbank, and waits outside for me to finish. He borrows my phone again to speak to his contact, and the price I was promised this morning – 25,000 pesos for three hours on the river – has gone up to 35,000 (around seven pounds sterling). At this point he hands me the phone, so I can speak to the boat owner, if I wish, just to prove he is not making it up. I decline. We stop a tuk-tuk and set off for the outskirts of town, downriver. When we arrive at the agreed spot, there is no boat. Lazaro, a little frantic now, borrows my mobile again and makes a call. He furrows his brow. I can tell this is not going to be good news. The boat trip is off: the other two passengers that were lined up have postponed until tomorrow. I have a friend, begins Lazaro, with a boat, good price ...

I have lost all interest in the boat venture, but we have to return to town anyway, so off we head in the same tuk-tuk, whose driver has been lingering in the shade of a tree as we confer. When we get to the Plaza San Francisco, Lazaro strides to the bank and yells across the wide river in the direction of a single farm building on the other side. Miraculously, a couple of minutes later, a man emerges and walks to the shore. He is accompanied by a second man, in a red shirt, and a child, a girl of around ten. After considerable discussion between the two men on the other side, they unrope a launch – basically a canoe with a small outboard attached, and cross the river. We fix a price, a quarter of which goes to Lazaro, who then departs, happy. I am not sorry to see him go.

Pedro, the boat's owner, introduces himself. He is courteous and sober. His companion, Edgar, seems exceedingly dim, until I realise that his exaggeratedly slow speech and movements are due to the fact he is somewhat the worse for wear, though whether through drink, as I first suspect, or else some profound and irreversible melancholy, it is difficult to tell. The girl sits on the prow, but is deposited on the far bank before we set off, first down, then upriver. It occurs to me that her father doesn't want her here, with a strange man, and I wonder if the budding tourist industry here has already been infiltrated by would-be sex offenders, as in Nicaragua. Pedro is astute, and good at pointing out animals and birds. Edgar is completely vacant, occasionally turning to me and asking if I speak Spanish, and when I reply in the affirmative saying no more, but nodding to himself sadly. He even ventures to ask me where I am from, and when I answer he again nods in his melancholy way, as though my provenance were a matter of profound regret. He is perched on the edge of the launch, a position he maintains majestically throughout the trip. I would have put money on him tumbling in, and several times he wobbles, but he is clearly an adept at this balancing act. He makes no further attempts at conversation, except when Pedro calls out the name of an animal or bird and Edgar looks at me and then shouts incoherently and points in the required direction, of which the only effect is to scare the creatures away. The biggest thrill comes with the green iguana, which I cannot see at first – it is so well disguised – and Edgar rouses himself from his moribund state to gesture frantically at the bushes adjoining the river bank. There is a lot of green foliage, and by the time I have the giant lizard in focus, it moves. Fortunately, it emerges a minute later on the bank, and I am able to get a clean shot.

The next evening, my last in Mompox, I wander along the banks of the great river. I am picking up something of the sense of the town, its mystery, as well as its historical association with commerce, especially gold and silver. The town has a long tradition of silverwork, and is renowned for its fine filigree jewellery, though this trade has declined in recent years. Along the riverside, some buildings, which once served as warehouses and workshops, look as though they are being turned into bars, but haven't opened yet. My unhelpful guidebook tells me the Zona Rosa is a pleasant place to take a nightcap, but I can neither agree not disagree, because it doesn't seem to exist. Perhaps Gabo's Bolívar was right, after all. However I have a flavour, I think, both of what Mompox once was, and what it might become when tourism gets a firmer hold, which no doubt it will. Certainly there were properties for sale that could well appeal to a certain kind of nostalgic and world-weary European or North American with an urge to sink into timeless reverie on the banks of the Magdalena.

On Tuesday at 4.30 a.m. Washington is outside the hotel with the pick-up truck, all set for the return journey to Cartagena. This time I get to sit in the front. I must have earned the privilege after our big night out, I think, but it turns out I am the only passenger. As we set off, there are rumblings of approaching thunder.

We are barely out of Mompox when the storm hits the ground with apocalyptic intensity, rain crashing down around us. In fact the downpour is so overwhelming that Washington has to stop the vehicle, as he can see nothing, even with the wipers on double speed. Then, very slowly, we edge forward along the mud road, which has become a river of sludge. Visibility is down to a few metres. An hour out of Mompox, the rain has not diminished; it is still dark, but there are streaks of lighter grey in the sky to the east and I glimpse a cyclist, dressed only in a vest and pants, utterly stuck in the alluvial mud, drenched, immobile on his bike. The water is running past him at knee-height. He is a still from a black and white movie, in which we – Washington and I – are the only other actors. We pass him, in slow motion, a lean statue balanced perfectly on a bicycle, beneath the torrential rain.

Two hours after setting out, we arrive at the ferry-crossing in Santa Ana de la Magdalena, where I spotted the conjoined dogs on the outward journey. The ramp that connects the ferry to the shore is now under several inches of fast-flowing rainwater and we are escorted down it by a man clad in a bin liner. Around 6.45, daylight filters through and the rain begins to ease. We join a covered road and start to make real progress. Casualties of the storm appear along the roadside, mostly dogs that have been struck by cars driving blind through the storm. I count six dead dogs on this stretch of road. In one place, as we slow at a junction, a cannibal hound is tearing at one of the canine corpses, pulling at a leg, as if dismembering a chicken. Further on, vultures are feasting on another body. The corpse of a donkey splayed on the verge comes as a vision from Chagall. There is plenty of other random roadkill, which I cannot identify, and whenever our truck approaches, the vultures scatter. Eventually, four hours out of Mompox, the sky clears and we look set for another warm day. At our breakfast stop, a green parrot hops onto the railing by my table, glares at me rudely, and wolf-whistles. It continues to stare at me while I finish my coffee, and when I get up to leave, it flies off, disgruntled.

Just after eleven we descend into Cartagena, as another rainstorm washes in from the Caribbean. Washington drops me off at my pension, the fondly named Casa Relax. It rains hard for two hours and the streets are flooded. I take a nap. When I emerge to look for some lunch, the sun is finally attempting another breakthrough. Setting off down the street toward the Plaza, someone calls out: "Oy, Blanco!" I do a double take – my surname, Gwyn, means 'white' in Welsh, and sometimes, in Spanish speaking countries, I introduce myself as Ricardo Blanco; but how can a stranger in Getsemaní possibly know my name? And then I remember that this a regular form of address for a white man. A black street vendor is beckoning me over: "Hey, Whitey!"

I originally planned to visit Cartagena in order to meet the poet Rómulo Bustos Aguirre, whose poetry, infused by a mischievous and occasionally sinister surrealism, had been one of the discoveries of my past year's reading. However, when I called Rómulo's cell phone from Bogotá, he told me he was actually in the capital, shortly to depart for Madrid – so we met up for a coffee there and then. I warmed at once to Rómulo, who, since our meeting, has arranged for me to give a talk and a reading at the University of Cartagena, whose most famous alumnus was García Márquez himself. I carry out my services to Cymro-Colombian relations on the evening of my return from Mompox, without Rómulo, who is still in Spain, but ably hosted by a pair of his colleagues, and over drinks, after my event, I learn from one of them that there is a crypt in the bar of the Santa Clara Hotel that appears in one of Gabo's novels. The Santa Clara is in the old quarter, not far from the university. After bidding farewell to my hosts, I go and investigate. The hotel was once a convent, and has been converted into one of the most luxurious establishments in the city. Gabo, having returned from Mexico to settle in Cartagena, published *Of Love and Other Demons* in 1994, and it is as much a paean to the city as *Love in the Time of Cholera*. It tells of a young journalist sent to report on the newly excavated site of Santa Clara, in 1949. The exhumed skeleton of a child marquise is adorned with a twenty-two metre stream of copper-coloured hair, and the tale of demonic possession evokes the grimly gothic mood that found its material expression in the Palace of the Inquisition, which I had visited the previous week.

When I arrive at the Santa Clara, a white-coated lackey, with top hat to match, opens the door for me. I am unused to such ceremony. I tell him I've come to see the crypt. He shows me in. "Here it is," he says, "here is the famous crypt." The drinks in the Santa Clara are exorbitantly priced, but the bar is vast and cool, so I sit there for a while and allow the opulence to soak in. When I leave, I pass other, smaller, boutique hotels and very chic eateries with exotic names. I walk past a group of six young English tourists – three couples – who resemble cast members of the TV show, *Made in Chelsea*. "Oh don't let's do the walking game, Fiona," says a boy with a Byronic kiss curl: "It's just *so* tedious." He wants to sit down. Fiona snorts with impatience. She wants to go on, as she has somewhere particular in mind: "But Charles, I *so* need to find that Daquiri place."

I wander down the street a while, marvelling at the gentrification that has taken place in this part of town. Later, I return past the same group of English tourists. They have sat down. Evidently Charles has got his way.

When I stroll back into Getsemaní, the difference is striking. First, after crossing the main road, you have to negotiate your way past a very obvious brothel, and a couple of its denizens hail me with an invitation to sample their wares. There is more dog-shit in the street here. More dogs too, obviously. The little plaza at La Santisima Trinidad is packed with a different sort of company: locals, Colombian tourists, budget backpackers, stoned travellers, students. A few middle-aged men, in shorts and baseball caps, stranded in a second adolescence.

On the southwest corner of the plaza a young white man sits outside the bar called *Demente*. A discreet bar, I might add, in defiance of its name; discreet to the point of being almost empty. Inside it is discreetly and expensively furnished. It stands out from the other local dives. I've seen the man sitting here before. I couldn't help but notice him, since he bears a passing resemblance to Leonardo di Caprio. He sits outside in an armchair, pulling on a fat cigar. At his feet lies a bulldog. The dog looks like he might fancy a cigar as well.

We nod a greeting to each other the second time I walk by. The third time I stop and speak to him, in English.

Are you the owner, or do you just look as if you should be?

He smiles. I am the owner, yes.

He is of medium height, blonde hair with a side parting, friendly face, perhaps too innocent looking for this game, but I might be mistaken. Looks can be deceptive. With old-fashioned courtesy, he stands to shake my hand.

Hi, I'm Nicolas. Pleased to meet you. The accent is slight, almost imperceptible, perhaps a trace of German.

Richard. And who is your friend? I gesture down at the pooch.

Ha ha. He is my partner. His name is Socio. Which in Spanish means partner.

How old is he?

Five years.

How does he handle the heat?

He does OK.

I want to ask what the local strays make of Socio, but it's too early for that.

Looks like a nice bar, I say.

Thanks, he says. We have been open one year now.

I peer inside. Three women have materialised, perched in a row at the bar. I've been past here on half a dozen occasions and it's the first time I've seen anyone inside.

I'll come and have a drink, but need to get some food first, I tell Nicolas.

Ah, we do food normally, but with this electricity cut, it's not possible.

That's okay. I'll see you later.

I go to eat at Trattoria di Silvio, at a table on the pavement across the narrow street, fifty metres up from the square, where, it would seem, they haven't been so disabled by the electrical outage as to shut down the kitchen. I have just finished my pizza when the second power cut of the evening strikes and the lights go out. I have a candle at my table. The three Portuguese at the next table do not, and they are still eating, with some difficulty, so I pass them my candle. A few minutes later the waitress brings me another. Nicolas walks past with Socio. I wave at him and he calls back a valediction. I guess the second power failure has proved too much for him. I would have liked to hear his story, and why he thinks it's a good idea to open a new bar in a place like Getsemaní. After all, the shop next door sells beer for 2,000 pesos (around 50 cents) and bottles of rum or aguardiente for a couple of dollars apiece. But once Getsemaní becomes a little more gentrified, Nicolas will be in a prime location.

I sit on the edge of the square and soak in the spirit of the place. I will be leaving Cartagena in the morning, and am reluctant to return to my hostel. The cat's pee scent of marijuana sits heavy on the air, overlaying the smell of the drains.

Three old aguardiente drinkers, a black man flanked by two *blancos*, sit in a row on the bench to my right, passing a bottle between them. The one in the middle is toothless apart from two protruding yellow canines. He laughs wheezily, before bursting into raucous song, singing the same chorus again and again, which his two companions applaud loudly at each rendition. The thinnest one – they are all three skin and bone, but this one is so gaunt he looks as if he would snap at the slightest touch – is shaped like a question mark. He stands and calls out every few minutes for *música música!* – looking around the square to see whether his plea will be heeded in some quarter, and then turns his head imploringly to the heavens, as if some celestial orchestra might appear to do his bidding, and when no response comes he cackles disdainfully and shuffles in a circle around the bench, dragging one foot as he moves. The third, the most desperate of these musketeers, is too far gone to do anything but gurn like a gargoyle at the world passing by, if indeed he can see it. His drunkenness is such that when they rise, he immediately stumbles, but his black comrade-in-arms – who can barely stand himself – has already extended a hand to steady him. After some hesitation and incoherent argument, the three eventually stagger off into the night, moving with extreme difficulty, as though struggling against the impossible tide of fortune, croaking and cackling their way towards oblivion. I have a vision of Macbeth's witches, reincarnated and transgendered as these three Caribbean drunks, wrecked beyond pity or purpose.

There is a ship in the middle of the desert.
A ship reclining on rocks in the desert and above it
the wrecked slab of the sky.

Raúl Zurita, 'Inri'.

Santiago – Valdivia, Chile, January 2015

The sixth floor of the Holiday Inn at Santiago de Chile's international airport is an ideal place from which to savour anonymity. From my room I can look down on the runway and the planes neatly docked in their aprons like Dinky toys. The hotel itself, a non-place for world travellers, offers its guests a veneer of self-conscious transience, and a restaurant where they might consume generic world cuisine in a habitat devoid of any specific cultural reference. As though both to confirm and deny this sense of displacement, the hotel lobby displays a full range of multi-coloured 'Welcome' signs in around a hundred languages, including Welsh. It is January 2015 and although the UK's Home Secretary and future Prime Minister, Theresa May, has yet to make her famous comment about citizens of the world being citizens of nowhere, I am certainly among them here, and presumably share with them – despite the synthetic bonhomie of the welcome signs – that sad brand of homelessness characterised, in May's estimation, by frustration, lack of purpose, and despair. In my hotel room, I am indeed above and beyond citizenship, or even identity, but can see everything going on down below: the passengers queueing at the carpark pay-booth; others dragging their wheelie suitcases across the tarmacadam towards the straggling expanse of Brutalist concrete buildings that house the Departures Hall ... and if I were to open the window – which I cannot, presumably to prevent me from hurling myself earthward in horror at my own anomie – I would no doubt be able to smell the fumes of the petroleum-laden day. Like almost everything else, modern travel is a consumerist project. The gringo in the foyer with his cargo pants and hiking boots, ready to head off into the Andes in emulation of Alexander von Humboldt, who is he trying to kid? What kind of a fiction is he trying to promote?

I have come to Chile to hunt down poems, on the final leg of what I now refer to as 'my research project.' I have, for reasons which may become apparent, left the Chileans to last. I am glad to escape the northern winter for a few weeks, but am also a little apprehensive, as this will be the last trip I undertake before settling down to the proper work of translation, whose stuttering preamble has now been underway for four years, since my first trip, to Nicaragua, in February 2011. The selection process, at least, is heading towards completion. No book is ever finished, however, even when it has gone to press and is done and dusted; it carries on reinventing itself in the heads of its readers, if not its creator.

I am staying at the Holiday Inn because my flight from Heathrow arrived too late for me to make a connection to Valdivia, in the south of the country, where I plan to spend the first couple of weeks of the trip with my friends Verónica and Menashe. Menashe is an Israeli chemist, painter and ceramicist: opposed to his government's policy in the occupied territories, he has settled in Valdivia and now has dual nationality. Verónica is a Chilean poet, who spent much of the Pinochet dictatorship living in London, and later Israel, where she met Mensahe. She is a dear friend, and has offered to help me in the selection of poets from her country, with which I have been struggling. She has also offered me introductions to several of these poets, and while I do not wish to be overly influenced by her preferences, it is undoubtedly a generous offer and one I am keen to pursue – although with reservations, where some of the poets are concerned.

I have visited Verónica and Menashe's house before, at the end of the 'Forgetting Chatwin' trip – Valdivia lying within Chilean Patagonia – and the Austral University, based in Valdivia, is one of the named sponsors of my tenure as Creative Ambassador, the title which has grown about me like moss on a stone, such that any underlying identity I may once have possessed has become lost to sight, to the extent that I am in danger of becoming the moss itself, which is equivalent to being the Ambassador of Nowhere, as the Colombian police sergeant, Eduardo, might have pointed out, had he been susceptible to metaphors of this kind. However, being Ambassador of Nowhere has certain advantages over being Ambassador of Somewhere, especially after the anonymity of the airport's Holiday Inn.

Valdivia is a small, bustling city: the architecture and names displayed on shop fronts and, notably, on the hoardings for upcoming elections, have a distinctly Teutonic flavour. Verónica, whose own origins are Polish and German Jewish, comes to meet me at the bus station and we drive out to her house on the edge of town, surrounded by green space and woodlands, an oasis of quiet, and a perfect place to gather my thoughts on the Chilean poetry of the past half century. It is the antipodean summer, and even this far south temperatures climb into the mid-thirties.

I hunker down for a week of reading, re-reading, discussion and translation. I have a list of Chilean poets born since 1945 and, as with the poets from the other countries I have visited, it remains my intention to communicate with the poets themselves where possible, and discuss with them the poem or poems I have chosen to translate.

My days begin with a breakfast of toast, avocados and coffee, with my hosts, and proceed in a regular and coherent fashion, mornings spent working alone, and afternoons in discussion with Verónica about the work I have carried out, all of it accompanied by coffee and cigarettes.

Over the first three days I do a first round of 'definites' – the poems I most want to include – and then the trickier task of filling the remaining vacancies. My problem is that, by the fourth day, I find a good deal of the poetry I am reading incomprehensible and formless. Not that I am great stickler for poetic form, but much of what has been written in Chile in the long wake of Nicanor Parra – who, more so even than Pablo Neruda, influenced the generations that followed him – strikes me as mechanistic, dull, and lacking in any structure, musicality or even rhythm. Maybe I am missing something, but it seems to me that

Parra's most substantive legacy has been to licence anyone who chooses to call him or herself a poet to do so, and to publish endless collections of diarrheic verse, on any topic, with the sole purpose of being seen and heard; heard and seen. I'm sure this tendency isn't limited to the poets of Chile; it's just that they're the ones doing it right now, inside my head.

I am so immersed in Chilean poetry that I begin to feel dizzy. I keep wondering about Roberto Bolaño's provocative remarks on the subject: "I have a vague suspicion that Chileans see Chilean poetry as a dog, or as dogs in their various incarnations: sometimes as a savage pack of wolves, sometimes as a solitary howl heard between dreams, and sometimes – especially – as a lap dog at the groomers." What did he mean? After all, he was a Chilean poet himself, and although he became far better known – and for good reason – as a novelist, always considered himself first and foremost a poet. He spent almost all of his life after the age of fifteen in Mexico and Spain and, on returning to his native country to judge a short story competition, was less than complimentary about his fellow Chilean poets, entering into a recriminatory dispute with Raúl Zurita, which descended into a mud-slinging contest. Since I have just been reading through Zurita's collected poetry, in search of something to translate for my anthology, I find myself returning to Bolaño's writings about Chile, among the essays, reviews and interviews in his book, *Entre paréntesis* (Between Parentheses), and begin to assemble a clearer idea of his conflicted feelings about his homeland. Bolaño's casual, cavalier approach in his nonfiction writings can be distracting to the reader, just as he is distracted, constantly, in 'Fragments of a return to the native land', in which he describes the trip he took to Chile in 1998, the first visit he had made there since January 1974. He is distracted on the flight out, for example, by the very idea, or fact of flying (which he has avoided for the past twenty years) and reflects, between "strange and vivid dreams" on the plane's engines drilling through the night, "the night itself a plane flying inside another plane ... a fish eating a fish eating another fish." He is distracted, too, by a woman in the row behind him, whom he "deduces" is a Chilean hooker returning home after some years in Europe, in order to buy property, a woman who talks in her sleep, uttering "unintelligible words in Spanish and Italian and German" and whose snoring is as loud as the engines of the plane that "miraculously" bring Roberto and his family to Chile.

Several pieces of writing emerged from that return trip to Chile, most notably 'El pasillo sin salida aparente' ('The corridor with no apparent way out'), in which Bolaño tells the story of a married couple's home at the time of Pinochet's dictatorship: she is a promising poet; he is a member of the Chilean secret police, and he, the husband, uses the basement of their big house in the suburbs as a torture chamber for political prisoners. In the evenings the wife holds soirées for writers, evenings of readings and wine, which sometimes turn into dinners. "One night," Bolaño writes, "a guest goes looking for the bathroom and gets lost. It's his first time there and he doesn't know the house. Probably he's a bit tipsy or maybe he's already lost in the alcoholic haze of the weekend. In any case, instead of turning right he turns left and then he goes down a flight of stairs that he shouldn't have gone down and he opens a door at the end of a long hallway, long like Chile. The room is dark but even so he can make out a bound figure, in pain or possibly drugged. He knows what he's seeing. He closes the door and returns to the party. He isn't drunk anymore. He's terrified, but he doesn't say anything."

The story reads like an allegory of some kind; perhaps, as suggested in the passage cited here, an allegory of Chile. And so it is; but it is also based in fact. The writer's name was Mariana Callejas, and she worked undercover for DINA, Chile's secret police. The husband was Michael Townley, an American businessman, who also moonlighted for the secret police. The literary workshops took place in their house in the suburb of Lo Curro, Santiago, that was procured for them by DINA. In the basement of their home, Townley interrogated leftist dissidents, prior to them being shipped to detention centres where they were 'disappeared'. Rarely have literature and political violence been so graphically intertwined, but then literature and political violence was a collocation which obsessed Bolaño throughout his writing career. For him, literature was a dangerous vocation, a matter of life and death: "Literature," he told Luis García-

Santillán in 2001, "has always been close to ignominy, to vileness, to torture."

Bolaño held in especially low regard any writer whom he deemed to be a sycophant or a 'courtier' (his term) – one whose work was moulded to fit in with or appease contemporary political or literary fashions, and anyone who wrote solely to accumulate fame and prestige. His later career is peppered with attacks on writers whom he perceived to have acted in this manner, but Chileans were his favourite targets, and chief among them was Zurita. In *Distant Star*, Bolaño describes the sinister career of Carlos Weider, who attends leftist poetry sessions as a young man and later reappears as an Air Force pilot under the country's dictatorship, writing sky poems in praise of death. Not coincidentally, Zurita once hired a biplane in order to write poems in the sky above New York, and carried out the stunt again above the deserts of northern Chile, and Zurita – unforgivably, in Bolaño's eyes – was one of the few poets of the left who rose to fame under the dictatorship, receiving laudatory reviews in the country's main newspaper and organ of the State, *Mercurio*, which, with President Nixon's authorisation, was funded by the CIA. Bolaño savagely parodied Zurita's aeronautic antics in *Distant Star*, which, along with *By Night in Chile*, is widely regarded as amongst his finest work. And yet, paradoxically, in the same article in which he likens Chilean poets to a pack of dogs, he is able to write: "Zurita creates a wonderful body of work ... for which he stands out among his generation, but his eschatology and his messianism are also the pillars of a mausoleum or a funeral pyre toward which almost all the poets of Chile marched in the 1980s."

Despite this barbed endorsement, I struggle to decide on which poem of Zurita's I should include in the anthology, but eventually settle on a sequence from *Inri*, a strange and moving sequence set in the waterless expanses of Chile's Atacama Desert, in which a stranded ship comes to rest, its iron hull rusting amid the blown sands. There seems be a special place, in Zurita's work, for metaphors of mechanised transport, and I am curious as to why, precisely. Then I remember that Zurita studied to be an engineer: aeroplanes and ships, machines for the delivery of poetry ...

As I read on, I learn that the enmity between Zurita and Bolaño festered until the latter's death in 2003, and even beyond, Zurita giving an interview with Chiara Bolognese for the *Anales de Literatura Chilena* in 2010, in which he claims – using the analogy of a schoolyard brawl – that he would have liked to have "had it out" with the "hepatic" Bolaño, which Zurita, as he himself concedes (he was by now suffering from Parkinson's disease) would probably have lost, especially as Bolaño was something of a brawler in his day, and his father was a semi-professional boxer. I can picture the bleakly comic scene: "In the blue corner, the poet with Parkinsons; in the red, the novelist with the knobbly liver." The idea of this literary tussle dissolving into a grotesque fistfight between two middle-aged literary invalids is one that makes me shake with laughter. I've been too long at my desk and need to take a walk in the garden.

 I wander off the path to follow a curious, irate bird with a long curved beak. Its behaviour fascinates me, as it huffs and faffs in frustration, strutting about in circles before setting off, as I now see, after another bird of the same type (which I later identifiy as a *bandurria*). I have walked in on their courting ritual. The male follows the female around in an obsequious manner, until she, and then he, disappear under a large bush, and I leave them to it.

In the evening we go out to celebrate Verónica's award, announced that day, to work on a major project about the poet

Gabriela Mistral, the first female Nobel prizewinner, and one of two Chileans to be so honoured (the other, of course, was Neruda) and we enjoy an evening on the restaurant's quiet terrace, looking out over the river, infused by the golden light of the sun falling over the southern Pacific. We are joined by Verónica and Menashe's daughter, Tamara, and we drink pisco sours and eat *papas bravas* and more *papas* with Roquefort, and a variety of fish, and the company is good, and the conversation lively, all of it brushing away the cobwebs of my day's slog through the dog-eat-dog labyrinth of Chilean poetics. On returning home, Menashe and I share a smoke on the balcony and then we all watch *Patience*, a documentary about W.G. Sebald's *Rings of Saturn*. I like the film very much, but have seen it several times before, and I fall asleep before it ends.

★   ★   ★

Many and varied are the approaches to translation, and numerous its unsought consequences. There are those who become obsessed by the *process* of translation, even at the cost of progressing to the end of a piece of work, and abandoning it in frustration, so bogged down have they become in the minutiae of the task itself, so abundant the permutations and dead ends of its untranslatability. They have reached a conclusion that has occurred to all translators, at some point: it doesn't matter how you try to stem the tide; sooner or later, you realise, everything becomes an act of translation.

At the weekend, we translate ourselves to the coastal park, the *Reserva Costera Valdiviana*. The land is given over to the Mapuche people and building is prohibited within the area of the reserve. There are eight of us on the trip – Verónica, Menashe, Tamara and myself, and four others, members of Verónica's writing workshop – and we have rented log cabins for the weekend. We arrive on Friday evening and are greeted by our hosts, Teodora and Julio, who prepare *pulmay*, a dish cooked in layers of pork, chicken, sausage, chorizo, potatoes, and topped off with a thick layer of two kinds of shellfish, cholgas and choritos. It is rich and tasty, but altogether too much: I prefer not to be bamboozled by flavours so much at odds with each other. After supper I take a walk under a canopy of stars, the like of which I have never witnessed, in part because I have never before travelled this far south, but also because here, the night sky, untouched by light pollution, is endowed with a unique clarity. I stand for a while, humbled by the majesty of the heavens, the miracle of the universe, and our place within it, on our blue planet spinning its course around the sun, one among the billions of stars, only a tiny fraction of which are visible to the eye.

In the morning we drive to Chaihuín, then south towards Laguna Colún along an unmade forest road for an hour, having to stop several times to move logs from the track, where the mud has piled thick. When the road runs out we park up and start off through the forest on foot, following a trail that curves down towards a broad expanse of high dunes, overlooking the sea. There is no one here, only miles of unspoiled, empty beach. What I hadn't counted on were the cows, grazing, it would seem – except that there is no grass. They come, apparently, for the algae: there are two main kinds hereabouts, cochayuyo (large, rubbery and octopoid) and luche, a variety of sea lettuce. The cows, unlikely beach bums, are relaxing between piles of seaweed, of which there is an abundance along the shore.

The only inconvenience are the flying insects known as tábanos, and colloquially as colihuachos. You must not wear dark clothes: if you do they will hunt you down and pester you incessantly. If you wear white, they will ignore you altogether. Almost every beautiful landscape, beneath a certain altitude, seems to harbour some resident bug whose only purpose is to pursue and persecute humans. My navy fleece attracts swarms of the stingy things; removing it, my faded tee shirt holds no interest at all.

We turn inland, past the lagoon, where the plan is to swim, although, in the event, the water is far too cold, a result of the famous Humboldt current, which keeps coastal water temperatures at around 11 degrees Centigrade, so instead we climb the adjoining dunes, a frustrating and exhausting venture in which we slide several metres down the dune for every one climbed; then, after following the summit of the undulating hillocks, we descend towards green pastures and a grotto, reassuringly called the cave of the vulvas, a dark cavern filled with fissures carved into the rock and daubed with aboriginal art. A battered lectern outside provides information in both Spanish and English, but omits to inform who originally made the drawings and carvings inside the cave, or why. The place has not yet been researched or carbon dated.

One of Verónica's students says it was used as an initiation chamber by the indigenous people of these parts in pre-Hispanic times. Climbing the dunes and sliding down the other side only to enter the cave of vulvas has made for a disorienting and slightly surreal experience. We eat our sandwiches before starting the long walk back, past the still motionless cows.

The region is famous for its extensive deciduous forests, La Selva Valdiviana, and the next day, a Sunday, while Menashe and Tamara go kayaking, Verónica and I visit Los Colmillos de Chaihuín, which contains among other trees, canelo (Winter's bark), alerce, and eucalyptus. The first two are indigenous, the last a moisture-hogging outsider, the villain of the piece in the local eco-system, imported from Australia and now being slowly replaced by the older indigenous varieties in a patient programme of replanting. The eucalyptus grows very quickly and self-regenerates once it has been chopped down; it can do this five times, and, given the opportunity, will grow to full height between each growth. South America's only marsupial, the monito del monte (little mountain monkey) may be found here but we are unlikely to see one as they are very shy, as is the pudú, a squat, dwarfish deer with a sweet face and dark, fearful eyes.

We stop to pay homage to an individual tree: this alerce (*Fitzroya cupressoides*, a member of the cypress family) is forty-five metres tall and at least 3,500 years old, according to our guide, Alonso. Its age is calculated by the girth of the tree, which is three and half metres in diameter. I reflect in astonishment that the Minoan civilisation was still flourishing on Crete when this tree was young. The forests hereabout were once filled with these trees, but the wood is good for making boats and houses, and the Spanish colonists cut down thousands of them to furnish their navy and build barracks for their troops, a practice continued by successive Chilean governments and licensed foreign companies. The trees have been protected by law since 1976, but they grow so slowly that it will be a long time before they ever repopulate the forests of Valdivia.

As we walk through this enchanted forest, I notice a bright yellow fungus, the size of a tennis ball, growing at the base of a tree, almost luminous in the dark of the woods. It is known, Alonso tells us, as *caca de duende*. Of course, as we have seen, there is some difficulty in rendering 'duende' into English: it can mean 'spirit', or 'creative force' as well as referring to a sprite, fairy or elf. Elf-shit sounds the most evocative translation, and the idea sticks.

> Next to the river of these skies
> dark green towards the coast
> we raise the house of Zulema Hualquipán.
> The foundations so many deaths ago,
> so many sons ago
> for the red dust of the road.
>
> Jaime Luis Huenún, 'In the House of Zulema Hualquipán'.

Valdivia – Santiago de Chile, January 2015

A few days later, I drive north with Verónica and Menashe to the Huerquehue national park, where we climb through temperate rainforest until we reach the zone of the Araucaria araucana (the national tree of Chile, known in English as the monkey puzzle tree) – which is only found above 1,000 metres – amid bursts of outlandish birdsong from the chucao and the huet-huet. I swim in a lake surrounded by the mountain peaks, and am immersed in the dense, moist odours of the Andean forest. I float on my back in the middle of the lake, enjoying a moment of absolute peace, astonished to find myself in such a place, and entranced by the pristine beauty of the forest, mountain peaks looming high to one side, the inisistent birdsong weaving a tapestry of sound around me.

I'm not sure how the topic arose, but driving back from our hike, Menashe begins to tell me the story of Paul Schäfer, who, in the 1960s, directed the 'Colonia Dignidad', a centre for the training and indoctrination of children into his very personal theology. Born in Troisdorf, near Cologne, in 1921, Schäfer joined the Hitler Youth as a boy and served in the Wehrmacht medical corps during World War Two. Following the war, he founded an orphanage and began preaching an apocalyptic vision of Christianity, influenced by the American preacher William M. Branham, one of the first practitioners of televangelism, and an advocate of charismatic healing. By 1959, Schäfer was already under investigation by the German police on charges of child abuse, and he disappeared for two years, surfacing, like so many ex-Nazis, (though the ex- in this case would seem redundant) in Chile.

Arriving at Colonia Dignidad, which had been settled by Germans in the 1950s as a kind of sanctuary where traditional German values and language were preserved against intrusion from the outside world, Schäfer soon re-shaped the place to fit in with his own designs, supported by others who had followed him from the Fatherland. Once in control, he encouraged members of the colony to adopt Chilean children from local communities, and established himself as an improbable Messiah, with his long grey hair and glass eye (sustained, improbably, after an accident with a dining fork). He prohibited marriage among new members, although he allowed those who were already married to remain so. All the colonists slept in dormitories, and were permitted few personal possessions. Babies born in the colony were taken from their mothers and raised by 'aunts', appointed by Schäfer. Colonists worked hard, in the dairy, mills or gravel factory, in the fields and in the hospital, where care was also extended to nearby villagers: indeed, local people were especially encouraged in this regard, and mothers were sometimes told that their children had died, when in fact they had simply been abducted, to be raised in the colony. The place even boasted a hydroelectric power station. When Pinochet came to power in September 1973, the colony received a new and lucrative form of sponsorship, as Schäfer forged a close relationship with senior figures in the dictatorship, and political prisoners were sent to the colony to be tortured by agents of the Chilean secret police, DINA. According to a report by Chile's National Commission for Truth and Reconciliation, around three hundred prisoners were interrogated and tortured at Colonia Dignidad, and at least one hundred were murdered there. Poison gases were developed in the colony's laboratories, for use by the military. None of this could have been done without Schäfer's connivance and support.

Even after the return to democracy in Chile, Schäfer continued to run the colony as a personal fiefdom. His abuse of children remained unchecked, and he used a compliant physician, Hartmut Hopp, to prescribe sedatives for children in his care at the colony's boarding school, children that Schäfer drugged and raped. He also continued to assault local Chilean boys until, in 1997 he disappeared, fleeing accusations of child sex abuse filed against him by the Chilean authorities. He was eventually tracked down, in 2005, to a villa in the outskirts of Buenos Aires, and extradited to face trial in Santiago.

In May 2019, the German state acknowledged the claims of many of his victims for compensation (which the Chilean government had been reluctant to award, so prolific were Schäfer's crimes). Many of these claimants had been held against their will and kept as sex slaves at Colonia Dignidad.

The Colony, renamed Villa Baviera, still exists, run by Schäfer's remaining acolytes. According to a report from May 2018, the colonists now draw their income from a poultry farm, which produces 30,000 eggs a day, and from tourism. The resort's Tripadvisor entry reads, in slightly off-key English: 'Cozy atmosphere for you to enjoy rest and silence in the midst of a surprising nature and first class attention.' Facilities include a manmade-lake with pedal boats, a small museum (that makes no mention of the disappeared) and a restaurant where vistors can enjoy such treats as venison, sauerkraut and smoked sausage: there is even a display of traditional dancing in lederhosen. All of this, even as the search for mass graves at the site goes on.

Relatives of the disappeared have demanded that Villa Baviera be closed, and the place honoured by a memorial to their dead.

Margarita Romero, president of the Chilean Association of Memory and Human Rights, is quoted as saying: "It is not possible that a place where serious violations of human rights such as torture, murders and disappearances should function as a tourist destination. Imagine a hotel built in a concentration camp in Europe – it would never be permitted."

I cannot help but link this singular abuse of the human environment – a cult led by a Nazi paedophile in the woodlands of the lower Andes – with the desecration of the geography in which it takes place. If we accept the term 'climate', as referring to the relations between human beings and the material conditions of their lives, then the desecration of the land and the abuse of its inhabitants – human, animal and arboreal – merge into a single sustained affront, and its reverberations touch us all.

★   ★   ★

Alexander von Humboldt is only now being given credit for having been the first to comment on deforestation as a destructive force, witnessing for himself, on his journeys around South America between 1799 and 1803, how the plundering of forests could not only despoil the wilderness, but wreak havoc in the ecosystem.

At Lake Valencia, in present day Venezuela, Humboldt observed that extensive tree-felling was having a devastating effect on the local ecology. Trees, soil and climate were all connected, Humboldt asserted, and the damage he witnessed being done to the environment might, he claimed, in the long run, cause climatic changes that would be impossible to reverse. According to his biographer, Andrea Wulf, "Humboldt was the first to explain the forest's ability to enrich the atmosphere with moisture and its cooling effect, as well as its importance for water retention and protection against soil erosion." Two centuries on, Humboldt's ideas are finally being taken seriously, but it may be too late.

When the Spanish arrived in the land that would one day be called Chile, they began to exploit the rich supply of timber, useful – as illustrated by the near-eradication of the alerce – in servicing the navy upon which the maintenance of their empire, and the delivery of its looted gold and silver, depended. It goes without saying that the approach taken towards the indigenous population was extended towards the land they lived on. The land was held as sacred by native American peoples, and the exploitation and degrading of the earth for material gain was utterly beyond their comprehension. But the colonial attitude towards exploitation of the land did not finish with the end of colonial rule. The governments of the new republics of Latin America – almost all of them dictatorships – continued in much the same vein as their colonial antecedents.

A dictatorship takes the tenets of colonialism and applies them to its own citizens: just as, under colonialism, the subjected peoples exist in order to serve the interests of the mother country, under a dictatorship the masses sustain the interests of the privileged few. Thus the exploitation of indigenous lands for profit (mining, logging etc), once carried out by a foreign colonial power, is discharged, under the dictatorship, by one's own rulers, as well as to whomever the country's leaders have sold off its assets, nowadays, predictably the USA or China, although historically Great Britain and France were among the principal beneficiaries.

In Chile, the Pinochet regime made sure that power was retained by the few, at the expense of the many: education was a resource to withhold in order to exercise greater control. The rail system was abandoned, in order to gain the support of road transport haulage companies and their drivers, who formed a phalanx of support for the dictator, in spite of the fact that Chile imports all its fossil fuels. An efficient rail system, it might be argued, in a long thin country, whose economic infrastructure is to a large extent determined by the geographical shape of the land, would seem an obvious solution. However the rail system in Chile remains unused, thirty years after the dictatorship ended. Never before had I so clearly perceived how a breakdown of responsible government affected the ecology of a country, especially in the way that logging, in this part of Chile, causes deforestation and the laying waste of the ecosystem: entire forests, that took thousands of years to grow, can be dismantled and destroyed in a matter of weeks.

On our trip to the Coastal Reserve, on the ferry across the Río Valdivia between Niebla and Corral, I witnessed the effects of this sylvan slaughter, as the largest container vessel I have ever seen was escorted downriver by three tugs. I asked a ferry worker standing nearby where they were headed. The vessels are unloaded, he told me, onto Chinese cargo ships sitting offshore, their hulls filled to the gunwales with wood pellets, the material output of Chile's depleted forests.

I know that I will miss Valdivia, and the comforts of my friends' home, but will not dwell on the impossibility of my staying here, even if, as places go, there are few I would rather remain. Instead, I haul my big blue suitcase, laden with books of poetry, and move on to the next place.

★ ★ ★

Arriving in Santiago from the south, I was invited by friends, the publishers Paulo Slachevsky and Silvia Aguilera, to attend a performance of *Exhibit B*, showing as part of the 'Santiago a Mil' theatre festival. *Exhibit B* is a theatre installation that replicates the grotesque phenomenon of the human zoo during the 19th Century, in which Africans were put on display like circus freaks for the titillation of European and American audiences under the guise of 'ethnological enlightenment.'

Holding the performance in the baroque setting of the nineteenth century Cousiño Palace in central Santiago was a provocative decision. The Cousiño Goyenechea family owned coal and silver mines, which employed slave labour, as well as the Cousiño-Macul Vineyards. The nouveau riche glitz of the palace, set off by classical music, provided a sinister but fitting venue.

The experience of *Exhibit B* was painful, as I expected it to be, and my emotions as I walked slowly around the exhibits were complex, and included a certain shame even in experiencing discomfort of any kind, given the extremes of discomfort, abuse and torture suffered by the subjects whose painful lives were being recreated by the actors. I was confused, as I was doubtless meant to be: should I make eye contact with the 'exhibits', for instance? Would I not be replicating the white man's gaze that the performance so vehemently interrogates? The actors weren't avoiding my gaze, that was for sure, as they surveyed us spectators with clinical interest, each one following our passage across the space in front of them, most memorably the replica of the man adopted by some Austrian prince in the eighteenth century who, when he died, had been skinned and stuffed and put out on display.

The show created something of a scandal when performed at the Edinburgh Festival in 2014: there were complaints that the actors were being subjected to a similar form of exploitation as the people whose lives they were reproducing, and its run at the Barbican in London was cancelled, on the grounds, according to the sociologist and activist Kehinde Andrews, "that it reinforces, rather than challenges the racism it stands as a commentary on." Furthermore, given that the exhibition's creator, Brett Bailey, was a white South African, critics argued that it was not his right to appropriate the experience of the black people whose sufferings he sought to document.

These views were not necessarily shared by the show's British perfomers. In an exchange published in the *Guardian*, one of them, Stella Odunlami, wrote in response to Andrews, who was active in getting the show shut down, despite not having seen it, as follows: "my fellow performers and I chose to be part of a production that exposed racism then and now. We have had to defend our decision to exercise our freedom of creativity to those who call us puppets. It is not your job to decide what is or isn't good for me; I am capable of doing so for myself."

The fictions we make are often ways of overcoming and ordering the disorders of reality, and the uncomfortable quality of a fiction, in pursuit of a valid goal, is less important than its effectiveness. In the case of *Exhibit B*, this was not in doubt: it was both effective and deeply unsettling.

This visit to *Exhibit B* lingered with me for a long time afterwards. My confusion, and the residual remorse which I had no power to resist, was exacerbated by a string of questions to which I could find no answers. But I was beginning to understand that the exploitation and systematic abuse of certain groups of people – captive African slaves, in this instance, but also refugees, impoverished migrants, the displaced, others of all description – are not to be treated in isolation, but as part of a larger and possibly terminal problem. The current era of world history has been marked, claims Bruno Latour, by three phenomena: Globalization – which effectively means economic deregulation; increasingly vertiginous inequality between rich and poor, and a systematic attempt to deny the existence of climate change —"climate," as Latour puts it, "in the broad sense of the relations between human beings and the material conditions of their lives."

It is these relations between humans and the material conditions of their lives that is at stake, and our leaders, cocooned from all risk of contamination, do not wish to address it. The primary reason for this is that the ruling classes and the super-rich have decided the world doesn't have room for them and for everyone else. Since the 1980s, the ruling classes have stopped even pretending that their role is to defend the greater good, and have instead focused on protecting their own interests, while sheltering themselves from the world. But, as Latour says, "the absence of a common world we can share is driving us crazy."

> Valparaíso has the smell
> of a crazy port,
> the smell of shadows, of stars,
> of moon-scale
> and fish-tail.
> The heart judders
> on the harrowing stairways
> of the bristling hills ...
>
> Pablo Neruda, 'To Don Asterio
> Alarcón, timekeeper of Valparaíso'.

Valparaíso, Chile, January 2015

A few days later, I leave the enormous blue suitcase stuffed with books at Paulo and Silvia's house, which has been my base during the Santiago leg of my trip, and take the bus to Valparaíso, a city that carries a host of fictions, some them my own. I arrive at midday and phone my friend Enrique Winter, a writer whose work I am including in the anthology, and a point of contact for other poets in the city – Carlos Henrickson, Carlos Decap and Jaime Pinos – whose work I am currently reading, and whom I plan to meet on this trip. Enrique tells me he is at his girlfriend's place, and will not be returning home for a couple of hours, so I deposit my rucksack in the left luggage office at the bus station and take a walk, looking for a clean, well-lighted place that might offer up a drink and a sandwich, maybe one of those huge Chilean sandwiches that contain a variety of colourful food: a *completo* or an *italiano*.

My current state of mind leaves a lot to be desired. I spent some time in Valparaíso the previous October, visited Neruda's house and did the things that visitors do in 'Valpo' on a first trip, and I was looking forward to returning, but am not comfortable in myself. Over the past two days in Santiago the temperature has reached 35 degrees centigrade; here it has dropped to around 19, and is overcast and humid. Dressed like a tourist, in shorts and a floral Hawaiian shirt, I feel ridiculous. I am dehydrated after the bus trip, have a headache, or rather a hangover, and am suffering from travel fatigue. I kill the first hour in pointless perambulation, and then, realising I am lost, attempt to orient myself. I set off towards the covered market, since markets are often useful places for one in search of food, but the stalls are shutting up and the little kitchen shacks outside also, and the whole place has the forlorn aspect of closing time, or even of time closing down. The street outside the market smells of fish, urine and rotting fruit.

I find a more promising street and follow it. The open-fronted shops selling herbs and fruit and meat give off an aroma that reminds me of Greece, specifically the smell of Xania market, in Crete. I try to identify precisely what the smell is, and fail to name it, or rather, the smell fails to trigger the memory that will provide the word or words, if indeed they are words, which now I begin to doubt, as there is something else, which remains tantalisingly beyond recall. It is a smell that combines mountain herbs, coffee and something else, something that will not be named, probably not the background stench of animal entrails, which, however, are there also, the ingredients, perhaps, for a *kokoretsi,* or Cretan haggis. And then it hits me, and I begin to feel a useless nostalgia for people I associate with that market in Xania, and whom I will never see again, and the ghosts of those years of reckless travel during the decade of my twenties – those human phantoms, once living, who shared parts of it with me – return in memory, and with a surge of remorse I conjure two of my dead, a woman I loved, and a man, a sweet shambolic friend who accompanied me on some of my most desolate journeys, and they walk beside me for a stretch, shadowy shapes flanking me along this shadowy side street on the other side of the world; but just as quickly they fade back into the oblivion from which they emerged.

Eventually I spot a likely café and cross the road. I take a table half way down the room. When I order, the waitress turns her head to one side, as some people do when confronted by a foreigner, as though the presumption of their foreignness will necessarily involve not understanding them. When she realises that there are no imminent communication issues, she smiles. Despite my command of the language, I am still a foreigner, and perhaps the waitress feels a degree of pity for me, or something like it. I have seen the other waitress carrying a plate with the kind of sandwich I require: meat, tomato, avocado, mayonnaise. I request the same. It doesn't take long to clock the fact that I am the only non-local in the place; I also seem to be the only customer not personally known to the staff. The sandwich arrives. It is pretty much what it sets out to be, and settles reluctantly in my stomach.

That evening, when I have shed my tourist garb and put on a disguise of black joggers, black tee shirt and a cardigan, all borrowed from my host, I venture downtown with Enrique, who is twenty-five years younger than me, and who remarks, casually, that the two of us might appear to be father and son, taking a turn out to the pub together. Enrique seems to enjoy this idea. My foreigner identity shifts temporarily into 'Chilean dad impostor' mode, an unfamiliar and unexpectedly reassuring role.

We wind up at the Colonial bar, near the harbour, a place redolent of bewhiskered sea dogs and cheap rum, even though the clientele is already veering into a pastiche of itself – a mix of local ruffians, scalliwags, dipsos, and the more adventurous of the backpacking crew, including a couple of fiercely inebriated young Irishwomen, one of whom is so red-raw with sunburn that she looks like a victim of radioactive fallout. They are with a very straight-faced Chinese guy, who clearly doesn't know what he's gotten into, and an equally bemused German, who is doing his best, but is likewise way out of his depth. The Irish girls – as one of them redundantly informs us – are *absolutely blutered*. Despite their entreaties, Enrique and I do not join them, and sit at the only remaining table, just as a couple of musicians take up their instruments at the front of the room, and a tall, ginger-haired man approaches us to inform us, in broken English, that he is part of a French TV crew, that they are filming inside the bar, and it would be very helpful, indeed it would make his day, if Enrique and I relocated to another part of the bar, or at the very least moved our table a metre to the right, so that they can get a good shot of the musicians. Why, asks Enrique, don't you want us in your show? Don't we look *Chilean* enough? The guy grins, though I'm not sure he quite understands Enrique's point, and says he'll pay for our beers. We agree to move. Strangely enough, and despite Enrique's jibe, we are part of the film, and when the documentary appears on French TV the following year – Enrique sends me the link – the bar scene closes with a shot of Enrique and I, watching the pair of musicians; one, animated enough, but wearing a bum-bag, the other, red-eyed, his mouth fixed in a melancholy smile.

Later, we go to eat at the Cinzano, a well-known cabaret restaurant. Enrique's girlfriend joins us, and the Irish women also turn up, along with their indefatigable suitors. They have swopped roles: the sunburned one seems miraculously to have sobered up, while it is her companion who now looks as if she is in need of a good long sleep. Soon after the cabaret starts up, Enrique and his girlfriend disappear, and the Irish pair also, along with their admirers. I stay on, entranced by Pepe de Valencia, a bald, diminutive singer of heroic and lachrymose ballads. After his set there is a break, and Pepe sits nursing a drink, so I go over and join him for a chat. We have met before, when I visited the Cinzano the previous year, and Pepe appears to remember me, or else he pretends to. He is in his late seventies, and came over from Spain as a very young man, so has spent all his adult life here in Valpo, but in the way of these things is still known as Pepe de Valencia. He launches into conversation as though we had just broken off, telling me a convoluted story – or more likely a joke – about a man with a wooden leg who owns a three legged cat, and I feel as if I have slipped into a gap between the worlds, or else a David Lynch movie, and Pepe's face, like that of a beardless, animated leprechaun, acquires an almost divine aspect. His seemingly endless anecdote is broken off, however, when he is called upon to get up and do another set, and so I leave.

I take the long way back, up through the steep streets towards Enrique's house. I'm not in a hurry; Enrique is staying over at his girlfriend's place and I have the apartment to myself. However, after wandering down the street called Esmeralda, and having taken the fork into Cochrane, I am joined by a big black dog, and then another. By the time we have reached Plaza Sotomayor, I have an escort of five large black or brown dogs. They seem to have adopted me, and whenever I take a turning, they follow. A sixth dog, which has been lurking beneath a shopfront, starts up, as if to join the pack, but the others apparently do not want him. The leader – the first to have joined me, an especially brutish specimen – attacks the newcomer viciously, and the others join in. I hear terrible squealing, but know better than to interfere with this territorial battle, and I walk on, quickening my pace. Just when I think I've lost them, a couple of hundred metres up the street, the pack rejoins me, at a run. I am beginning to feel like some lone caped warrior, or the lead singer of a heavy metal band, with my thuggish canine bodyguard now spread around me, the boss dog leading the way, and the others to my side and rear. We climb through the Cerro Alegre and, with the dogs showing no sign of leaving me, I decide to stop off for a nightcap. I spot a likely bar on a side street, with a couple of tables on the pavement. It is past midnight; there is no one outside, but in the bar a few late drinkers are chatting loudly. I go in to order a beer, and return to find my escort has taken up position; the dogs are sitting around the table on the pavement, waiting for me. When I take my seat, they lie down, one by one. All five of them, lying there, watching me.

I take a sip of beer, and remember Alastair Reid's piece about the foreigner, and how one might find a place into which one could sink with a single, timeless, contented sigh. Could mine be here, outside a bar, at midnight, surrounded by a pack of large, feral street dogs? Could this be my vocation, my *function*; to pass the rest of my days as a crazy street person, the dog-man of Valparaíso? Again, I think of Bolaño, and his remark about the poets of Chile as "dogs in their various incarnations ... sometimes a savage pack of wolves, sometimes a solitary howl heard between dreams."

I am lost in these reflections when the bar's owner appears and invites me to come inside. It is not right, he says, for me to be sitting outside, alone. The big dog at my side growls at him. For some reason, the bar owner, whom I have never met before, wants me to meet his friend, a local restaurateur. I leave the dogs and step inside. The restaurant man is a Sicilian called Luigi and he is a big talker. Both he and the guy from the bar are pretty drunk, and the conversation is hard to follow, but I do my best to join in. The bar owner keeps us supplied with Pisco sours, on the house. Luigi insists that I visit his restaurant before leaving Valpo, and sample his incomparable Pasta alla Norma. When eventually I leave, at around three in the morning, the dogs are gone.

> If they tell you that I fell
> it's because I fell.
> Vertically.
> And with horizontal results.
>
> Beatríz Vignoli, 'The Fall'.

Buenos Aires, April 2015

Buenos Aires kept calling me back. The city held a perennial fascination that I shared, after a fashion, with the late Nobel Prize-winner and fantasist V.S. Naipaul. In 'The Brothels Behind the Graveyard', an essay published in the *New York Review of Books* in September 1974, Naipaul developed a thesis about the Argentine national psyche that led him toward some surprising conclusions; or else, it might be argued, he made some wild assumptions and then developed a thesis around them. Whichever way you read it, the piece has an interesting history, and it provided context for a section of Phillip French's official biography of Naipaul, as well as a review article of that same biography by Ian Buruma, a friend and admirer of the Trinidadian author. It also inspired a short piece discovered on Roberto Bolaño's computer and subsequently published, a decade after the Chilean author's death.

The essay by Naipaul, described by Ian Buruma as "beautifully and passionately written", is offered as a reflection on the legacy of General Juan Domingo Perón, who had died two months before it was published. First, Naipaul asserts, "Argentina is a land of plunder, a new land, virtually peopled in this century. It remains a land to be plundered; and its politics can only be the politics of plunder" – 'plunder,' as we shall see, is a word reiterated insistently throughout the article. Despite the limitations of this assertion, Naipaul goes on, in the next sentence, to claim that "Everyone in Argentina understands and accepts this." Really? Everyone? By the same logic, would such a claim about the centrality of plunder not be true, historically, of the United States, for example, or the British Empire? Or of Rome? But this is only the first in a number of extraordinary pronouncements. A couple of pages on, we are told that Argentina is a country "where the political realities, of plunder and the animosities engendered by plunder have for so long been clouded by rhetoric. The rhetoric fools no one. But in a country where the government has never been open and intellectual resources are scant, the rhetoric of a regime is usually all that survives to explain it." Surely there is more to the matter of political analysis than this? And where precisely, one might ask, *has* the mechanics of government been 'open'; and what, indeed, might the consequences of such a state of affairs resemble? Regardless, he continues, despite the country having "the apparatus of an educated, open society" – surely a rebuttal, if not an outright contradiction of the previous claims about both the government and the country's lack of "intellectual resources" – as well as newspapers and universities and publishing houses and "even a film industry", yet, he claims, "the country has as yet no idea of itself." Lacking this self-knowledge, Naipaul decides to provide one, and it comes down to sex; more explicitly, to buggery.

Discussing the macho attitudes that dominated Argentinian society at the time, and the brothels which, he writes, lined the street behind the famous Recoleta cemetery, Naipaul – who would know, as he was a frequent visitor to such places – warns that "Every schoolgirl knows the brothels; from an early age she understands that she might have to go there one day to find love, among the colored lights and mirrors." As though this outrageous claim were not enough, Naipaul goes on to assert that the Argentine male is besotted by the act of sodomising women; and then, as though producing a rabbit from an especially stained and soiled top-hat, offers his coup de grâce:

> The act of straight sex, easily bought, is of no great moment to the [Argentine] macho. His conquest of a woman is complete only when he has buggered her. This is what the woman has it in her power to deny; this is what the brothel

game is about, the passionless Latin adventure that begins with talk of *amor*. La tuve en el culo, I've had her in the arse: this is how the macho reports victory to his circle, or dismisses a desertion. Contemporary sexologists give a general dispensation to buggery. But the buggering of women is of special significance in Argentina and other Latin American countries. The Church considers it a heavy sin, and prostitutes hold it in horror. By imposing on her what prostitutes reject, and what he knows to be a kind of sexual black mass, the Argentine macho, in the main of Spanish or Italian peasant ancestry, consciously dishonors his victim. So diminished men, turning to machismo, diminish themselves further, replacing even sex by a parody.

Armed with this discovery – notwithstanding the odd suggestion that encounters in any brothel are initiated with talk of love (*amor*) – Naipaul feels he has finally understood the Argentinians, with "their violence, their peasant cruelty, their belief in magic, and their fascination with death, celebrated every day in the newspapers with pictures of murdered people, often guerrilla victims, lying in their coffins." However, Naipaul is mistaken in his depiction of these famous 'brothels'. Neither at the time Naipaul visited Buenos Aires nor since have there been brothels behind the Recoleta Cemetery. True, during the 1970s, there were a number of 'albergues transitorios', or 'hoteles de paso' which were the equivalent of today's 'love hotels', where couples might enjoy sexual encounters, in rooms paid for at an hourly rate. But they were generally used by young people who did not have their own place, and lived with their parents, or else for illicit liaisons with someone other than one's spouse, or even for married couples with children whose small apartment compromised their opportunities for sex. But they were never, or only rarely used by prostitutes, and were certainly not brothels. In this short extract Naipaul also displays a faulty command of Argentine Spanish. *La tuve en el culo* is not an expression that would be uttered by any Argentinian (in any case, it would be 'por', rather than 'en' el culo). Specifically, for the practice that Naipaul is describing, the phrasing would most likely be 'le hice el culo,' or even 'se la di por el culo.'

Many years later, Roberto Bolaño wrote a short, somewhat chaotic retort to Naipaul's article titled 'Scholars of Sodom' – which, to be fair, he never himself released for publication – in which he claimed of Naipaul's time in Argentina, that "[as] the days went by, he came to find not only the city [Buenos Aires] but the country as a whole insufferably aggravating. His uneasy feeling about the place seemed to be intensified by every visit, every new acquaintance he made."

Bolaño was especially taken aback by the passage in Naipaul's essay in which he ascribes the historical origin of the Argentine habit of sodomy to its predominantly Spanish or Italian peasant ancestry: "The explanation has no basis in historical or social facts," writes Bolaño. "What did Naipaul know about the sexual customs of Spanish and Italian rural labourers from 1850 to 1925? Maybe, while touring the bars on Corrientes late one night, he heard a sportswriter recounting the sexual exploits of his grandfather or great-grandfather, who, when night fell over Sicily or Asturias, used to go fuck the sheep. Maybe." Bolaño then riffs on the theme with some delight, as in his imagination,

> Naipaul closes his eyes and imagines a Mediterranean shepherd boy fucking a sheep or a goat. Then the shepherd boy caresses the goat and falls asleep. The shepherd boy dreams in the moonlight: he sees himself many years later, many pounds heavier, many inches taller, in possession of a large moustache, married, with numerous children, the boys working on the farm, tending the flock that has multiplied (or dwindled), the girls busy in the house or the garden, subjected to his molestations or to those of their brothers, and finally his wife, queen and slave, sodomized nightly, taken up the ass—a picturesque vignette that owes more to the erotico-bucolic desires of a nineteenth-century French pornographer than to harsh reality, which has the face of a castrated dog. I'm not saying that the good peasant couples of Sicily and Valencia never practiced sodomy, but surely not with the regularity of a custom destined to flourish beyond the seas.

The danger in theorising outward from a single sexual act (and one, incidentally, which seems to fill Naipaul with self-righteous disgust) is that, to put it mildly, it creates a somewhat lopsided simplification of Argentinian culture. Although an early fan of *A House for Mr Biswas* and some of the travel writing, it is a long time since I enjoyed Naipaul, and reading this demented essay, alongside Bolaño's response to it, reminded me why, in spite of the vicarious pleasure offered up by a writer in thrall to outbursts of almost comically vindictive spleen.

A passage in Phillip French's biography of Naipaul summarises the longstanding relationship his subject sustained with his Anglo-Argentine mistress, and the very special role of buggery within it. The story is taken up by Ian Buruma, in his review of French's biography: "In Buenos Aires, at the apartment of Borges's translator, Naipaul met Margaret Murray, a vivacious Anglo-Argentinian: 'I wished,' he told his biographer, 'to possess her as soon as I saw her.... I loved her eyes. I loved her mouth. I loved everything about her and I have never stopped loving her, actually. What a panic it was for me to win her because I had no seducing talent at all. And somehow the need was so great that I did do it.'" Buruma continues:

> Margaret left her husband and children, and for the next twenty years would be at the beck and call of her master, who was finally able to do all the things that had horrified and fascinated him before ...[T]he more Naipaul abused Margaret, the more she came back for more. She wrote him letters, paraphrased by French in his biography, about worshiping at the shrine of the master's penis, about "Vido" as a horrible black man with hideous powers over her. Her letters were often left unopened, and certainly unanswered, adding to her sense of submission. According to Naipaul himself, he beat Margaret so severely on one occasion that his hand hurt, and her face was so badly disfigured that she couldn't appear in public (but the hurt hand seems to have been of greater concern). But Naipaul claimed, "She didn't mind at all. She thought of it in terms of my passion for her." And then there was the mutual passion for anal sex, or as

Margaret herself put it: "visiting the very special place of love."

How interesting to discover that – despite his volley of splenetic accusations at the Argentines – when not beating her up, sodomising his Anglo-Argentinian mistress was Naipaul's preferred occupation of an evening, as the cockatoos sang and the sun went down over the Pampa. Margaret Murray herself, abused and neglected by Naipaul, commented on the matter, with devastating brevity, in a note written to the *New York Review* following the publication of Buruma's article: "Vidia [Naipaul] says I didn't mind the abuse. I certainly did mind." Paul Theroux, whose own memoir of Naipaul, *Sir Vidia's Shadow*, comes under attack in Buruma's article, also chipped in: "Mr. Buruma speaks of Naipaul's 'great modesty.' In thirty years of knowing the man I was never privileged to observe this. I mainly saw his sadness, his tantrums, his envy, his meanness, his greed, and his uncontrollable anger. But I never saw Naipaul attack anyone stronger than himself; he talked big and insultingly but when he lashed out it was always against the weak – women who loved him, his wife, and waiters: people who couldn't hit back, the true mark of the coward."

Naipaul's egomania, cruelty and racism – his preferred term of denigration was the N word – are by now well-documented, but his article on the brothels behind the graveyard marks a new low in hypocrisy and doublethink. Nor can his analysis of Argentine politics in the 1970s, when that country truly was a broken state, be taken seriously, given that it devolves into such a reductive farce. And nor, decades on, even though his account reveals much that was repellent about Naipaul, does there seem any cause to approve Ian Buruma's mendacious apology for his friend, revealingly titled 'The Lessons of the Master'.

I was pondering this sorry tale while flying over the Atlantic, en route to Buenos Aires. It was April 2015, and I was on my way to the international poetry festival that takes place as part of the city's annual Book Fair. We, the festival poets, were put up at the cheerfully dilapidated Hotel Castelar, where Federico García

Lorca stayed during his six-month visit in 1933-4. His room, number 704, has been preserved as a kind of mausoleum for poetry groupies, but it never seemed to be open and consequently I didn't get to see the poet's burgundy silk pyjamas.

I had travelled to the Argentine capital only the previous October, while en route to Chile, in order to give a lecture for the British Council, and Rose, my wife, had accompanied me. On that earlier occasion we were put up at the grandiose Plaza Hotel, overlooking Plaza San Martín, and I had taken to visiting the darkly seductive oak-panelled bar, fittingly situated in the bowels of the hotel and serviced by inscrutable waiters in tuxedos. It was the perfect place to drink martinis and pretend to be someone I was not. My fondness for this bar, my utter capitulation before its decadent charms, had not escaped Rose's notice, prompting her to remark that I needed to address 'the elephant in the room' – an observation to which I had no reponse, as I knew beyond any doubt that she was right – yet I seemed incapable of taking steps to tackle the problem of my drinking.

On this latest visit to the city, I returned to the Plaza bar, enacting a role that resembled Jack Nicolson's in *The Shining*, when he converses with the sinister barman, Lloyd, and although my interlocutor behind the bar was equally well turned out, and shared with Lloyd a knowing and conspiratorial manner, he did not counsel me to murder my family with an axe, although he did once refer nostalgically to the regime of the late 1970s, thereby intimating that he had been a supporter of the country's military dictatorship. I was, however, beginning to commit a kind of murder against myself. My deterioration may not have been noticeable to those who did not know me well, but it had provoked a concerned interrogation from Jorge, who knew me better than most.

I was heading for a fall, and knew it. A few days into my stay, my active participation in the festival mostly done, I spent an afternoon in the bar at the Plaza. I had dropped in for a martini, on my own, having arranged to meet up later with some of the other poets from the festival. As I was checking my phone for messages, I noticed someone sidling up and claiming residence of the bar stool next to my own, and it was with a mixture of curiosity and alarm that I recognised my old adversary, Gaston.

The years had not treated him kindly, it must be said. The lines on his tanned face resembled deep crevasses and had, I suspected, been well-earned. Add to that the washed-up, wasted quality of his demeanour – the lecher's leer, the fake concern of his fraudster's frown – and one might have been forgiven for writing him off as a craven degenerate, were it not for a hint of sadness, or perhaps remorse, about the eyes; a remorse I did not care to indulge, because at that moment he so thoroughly embodied a version of my shadow self that I was beginning to feel sick. I could sense his corporeal presence, both next to me, and, if this were possible, within me.

What are you drinking? I asked him eventually. It's the question one always asks one's doppelgänger.

He gestured to my glass. The same as you, obviously.

I made eye contact with Lloyd – or rather, Lloyd's double, Alfonso – who moved down the bar in a single fluid movement, as though swept along on invisible runners. He glanced ever so discreetly at Gaston, and if there was the merest flicker of disdain in his appraisal you would have needed to be in possession of the most finely-tuned apparatus to register it, but Alfonso's subsequent and equally fleeting glance at me was sufficient to convey his disapproval.

Never mind all that, Alfonso, I said, – get my friend one of your specials.

Por supuesto, *caballero*. And there was not the flake of a suggestion that he could be anything other than the perfect servant. Or the perfect savant.

What brings you to Buenos Aires? I said, turning to Gaston.

You know perfectly well, he replied. I don't want to miss the action. He smiled – not quite a smirk, he was not so brazen; more a suggestion of sly self-assurance, as though reading my mind.

I looked him over, pondered the ineluctable fact of him, interested now in his material attributes, rather than attempting to deny his existence. He was dressed, as he had been in Veracruz, a year ago, in bomber jacket and jeans. There was an odour emanating from him, both acrid and earthy, pungent and putrid.

The black leather cord around his neck, and the silver ouroboros. The scar on his cheek, acquired one dark night outside a hostel for the homeless in Avignon, following an altercation with a crazed, knife-wielding clochard (I know, I was there).

I was brought back to the present by Alfonso, who placed two fresh martinis in front of me. I pushed one of them to my left, towards Gaston. Alfonso blinked, and looked at me for a second longer than was necessary. Then he sniffed, unmistakably.

Anything wrong, Alfonso? I asked.

No, *caballero*. Todo perfecto. He glanced briefly heavenward, and I could have sworn he muttered a little prayer, bless him, and then he took up his cloth and started polishing the immaculate oak of the surface, dallying a little, until he spotted a customer in need of refreshment at the far end of the bar. I was relieved he had been called away.

I took a sip of my drink, then drained the glass in one. I could feel it course through my veins, like a homecoming, the blissful draft in which all doubt is flushed forth, and a deeply familiar animal warmth washed through me; and for an instant I was entirely, utterly free of all thought, and some furious element within the reptile brain screamed: *Yes*, this is what you are for, *this is your function*. The floor opened like a cavernous vault below me, and I hovered above it, omnipotent, lost to the world, afloat in time. When I returned to the present, aeons later, the warm glow lingered, but had begun to dissipate a little, and already I knew that I must replenish it, although there was no sense of urgency, yet, to this demand. That would come later. For now, it was tucked away deep in my limbic system, a euphoric memory, a token of love, or else a debt that I must one day pay, a debt laden with the threat of imminent and recurring panic. Like so many other things that are locked away.

Alfonso was before me again, an impenetrable half-smile on his face. *Another one, caballero?* He whisked my empty cocktail glass from under my nose, and went about his business with the silver shaker. I looked over at Gaston, who was fiddling with a cocktail stick, which he had removed from his glass, and on which was impaled a single green olive. He looked at it, wistfully. I knew that he was remembering.

We had some larks, cut some capers, hein? he said, looking up at me, sideways, but it was not a question. He began to laugh, then stopped, shaking his head slowly.

What do you remember, Gaston? I said.

The same as you, mon capitaine, he replied at once, – but with slight, comment dit-on? ... variations. One set of memories is the distorted reflection of the other. The far side of the mirror, let's say I remember the parts that you choose to forget.

All those years of aimless wandering, you were at my side? I asked, though I already knew the answer. No wonder my life was a perfect shitstorm.

Sí señor, I was always around, he says, ignoring my last remark. In Izmir, in Saloníki, in Xania. And of course, across le grand sud-ouest.

The memory of my vagrant life in the south-west of France roused in me an indefinable sense of grief and loss. I hastened back to the present, but could already feel the incipient stirring of some other presence, some other unwanted visitor crowding in on me from the other side of nowhere.

On the wall behind Gaston hung a display of black and white photographs from the seventies, of some tuxedoed crooner, hand clutching a microphone, mouth open to reveal perfect teeth, eyes closed in the ecstasy of song. A Latin Perry Como. The same singer, no doubt, whose song was playing softly on the sound system. The ideal music to accompany the downing of martinis as the Argentine air force captain who once sat where I was sitting – and with whose memories my own seemed to be merging – recalled the screams of his prisoners as they were dispatched, one by one, from the hatch of the plane, and descended like flapping insects towards the dark waters of the South Atlantic.

I shook my head, hoping to dispel this new, unwanted vision. From what precinct of hell had it appeared? Had I become the conduit for some kind of malevolent energy, under the mephistophelian gaze of Alfonso? And with the thought of him, he returned in person, carrying not one, but two fresh martinis, which he placed before me, then turned, clicking his heels in a mock military gesture, and set off down the bar once more. I took a sip of my new drink.

Why these images of violence? I asked, turning toward Gaston, as if he, of all people, would know. But Gaston was not there. When I looked to my left I saw a Catalan poet from the festival, Àlex Susanna, whom I had invited to meet me here. Alfonso must have brought the second martini for him.

We were joined by two other poets, both Colombians. I vacated my place at the bar and we took our drinks to a table in the centre of the saloon; but for the rest of the afternoon I was absent, lingering in a realm of memories that I only half-recognised as my own.

That evening I attended an event at a bar in San Telmo called *La Poesía*. The poetry bar. I had visited the place before, with Rose, on my last trip to the city, and had observed how the downstairs bar was stacked with a fabulous arrangement of spirits and wines; row upon row of colourful bottles, the shelves ascending to the ceiling in a most picturesque and alluring way; a display to delight any dipsomaniac.

The tableau brought to mind the fantasy imagined by Lowry's consul, as he reflects on his own desolation, and conjures, in his memory, the countless bottles – "of aguardiente, of anís, of jerez, of Highland Queen, of Calvados" – that he had consumed or dropped and broken or flung into the sea, as he considers the possibility that he may have lost himself in one of them, that "in one of those lost or broken bottles, in one of those glasses, lay, for ever, the solitary clue to his identity."

The wall of bottles was so impressive that I had photographed it, little thinking that I would return to the same bar six months later and come close to killing myself, plummeting headlong down a full flight of stairs and remaining unconscious until revived by the two paramedics who had been summoned to the scene, but who, nonetheless, I stubbornly refused to accompany to hospital for a brain scan. However, even this warning, and my escape from serious injury – an intervention, I conjectured, on the part of Saint Jude, the patron saint of lost causes – was not sufficient to arrest an ongoing downward trajectory.

The basement of the Hotel Castelar was given over to an ancient system of Turkish baths. The following afternoon I booked in for a session, hoping to sweat out some of the week's accumulated toxins. As I lay covered in towels, reeking of poison, my limbs like twisted plasticine, heart pounding, I drifted into a restless sleep in which I was once again falling, falling into the void, just as I had fallen the night before and in countless recurring dreams.

Over the past five years, I had maintained a limited sort of control over my alcoholism, at least at a superficial level. I could break off for weeks at a time, but would always return, and with increasing frequency, to self-destructive drinking. I had compartmentalised this habit so that it took place, for the most part, away from home and the workplace, and usually in solitude. On too many nights of my Latin American journey I would wake in my hotel room at 4.00 a.m. in a state of panic, thinking *I have to stop drinking I have to stop drinking.* In the daytime it wasn't so bad, and I would take a drink or three to keep ticking over, and I'd temporarily feel better, until the evening, when I'd drink to excess once again, and at 4.00 a.m. the next morning I would awaken from blackout, sweating profusely, in a state of existential horror, aching from unknown wounds. I was caught in a double bind. That same old quandary: if I admitted to being an alcoholic I would forfeit the right to drink, that was the deal I'd made; and even though I knew I was an alcoholic I couldn't admit to it because that would make me a liar for pretending that I wasn't when I was; admitting I was an alcoholic would mean I couldn't drink at all and even though I claimed I could quit at any time, in reality I couldn't, so I was a liar either way.

The remainder of my time in Buenos Aires passed in a state of remorseful confusion, but I do recall making an abject visit to the Book Fair, to attend one final event, which necessitated taking a metro journey. It was a route I knew well, since it was the same one I took to Jorge's apartment, and for this reason the poet Beatríz Vignoli asked to accompany me, since she too had an appointment at the fair, and being from Rosario, was unfamiliar with the Buenos Aires metro system, and did not feel confident to negotiate the transit across town on her own. When we arrived at the labyrinthine building in which the Book Fair was held (and which, on other occasions, hosts the annual Argentine Agricultural and Livestock Show) I spent an age trying to find the correct venue. Realising that we were going to be late, I stopped before a large map of the site. I was disoriented and in a state of acute anxiety. Noticing Beatríz behind me, waiting for directions, I quipped: "Don't follow me: I'm lost as well" – a phrase that Beatríz thoughtfully replicated on the title page of her latest book of poems, which she left for me at the hotel reception on the day of our departure. It might have served as a motto for my sojourn in the city that year.

> I am not sure if there is any such thing
> as the true measure of death
> until the house is empty, because
> what once had a meaning and, of course, a story
> can barely be summarised in an inventory
>
> Jorge Fondebrider, 'Closing up the House'.

Crickhowell, Wales, May 2015

In the family home, my father locked every door at night, all of them, except the bedrooms and bathroom. I'm not sure why he did it; I guess he must have been worried about burglars. I am thinking about this, and other of my father's particularities as I pursue the winding roads across the wild expanse of mid-Wales. It is May 2015, a couple of weeks after returning from the ill-fated trip to Buenos Aires. I have spent the afternoon examining a PhD at Aberystwyth University, a strange and darkly perplexing experience, since the thesis concerned a novel called *Gretel and the Dark*, loosely based on the Grimm brothers' account of Hansel and Gretel, and set in the Nazi prison camp of Ravensbrück. Driving towards Rhayader on this sun-dappled evening, my thoughts linger still with the damaged characters of the novel, drawn from fairy tales and interposed within a brutal historical reality, a story within a story. And then, fast on the tracks of this, the memory of my family home, and of my father passing from door to door and locking each room in turn before retiring upstairs to bed. It replays in my mind's eye like the opening sequence of a film in which one knows something terrible will happen.

I will be stopping over at his place tonight. He still lives in the village, though not in the family home; he sold that when my mother started to show the first signs of dementia, and they moved into a bungalow, where he looked after her with single-minded devotion until she died, seven years later, in 2003. Father has recently been unwell, although no one is sure exactly what is wrong with him. My sister, who lives nearby, is concerned; he has talked resignedly about being ready to die, or at least of being tired of living. He is ninety-one, but suffers from no obviously life-threatening condition.

I approach the village from the north-west, following the valley of the River Usk. On the radio, Bruce Springsteen too is going down to the river, as the sun dips behind the Llangattock Mountain. I park outside my father's bungalow. Looking out across the road and beyond the cricket ground, the view is so imprinted in memory that despite the many years that have passed, it remains the single most familiar landscape I own, pretty much the same view as that from the kitchen window in our childhood home, five minutes' walk down the road. The broad elevated ridge beyond the river, crowned by the limestone escarpment of Mynydd Llangatwg, has been a constant backdrop to my memories and my dreams, its lower reaches dotted with sheep and shaded by patches of woodland and the occasional farm building, notably, half way up the mountain, a solitary white farmhouse that always draws the gaze, and which, as a small child, I was convinced belonged to Bo Peep, who had lost her sheep, and knew not where to find them ...

My father has taken to his bed: this is unprecedented, as he has always insisted on the importance of remaining active. Chris, his carer, is in the kitchen when I arrive, and explains cheerfully – her default mode – that my father has simply refused to get up for the past two days. Then she leaves, after telling me she will be in as usual the next day, and that Dr A, one of the local GPs, is due to visit in the course of the morning. Father seems genuinely glad to see me, but there is, as I soon discover, an unfamiliar patina of melancholy about him. In the past, he would not have come across as a dispenser of sorrows, but recently – the last five years or so, since he became less mobile – he has taken to introducing, after an initial exchange of pleasantries, a litany of woes concerning the pain he feels in different parts of his body, especially his back, along with routine accounts of visits to the dental surgery or hospital, complaints relating to the failings of the telephone and internet providers, the bank, insurance companies, gas and electricity services, the general incompetence or incivility he endures in exchanges with the representatives of these agencies, the numerous unsolicited sales calls he receives, and the shortcomings of the National Health Service to which he dedicated his working life. He is upset by almost everything, but especially by these interactions with service providers, by the vulgarity and vindictiveness of the news media, and by the contemporary world's grotesque mix, as he sees it, of neediness and confessionalism. Other concerns are of a more ontological nature: he is lonely, I think, although he never says as much. He misses his wife, my mother. It is not that he feels abandoned: Chris comes in twice a day, to help him get dressed in the morning – humiliating, but necessary – and to prepare him for the night, as well as to shop, clean and wash for him. My sister also comes in most days, although, unusually, she is away this week. My brother drives down from London once a fortnight and stays the weekend. I come up from Cardiff from time to time, though not as regularly as I might so it is not that he feels neglected. No, the problem with Father is more deeply rooted: he feels as though he has nothing to live for. He has given up caring about the future. Everything that has meaning for him lies in the past.

    The next morning I rise early, to work on a translation. Chris arrives and attends to my father, helps him dress, and gets him ready for breakfast. When she has left I take a shower. From the moment that I emerge from the bathroom, the morning accelerates into high drama. I sit with Father in his bedroom and he tells me, calmly, out of the blue, that he thinks he may have 'a day or two' – but without offering any explanation. I am uncomprehending at first: he doesn't say 'a day or two to live', but that is what he means. Despite being a fine diagnostician in his day, he fails to furnish any detail as to why, precisely, he is going to die. Perhaps this information is code; what he really wants, but is reluctant to ask, is for me to contact my brother and sister. My brother is on a cycling holiday in Sicily; my sister is in London. Paradoxically, as I have been easily the least attentive of his children over the years, I am the only one to hand when he decides he is ready to set out on the definitive journey.

However, I put off making any phone calls until Dr A has visited.

When, an hour later, the doctor, who, decades ago, was one of my father's trainees, emerges from the bedroom, his eyes are filled with tears.

He says he's going to die, he says, visibly failing to control his emotion.

I, in turn, am alarmed by the doctor's distress.

I know, I say. He's convinced of it. We can only hope his diagnosis is incorrect.

Haven't known him make too many of those, says Dr A.

The whites of the doctor's eyes are red. He rubs them, hastily. I barely know him, but feel a surge of warmth towards him.

We are standing in the front room, out of earshot of my father. The bedroom door is shut.

The doctor wipes a tear from his cheek.

He was the kind of doctor we all aspire to be, he says, his voice breaking.

I can tell he means it, and try to say something in return, but cannot find the words. So I thank Dr A. and see him out. He tells me he will return later in the day. He seems not to question my father's prophecy, even though he tells me that he can find nothing to support his prognosis.

I return to the bedroom. My father is lying peacefully, uncomplaining. All at once, I know that he has made a decision, and like most of his decisions over the years, it is set in stone. He might conceivably have changed his mind before today, but since telling Dr A, there is no going back. There should be a name for the point just beyond that of no return. In any case, we are in it. Time loses all sense of flow on these occasions, and yet it is because of time's relentless *ongoingness* that I stand here, a middle-aged man, before my apparently dying father. I feel an upsurge of conflicting emotions. The one that rises uppermost is this: I wish I had been less impatient all those yars ago, had taken things more slowly and been prepared to listen more; I wish I had taken the time to know my father better, and learned to love him in spite of everything. I wish I had been a better son ... I wish ...

My father, by contrast, is focused on the present. I later realise that he wants to organise the present so as to settle into the more reassuring territory of the past. The most pressing task for him now is to ensure that his three children are nearby, so he can die with them by his side. He seems to relish the small victory that his own diagnosis has prevailed in the meeting with Dr A. Perhaps he knew that this doctor, who has always regarded my father as 'the senior partner' – even though Father has been retired for over thirty years now and Dr A must be nearing retirement himself – would not contradict him. It occurs to me that we need a second (or a third) opinion, but I do not say anything at this point. Instead I sit in the pale blue wicker chair at his bedside as he slumbers, surrounded by photographs, on the dressing table and the walls, of his children and grand-children. A triptych of photos in oval frames of my sister, my brother and me as small children. My siblings' children. My own daughters. An old bear, its stuffing knocked out, lolls atop the chest of drawers, alongside a grinning hedgehog. I feel that now, more than ever, I need to be helpful. Ours has been a troubled relationship over many years, but right now he needs me here.

At midday Chris returns and we change his incontinence pad. Since when did my father start using incontinence pads? Some realisations, rather than simply serving as reminders of our frailty, and our mortality, simply take us by surprise. Chris pulls off the used pad and we roll him over gently, first to one side, then the other, and we pull the clean one on, and I note the ruptured and horribly creased skin of my father's thighs and buttocks.

Like all people, my father has his faults. He can be controlling and judgemental, but these less desirable qualities are countered by a profound sense of justice, and a belief that everyone should have a chance. He is utterly committed to the principles of his calling as a doctor and the ethical impartiality that goes with it. For instance, he took a public stand against the government's closure of small community or 'cottage' hospitals in the 1970s, even appearing on BBC's *Panorama* and various news programmes, something which he hated doing. But he believed – and was proved right in this belief – that the construction of vast centralised 'factory' hospitals was dehumanising, especially for those who had lived their entire lives in close-knit communities like those of rural Wales. I also heard him speak out against the scaremongering moral outrage directed at people with HIV/AIDS in the 1980s, and I remember him telling me how, for instance, HIV patients could be infected by the thoughtless actions of others; for example by taking holy communion from a chalice infected by someone with a cold. He took the tenets of the Hippocratic oath very seriously indeed.

Father is becoming accustomed to my presence at his side, and I can feel his defences – the defences built over a lifetime of difficult relations between us – slip away. And while everything is not on display, he is ready to talk.

Occasionally I feel my eyes well up. I begin to remember the way things were between us in the bad times, and I am bereft. The version of him I carried around with me for years, and my feelings towards him, so bitter and ungracious, were at odds with the way he was regarded by others. Such as Dr A, for one.

The doctor we all aspire to be.

I make the necessary phone calls to my sister and brother. My brother will cut short his cycling holiday, my sister will return from London. Word gets out. One of my nieces, Lucy, calls from Los Angeles. Her grandfather is sleeping. She speaks through her tears: Can you tell him, when he is awake, that I'm thinking of him? I always wanted to tell him that I loved him, but he would feel uncomfortable ... so I didn't.

I know the feeling. Though when I was her age these weren't precisely the sentiments I wished to express.

As Father sleeps, I work for an hour, editing lines by the Colombian poet Darío Jaramillo:

> If anyone asks after him,
> tell them that perhaps he'll never come back, or else
> on returning no one will recognise his face ...

Chris comes in with some groceries. We go through the pants procedure again. Father doesn't want to eat. But once Chris has gone, he does want to talk. In Latin.

It's funny, he says, how when the mind is blank it fills with old tunes and Latin tags.

This is not something I have ever experienced, so I ask: Such as?

Alea iacta est – though that is rather obvious, the die is cast. No, I was thinking of *mulier est hominis confusio*. I don't agree with it ... I don't think for a moment that woman is the ruin of man ...

And then: *Prosim* – what is *ut prosim*? That I may serve?

I guess he means to tell me that's what he believes, what he has always believed in: a life of service.

He is away now, reaching back into distant places, Ludlow Grammar School perhaps, circa 1934:

Peccavisti? Was it? Or *Peccavi*? I have sinned. It was what the General – what's his name? – was supposed to have said when he conquered Sind. The country. A pun. I have sinned. *Dominus illuminate mea*. Although he probably didn't send that telegram at all. It was an invention, that story ...

And then:

It's good to have family close. Family is important.

I'm not going anywhere, don't worry.

Good. I understand why. I saw my mother out, and I saw my wife out.

He says this with something like pride, bordering on defiance, as though anyone were about to contradict him. After a pause, he starts making mumbled sounds, which I identify as perhaps one of the old tunes that he has said accompany the Latin tags. He hums on tunelessly for a few minutes.

Curious how blank one gets, he says. I forget them for a moment, then they spring up. It's very strange not being able to control your limbs. My legs especially, and my neck. The spinal ... I can't hold my head up.

His voice becomes indistinct, then silent. I am sure now that his diagnosis of imminent demise will turn out to be accurate. I don't wish to be alone with him when he goes. I know that he wants all three of his children here.

I am intrigued by my father's little forays into Latin and song. It is as if time has concertinaed and the contents of ninety years have spilled randomly from the luggage rack of memory, or as if history were merely an uninterrupted progression of present moments, past and the future co-existing within the continuum of the present. I am reminded of Einstein's letter to the family of his friend Michele Besso, shortly after Besso's death. He wrote: 'Now he [Michele] has departed from this strange world a little ahead of me. That means nothing ... People like us who believe in physics, know that the distinction between past, present and future is only a stubbornly persistent illusion.' In recent years, my father has read widely in quantum physics, about string theory, black holes, dark matter, the multiverse, and he has found occasion, during my visits, to discuss these topics with me, or rather, has attempted to explain them to me. Some of it has rubbed off, though my intellect is not as sharp as his in attuning to such abstruse concepts.

Father's present has become infused by his past, so that the two have become indistinguishable. I think he likes it this way; moreover it allows him to feel closer to my mother, with whom, he seems to believe – or so he has said – he will shortly be reunited.

Finally, around midnight, he settles, and I move from the wicker chair at his bedside to the more comfortable armchair with footrest, and try to sleep. I am agitated, and so is my father. He stirs constantly, and occasionally speaks out in his sleep. I cannot help but be struck by the terminal symmetry of our situation; of caring, in what may be his final days, for the man who, once upon a time, looked after me, or looked out for me, who mapped out, or attempted to map out, in all its frail logistics, what I was to be, where I was to go, what air I breathed, never guessing that all I wanted was to escape, my only concern the adventures I might contrive as an antidote to long-term incarceration in boarding schools and a repressed and emotionally parched family home; hence the dark and hallucinatory places I would seek out in my vagrant years, and the terrible regrets I would later endure. But all of this dissipates under the blanket of something like tenderness, something like love.

Five days later Father is still with us, although very much weaker. He is cheered by the arrival of my daughters and of Rose, and of my brother and sister, who take over the vigil when I have to return to Cardiff for a couple of days. By the time I am back in the village all three of us – my brother, sister and I – are staying over, taking it in turns to sleep in the armchair, while the other two use the spare room or camp out in the living room. My sister, who was a nurse in an earlier life, takes charge of his care with calm eficiency. In the evenings we sit in the kitchen and talk while Father sleeps. He is sleeping a lot. My siblings and I drink gin and tonic or red wine, order food in or cook easy meals and reminisce about our childhood, and we exchange stories that we heard our father tell.

Some of these stories we all three know, others are only known to one or two of us. It is always a surprise when one of us doesn't know a story. We recount our favourites, such as his encounter with Rommel's tailor, when he was the medical officer at a Prisoner of War camp in Dover shortly after World War Two. He was holding a surgery, and one of the German prisoners, flanked by a guard and an interpreter, made a comment to him, gesturing at his uniform jacket. Father asked the interpreter what he was saying, and was informed that the man considered the state of the Herr Kapitän's uniform to be a disgrace. Father's curiosity was aroused, and he asked the man on what grounds he was passing judgement on his sartorial status, and the soldier replied, via the interpreter, that he had been Field Marshal Rommel's personal tailor, and for the price of two packs of cigarettes he would render my father the most smartly turned out officer in the British army, as smart, indeed, as the 'Desert Fox' (the sobriquet by which Rommel was known). As a non-smoker, this was an offer not to be missed. He had himself measured up. The prisoner was as good as his word, and a few days later Father enjoyed the unusual privilege of sporting a uniform that fitted him like a glove.

I recount a story that my brother and sister have not heard before. I think the event took place in the late 1950s, though Father had only told it me quite recently. On one of those cloudless and pristine winter days after snow has fallen, a Sunday, he was called out to Cwmyoy, in the Ewyas valley, on an urgent call. He was ushered into the church, where the priest had suffered a fatal heart attack. The unfortunate man had fallen, arms outspread, upon the altar, and was in this Christ-like posture when my father arrived, since no one in the congregation had dared to move him. My father described the scene with extraordinary clarity, and the sense of timelessness that overcame him on witnessing it, before stepping out into the snow-dusted graveyard, facing Twyn y Gaer and the Black Mountains beyond, against the bluest of skies.

Although I was not with him on that occasion – I would have been too young – I often accompanied him on his rounds as a child, and got to know some of the most secluded farmhouses in the old county of Breconshire. One memory is of watching him through the windscreen of the car, as he attempted to negotiate the deep mud at the edge of the farmyard and then dance, hopping, through a pack of feral sheepdogs, when visiting a patient somewhere above Cwmdu. I remember offering him a thumbs up when he arrived at the porch of the house and rang the bell, before settling back into my book and awaiting his return.

It is comforting to spend this time with my sister and brother, and to share memories, however many of them are confused or worrying. Like all siblings, we each of us have different and at times conflicting memories of childhood. Most notably, my sister has a good deal of empathy for our mother, whereas my brother and I have more ambivalent memories of her, as of someone disengaged, and no doubt clinically depressed. As these evenings progress, waiting for Father to die, I begin to feel the seductive draw of the gin bottle, brought on, in no small degree, by these memories of our childhood, and of my mother in particular. Oblivion, towards which my father is so evidently headed, becomes, for me, the main lure of those sessions around the kitchen table, so that rather than remember what was actually said, I can only recall the drift of my own emotions, and the familiar immersion in the warm waters of forgetting, or *Lethe*, as though I only wished to smother the intangible, inaccessible pain of childhood memory. But Lethe, it might be remembered, forms the middle part of the Greek word *Aletheia*, truth; so that truth is a kind of anti-oblivion, an un-forgetting and an opening up to the world – which, of course, is the motivating idea behind psychoanalysis. However much I contrive to forget, and however unreliable the stories we tell each other, the past is ever present. What we are doing around the kitchen table is a kind of therapy. We talk, and share memories, and insights into how the years have changed us, the variously inflected ways in which we each regard childhood and the adults who surrounded us then, the dominant figure of which was the man dying in the next room.

When Father is awake, he is frequently unsettled, although his speech is at times barely decipherable. He tells my sister again to cancel his subscriptions to various magazines and newspapers and to stop his direct debits and insurance payments. This seems like a disappointing, unheroic way to spend one's final days, caught up in a litany of financial trivia. His mouth is dry and he asks my sister to 'dilute the water' he is drinking. It is too strong, he says. No Latin now. Down to the perennial worries of money and survival. And the need to dilute the water.

I try to sleep in the expanding armchair in the bedroom again, but now he is talking almost constantly in his restless slumber, making demands, only some of which I can understand. I keep repeating to myself a line from T.S. Eliot's *The Waste Land*, a poem I studied and learned by heart for my 'O' level examinations, at the age of fifteen. I say the words again and again, when thinking of my father, and do not quite understand why, but still, they bring me comfort: 'These fragments I have shored against my ruins.' Around six in the morning, my sister comes in from the spare bedroom in response to one of his calls – I must have dropped off – and he asks for his face to be washed, which she does, and then I brush his teeth, a delicate operation, moving the toothbrush ever so gently over his yellowed teeth, his sore gums, though he cries out when I drop some cold water onto his chest; he cries out as if he has been burned. He has become very sensitive to discomfort of any kind.

The bedroom has become a terminal zone, an ending place. It is where our mother died, though none of us was here, except for him, and now he is preparing to die here also. There is a black, sealed 'Just in case' box on the table to the side of the bed, which contains Diamorphine, against pain and shortness of breath, Cyclizine (against nausea), Hyoscine (against the build-up of excessive moisture in the throat or chest) and Midazolam (against restlessness and anxiety). I was wondering about giving him some of the last of these during the night, but the black box comes with a leaflet that warns: 'The medicines can only be given by a nurse or doctor.' At four in the morning, alone with the dying man and the black box, such considerations seem academic.

He has turned a corner, or has passed a point of his own choosing – because there still remains no real medical rationale for his dying – from which there truly is no return.

Dr A has been replaced by Dr B, a kindly and conscientious man, who is younger and therefore less conflicted by an earlier relationship with my father. However, Father does put Dr B in an awkward position: now that he has convinced everyone around him that he is going to die, he wants the process to take place as speedily as possible, but because of the laws governing prescription and care of the dying, it is not that easy. Dr B is in a quandary. He visits three times in a single day, caught in an ethical impasse, with Father demanding an injection which Dr B cannot administer. But he does order a Diamorphine driver, a contraption that delivers a slow and steady drip of heroin and Cyclizine into his body but which hasn't yet had the effect of knocking him out, which is all he wants, or at least is what he says he wants, when he speaks in sentences. Given the legal labyrinth facing his carers, it is the best he can expect – and he must know it – but he still manages, in his more lucid moments, to voice a few grievances, specifically about the special adaptable bed that should have been delivered a few days ago. He worked for the NHS from its inception, and believed in it. In recent years he has witnessed it falling apart through a lack of funding, and the failure of the bed's arrival brings the dismal fact home in sharp relief: it feels not only like a failure, but a personal insult. Nevertheless, his complaints carry an edge of dark humour; even now he can see the pathos of his situation.

What impresses me most about my father over these days, however, is his stoicism. Despite the occasional grumbling, despite his railing against the world he is departing, he is steeled against his fate, and now that I am older I feel increasingly drawn to those qualities of stoicism and discretion which I once found so insufferable in him, and chose to see only as parsimoniousness and rigidity.

The special bed arrives, finally, at long last. My sister and brother and I are exhausted by the long vigil, now into its second week; physical tiredness exacerbated by emotional fatigue. Long evenings spent around the kitchen table while he slumbers restlessly in his bedroom, in which we go over episodes from childhood, disagree over points of detail (as we always have) but in most regards seem to be building bonds of love rather than finding differences. The district nurse visits and tells us that it might be an idea to call in a palliative care nurse for one night so we can all get some sleep. We agree to this, and on the following evening the specialist nurse arrives and settles into the armchair in Father's room. She has an air of impenetrable calm and we all feel at ease with her, Father too, as far as I can make out. He surfaces into semi-consciousness from time to time, but mostly he sleeps. It is no longer possible to have a coherent conversation with him, although my sister, miraculously, seems to understand his instructions, while I cannot make out a word he is saying. I settle on a camp bed in the living room, and get up at six in the morning in order to drive to Cardiff. I need to be in work today. I drink a coffee, and am standing in the driveway, about to get into my car, when the nurse appears on the porch and calls out to me: I think you may want to come back in. Your father's breathing has changed.

Within a half hour of my return to the bedroom, he has left us. The three of us are at his side, the nurse having discreetly withdrawn from the room.

Father's breathing, in a series of irregular gasps, is barely audible. I hold one of his hands, as his exhalations become shorter and then cease. When he is finally still, the presence of a living being disintegrates abruptly, and vanishes like a wisp of smoke, and a palpable absence descends upon the room in which the three of us remain. A wave of inexpressible sorrow washes over us, temporarily submerging all other emotions, and I experience the almost cinematic sense of unreality that accompanies those moments one recognises as life-defining. Loss and love. Regret, yes. In the draft eulogy that my brother sends me a few days later, I find the following words: 'He said that as he got towards the end, he was increasingly prone to regrets. I don't know what – he never elaborated.' In respect of my father, I identify with those words more than I care to admit. He never confessed any regrets to me, but I have my own, and always will.

For a long while after my father's death, every time I feel the stab of loss, regret follows close behind. However, four years on from his death, I begin to compose a letter to him, an ongoing text to which I return from time to time – I am writing it still —as though sharing in a conversation in which I have the only voice, and yet am strangely comforted by another, invisible presence as I write. My father, somehow, has become the ghost in the machine, and slowly, like pack ice melting, the regrets ebb away.

> The tiger leaps
> from a cloud of smoke into transience.
>
> Pedro Serrano, 'Dark Ages'.

Cardiff – London - Guadalajara – Buenos Aires – Santiago de Chile – Valdivia – Buenos Aires – San José de Mayo – Buenos Aires, 2016-17

I spent the year following my father's death completing my translations of *The Other Tiger*. I settled into the work obsessively, spending many hours each day absorbed in the curious alchemy of translation.

Late one evening, I was lying in bed at my home in Cardiff, reading John Berger's lyrical meditation on love and mortality, *and our faces, my heart, brief as photos*. I began to drift off, as happens all too frequently when reading at night, or in the daytime for that matter, and the words I read took on other shapes, that is, the eye, although closed or half open, conjured phrases, lines, sentences; I could see them, they were relayed to me in semi-slumber as though they were print on the page, but when I returned my gaze to the page, no such lines existed; they were pure invention on my part, and I had taken the story off at a tangent, into a kind of dream zone, in which I rewrote the text, not as image, merely, but as words which were unrelated to the text before me or to anything else the author actually wrote.

Now, this is something, as I said, that I do quite regularly when very tired; it involves a shifting from what is 'real' – on the page – to something which I have invented, which comes from me (I imagine) or to which I am distracted or called towards as if by a force outside myself or the text itself. Waking, and reading on, I came upon an especially arresting passage: Berger is in the post office collecting a Poste Restante letter from the woman he loves, and to whom the essay appears to be addressed, and he says this: "When I saw your handwriting on the envelope, which the woman behind the counter was still holding in her hand, I heard your voice ... A voice belongs first to a body, then to a language. The language may change but the voice stays the same. I recognise your voice before I know in what language you are speaking. In the post office you pronounced the name you had written on the envelope, yet it was not the two words which I heard, it was your voice." The voice, Berger goes on, coexisted with all the other events taking place around him in the post office, "the Tunisian trying to phone his family in Djebeniana, the woman coming to fetch her mail-order parcel, the office clerk posting a hundred letters, the old man drawing his pension."

And when I read that, I thought: yes, that is exactly what happens. I saw Berger's account as a direct confirmation of the experience I had just had, interjecting my imagined words onto the words of the text. Berger is in the post office, he hears the young female clerks talking, and he superimposes the voice of his beloved onto the text of their words. It echoes, analogously, with what I have just written: the text (any text) is there in front of you, but you see (or hear) something quite distinct, authored by some(one) other.

Perhaps translation is like this too: perhaps translation is, in its way, hearing a particular voice amid the cacophony of the surrounding world, and being loyal to it.

One of the things that delights me about the work of John Berger is that you can dip in at random and find a few lines that will provide a context for almost any idea you care to name. One morning I try the trick with *Confabulations*, a gathering from his late notebooks:

> What has prompted me to write over the years is the hunch that something needs to be told and that, if I don't try to tell it, it risks not being told. I picture myself not so much a consequential, professional writer, as a stop-gap man.
>
> After I've written a few lines I let the words slip back into the creature of their language. And there, they are ... instantly recognized and greeted by a host of other

> words, with whom they have an affinity of meaning, or of opposition, or of metaphor or alliteration or rhythm. I listen to their confabulation. Together they are contesting the use to which I put the words I chose. They are questioning the roles I allotted them.
>
> So I modify the lines, change a word or two, and submit them again. Another confabulation begins.

What a canny and insightful way of summarising the process of writing! Firstly, that if you don't write something, it risks not being told. This might not be the greatest of losses to humanity, but one rarely knows the potential of what one wants to say until one has said it, so the point is valid. Secondly, the idea of "letting the words slip back into the creature of their language." Berger considers language as an animate being, back into which words can mysteriously slide. This idea of the creature of language is much more attractive, as a metaphor, than the 'virus' of language which fascinated William Burroughs (and which might be traced to a reading of Chomsky). It also informs our understanding of the process of translation, by which the translator interacts with the living creature of language offered up by the original text.

And thirdly, the notion of words forming a community, a host of other words lying in wait, to align themselves or dissociate from those returning; a fluid body of words, a jostling mass of words as subparticles, contesting the writer's choice, questioning the decisions of their creator (who is, however, not uniquely their creator, as the writer only ever borrows words) and which, as animate forces, confabulate among themselves as to where they want to go, what they intend to mean.

My reflections on John Berger inevitably return me to his writings on translation, which encapsulate a view I have adhered to since beginning my Latin American project: He says:

> True translation is not a binary affair between two languages but a triangular affair. The third point of the triangle being what lay behind the words of the original text before it was written. True translation demands a return to the pre-verbal.

One reads and rereads the words of the original text in order to penetrate through them to reach, to touch, the vision or experience that prompted them. One then gathers up what one has found there and takes this quivering almost wordless "thing" and places it behind the language it needs to be translated into. And now the principal task is to persuade the host language to take in and welcome the "thing" that is waiting to be articulated.

This practice reminds us that a language cannot be reduced to a dictionary or stock of words and phrases. Nor can it be reduced to a warehouse of the works written in it. A spoken language is a body, a living creature, whose physiognomy is verbal and whose visceral functions are linguistic. And this creature's home is the inarticulate as well as the articulate.

Which reminds me, in turn, of Alastair Reid's claim, during our conversation at the house in Galloway, that translation was a kind of bewitchment, not a business simply of transposing something from one language to another, but about getting to "the very edge of saying," as Alastair put it, "where you look and you see the curious unspoken depth that is being touched by one or two words."

★   ★   ★

Eventually, in October 2016, the anthology was published, and launched at the Argentine Ambassador's residence in London. Jorge Fondebrider was present, as were Marina Serrano from Argentina and, from Mexico, Carlos López Beltrán and Alicia García Bergua, whose Embassy had flown them over for the event and subsequent tour. Jorge had been the first to hear of the anthology, back in Nicaragua, five years before, and had acted as guide and critic throughout the project, offering practical help and advice along the way, as indeed had Inés Garland, Pedro Serrano, Verónica Zondek, and many others I met on this long pilgrimage.

The London launch was a modest affair – this was the world of poetry in translation, after all – and we went for a drink afterwards in a quiet Belgravia pub; the poets, Stephanie Black León (the helpful and effusive cultural attaché from the Mexican Embassy), and a few members of my family. In the week that followed, the visiting poets and I went on tour with the book to other launch events in Cardiff, Cambridge, Newcastle and Edinburgh.

In every country I had visited during the five years of poem hunting I had been met with a generous welcome and endless, enthusiastic conversation. I had made many friends. The experience had changed me, too. Bringing the project to a close, it seemed to me that it could never be concluded, any more than poetry itself, or a single poem, truly ends. But there was also a deep sense of anticlimax, which was almost overwhelming. I worried about the many voices that would not be heard, in spite of my efforts, especially those from the neglected indigenous communities of the Americas. In late November, just before travelling to Mexico for the launch of the book at the Guadalajara Book Fair, I was filled with trepidation and a sense of foreboding. How had I committed the hubris of attempting to map a continent's poetry?

There are always parts of the journey that are not on the map. The trip to Guadalajara did not go according to plan. Even Gaston didn't show up, or else by then I had merged with him, and we had become a single person. The struggle with addictive illness is hard to relate, because we addicts lie, exaggerate, or else we forget things. The Guadalajara visit, much of it spent in a tequila blackout, interspersed with moments of fitful lucidity – which included a long conversation or confessional outburst with a very kind and understanding woman in her eighties who, although I was unaware of this at the time, turned out to be Elena Poniatowska – might have been the cause of despair and humiliation, had it not also been accompanied, paradoxically, by a profound sense of relief, of epiphany, even.

Shortly after returning from Mexico, I dreamed that the skin was being peeled from my body, sloughing off like a snake's, and then of myself actually being *without a skin*, flayed alive. In games that children play, the participants sometimes have to choose between two impossible choices of comparable severity: *would you rather be hacked to death by a mad axeman or be left to starve on a desert island with no water? Would you rather be made to eat slugs or drink a cup of sick?* Leslie Jamison recalls, in the account of her own alcoholism, one such question her sister asked her when they were children: *would you rather have no bones or no skin?*

To have no bones or no skin! Bad enough to be without the one or the other, but what if you were deprived of both? As an addict in meltdown, you are in a state of continual exposure, lacking both architecture (bones) or any sense of where you end and the world begins (skin). On the one hand, you are without structure or inner strength; on the other, you are completely unable to assess boundaries. How to describe the creature without either bones or skin? For Jamison, the addict's bewildered response is: *just totally fucked.*

For much of my life I had been repeating to myself the same stories, or fictions of the self, over and over, especially during the most desperate phases of my drinking; those times, as in Buenos Aires the previous year, or in Guadalajara that November, when I was *just totally fucked*. But now I was beginning to understand, at long last, that I did not need to repeat those fictions, and if I did, if I forced myself to re-live them, they at once felt stale and overused, the oft-repeated stories that drunks tell, to everyone's embarrassment, as though the teller were trying to convince someone, or himself, of their veracity.

Among the plurality of lives that I had lived, there was one that needed addressing, definitively. It was time to confront the addicted self and scoop out the poison from its hollow, rotted carcass. It was time to burn all my lost lives to ashes. Burn them to ashes, and commit, once and for all, to some careful self-examination. When I returned home from Mexico in December 2016, something in me had changed. I sought out help and got sober, to the relief of those I loved, and who most cared about me. By acknowledging the fact of my addiction, but choosing not to drink, I achieved the kind of surrender and acceptance that I had not managed before, for years of trying.

★   ★   ★

Fortunately, Guadalajara was not the final sending-off for *The Other Tiger*. The following year, in September 2017, the indefatigable Jorge Fondebrider brought together a group of the poets included in the anthology and organised a promotional three-nation tour, which started at the Goethe Institut in Buenos Aires, continued on to Chile, and then, via Buenos Aires again, to Uruguay, where we were due to attend a Book Fair in the small provincial city of San José de Mayo.

Returning to Buenos Aires, and catching a taxi to my Palermo hotel, I was suffused by an unwelcome melancholy, tinged with a nostalgia that was, I recalled, the mood of many of Borges' early poems, set in that barrio, and which is echoed, but now as parody, in countless blogs by visitors smitten with a love of the city and enthralled by its smoky tango bars – the milongas I too had attended, entranced, on previous visits – and by the flowering of the jacaranda trees in springtime or the ghostly, deserted summer streets. I was not expecting to be enfolded by such doleful dereliction that Sunday night, as Andy Ehrenhaus drove us – Jorge, Carlos and me – on an excursion from Palermo to the city centre and back again, taking in Belgrano, Recoleta, Plaza de Mayo, and the Casa Rosada, en route. There was a light drizzle in the air and it seemed that everyone had decided to stay in; the streets around the centre, usually gridlocked, were practically empty. Where was everyone? *Donde están los otros?*

On our return to Jorge's apartment there was a power cut, so we were unable to cook an evening meal. We set out on the streets again – though I was by now, as if to exacerbate my wretchedness, beginning to feel the effects of jet lag, having only arrived from Heathrow at eight o'clock that morning – until we found a friendly *parrilla*, La Popular de Soho, and were served, by our absurdly jovial host, platefuls of grilled beef, including glands from somewhere on the beast that I didn't know it had, far less that they were edible. Jorge's epicurean delight in this feast was contagious, Carlos too was in fine form, and my mood lifted. Green vegetables, which I craved, are something of a rarity in such restaurants, but you can hardly criticise a place for something it doesn't set out to do.

The following day, at Buenos Aires Aeroparque, when we checked in for our flight to Santiago, the young woman at the

Aerolineas Argentinas desk, who I assumed was new to the job, stared long and hard at the cover of my passport. I could tell she didn't like what she saw. Immediately three possibilities came to mind: (a) she believed the Falkland Islands or Malvinas belong to Argentina and disapproved of my UK passport on principle; (b) she disapproved of the passport's battered and faded state, the extremely faint image of the lion and unicorn, not to mention the words accompanying them; (c) she disapproved of me. Or a combination of these. She asked her colleague – as though I wasn't there – whether the bearer of such a document (which she waved beneath the other's nose) required a visa to travel to Chile. Her colleague shook her head. The first official seemed disappointed, but checked in my luggage before haughtily dismissing me.

I was beginning to think about the state of my passport as a metaphor of some kind. Following on from Alastair Reid's theory of the foreigner, I started wondering whether what was happening to my passport could be made to happen to me, so that I too – my identity, that is – might gradually fade to a point of being barely discernible, thereby achieving the ideal state for the foreigner of not belonging anywhere, which reminded me in turn (though I would rather not have been) of Prime Minister May's remark that *if you believe you are a citizen of the world, you are a citizen of nowhere*, which she had made the previous October. I could not, at that moment, in the wake of the Brexit referendum, think of any statement with which I disagreed more, or a mindset with which I could feel more at odds. After all, as I had learned on my travels, Nowhere is a place, unlike any other.

We spent a single day and night in Santiago, where I delivered a lecture at the Diego Portales University on 'Roberto Bolaño, Memory and the Episodic Life'. It went well enough, despite coinciding with one of the student strikes that so often take place in Chile, but I felt as though I were delivering coals to Newcastle, since everyone in that department, or in that lecture hall, was an expert on the novelist. The night following my talk I dreamt that I met up with the young Roberto, just as he was when I met him while grape picking in the Corbières in 1979 – an episode that appears in my book *The Vagabond's Breakfast*, and which had featured in my talk that day. We were in a city that felt like Barcelona, but might have been Mexico City or even Guadalajara. It was cold. We were walking back from a party, at dawn, and somewhere along the way were joined by two friends, Andrés (Neuman) and Juan (Villoro). A car pulled up. The driver and the passengers – there were four of them also – all wore masks; a wolf-mask, a pig-mask, the V for Vendetta mask, something else. They offered us a ride to the next party; Andrés or Juan, I forget which, said we'd rather walk. I said I hadn't known we were going to another party, and that I, for one, didn't wish to go, but Bolaño apparently did, and jumped into the car, telling the three of us that he would meet us there, at the next party. Near the cathedral, a river – the Taff, transposed from Cardiff with the scant regard for geography typical of dreams – was rushing by, and in the filthy, fast-flowing water was all the furniture of the city; desks, bookcases, refrigerators, lampshades, sofas, kitchen tables, dishwashers. I was thinking, in the dream, that I should remember all of this, but when I woke up I could not imagine why it might be important, nor could I remember what had happened next. But the dream had left an aftertaste of mystery and sadness that persisted throughout the following day.

In the south of Chile, early September means late winter, and the weather was cold and damp. Driving from the airport into Valdivia, the fields and surrounding woods were draped in mist, and the melancholy that I described on the Sunday evening streets of Buenos Aires returned, but in milder, pastoral mode.

We walked along the river through early morning fog, up to the Pedro de Valdivia bridge, named after the conquistador of that name

(1497-1553) who was the first governor of Chile under Spanish colonial rule. Valdivia met with resistance from the Mapuche people when attempting to conquer the south and, his army defeated, he was captured. Stories about how he met his death vary, but one contemporary account suggests that offers of a ransom, and the return of all occupied lands, were rejected by the Mapuche, who cut off Valdivia's arms, roasted them, and ate them in front of him before finally dispatching him.

A pair of sea lions lounged on a floating jetty. As we passed by, the male rose awkwardly on his front flippers and roared at the sky. From the bridge – with the awnings of the fish market stalls and a few fishing vessels arraying its left bank —the river appeared to dissolve into a wall of mist, beyond which I imagined a world, entirely hidden from view, in which strange and terrible things might happen. It was a vision from the beginning of *Heart of Darkness*, or from Juan José Saer's novel *The Witness*, which, like Conrad's, is a novel of European paranoia and dissolution. The reader is warned in both stories that the view ahead presents possibilities that are as grim and harrowing as anything that can be imagined on a wide river shrouded in white mist; the Paraná in Saer's case, and for Conrad, at the start of his story, the Thames.

At the Universidad Austral, we had a long day of presentations, literary discourse and performance, much of it concerning our anthology. In the evening, the poets Jorge Aulicino, Marina Serrano, Carlos López Beltrán, Jaime Pinos, Jorge Fondebrider, Pedro Serrano, Verónica Zondek and Damsi Figueroa, read their poems, and students from the university performed my English versions with great intelligence and fine dramatic emphasis. After dinner, as guests of the University Rector, Óscar Galindo, we returned through a freezing downpour to the hotel. I fell asleep to the sound of the rain pattering on the glass dormer window above my head, a familiar, comforting sound, and a percussive portal to a night in which I dreamed, once again, of rivers.

Returning for a single overnight stopover in Buenos Aires, we set out early the following day for Uruguay. On our way to the ferry terminal, we – Jorge, Pedro and myself – were waiting at Santa Fe, the main thoroughfare connecting Palermo to the centre of Buenos Aires, trying to hail a taxi, when three young women, on the way back from a night out – or rather, still on a night out at seven in the morning – accosted Pedro and me as we pulled our suitcases unsuspectingly towards the kerb. Pedro, informing them he was Mexican, proved of little interest, but on learning I was British, the partygoers engaged me enthusiastically in conversation on a range of interesting topics, and at full, inebriated volume: my favourite Argentine food (I went for medialunas rather than raw steak, to their obvious disapproval); my favourite Argentine beverage (theirs was Fernet with coke, which I have never tried and almost certainly never will), and lastly, with considerable ardour, my opinion on the political status of the Falkland Islands or Malvinas. In the opinion of their most articulate and animated spokesperson, there was no doubt on this issue, although I expressed scepticism, recalling, to my listeners' evident confusion, something that Borges said about two bald men fighting over a comb. When pressed on the issue of whether the Malvinas were Argentine on a purely geographical basis, I suggested that the islands should probably belong to Antarctica. These kids can't have been much more than eighteen; they weren't anywhere near being born when the Falklands War was in progress, and in its own ugly way, resolved, and yet the wound to national pride still festered.

The ferry, or buquebus, crosses the wide estuary formed by the Río Plata from Buenos Aires to Colonia del Sacramento, on the Uruguayan side. I'd done this before, on my 2011 trip to Montevideo, but today we were going to the town of San José de Mayo, to attend the Book Fair and Poetry Festival, where I was due to present *The Other Tiger* for the third time on this whistle-stop tour, along with the rest of the gang – the Argentines and Mexicans who had been on tour with me for the past week. We would be joined by Laura Wittner, Marina Serrano, Mercedes Álvarez and Silvia Dabul, from Argentina; Darío Jaramillo, who had flown in from Colombia, and two of Uruguayan poets included in the anthology, Rafael Courtoisie and Roberto Appratto. Inés Garland joined us on the ferry; she was attending the Book Fair separately, in her capacity as a novelist.

The weather was frightful. From my seat on the ferry I watched a grey sea against a slowly unfurling grey sky. The voyage seemed endless, despite the relatively short distance travelled. On the Uruguyan shore, we piled into a minibus and, as the rain hammered down, sped past green fields and scattered woods. Arriving at San José, we settled down to a very slow lunch, its duration exacerbated for me by a piece of meat from the *asado* that went down the wrong way. Immediately I sensed that I was in trouble, started choking, and couldn't breathe. The only remedy for this was the Heimlich manoeuvre. I knew, without thinking about it for very long, that of all the people in the dining room, Andy Ehrenhaus was the one to ask – by means of some frantic gesturing on my part, interpreted fluently by Inés – to perform the task. Which he did, instinctively and without hesitation, although he hadn't done it before, nor ever considered it, grasping me from behind, delivering a few sharp blows to my back, and then hugging me around the midriff and pulling his fist into my navel. I spat something out, and breathed again. I never could account for the certainty with which I had selected Andy, an especially laid-back type with no more than a rudimentary grasp of first aid. I returned to my hotel room, and watched the rain through my window, and from the distance came an almost continuous rolling of thunder. Although only my first afternoon in San José, it felt as though I had been here too long already.

That evening, after an unsatisfactory siesta, I left the hotel and walked in strange amber light towards the theatre in the town's main square. Everything seemed to happen in slow motion here. Even the dogs shuffled arthritically down the pavement. One especially decrepit mutt made an effort to accompany me on my way, before giving up and slumping to the ground.

I wanted to find a reason for being here, other than the fact of having being invited, but drew a blank. I knew it was for the anthology's sake but, to be honest, I had left the anthology behind a year ago. My mind was on other things, especially now that I had recovered the energy and focus that sobriety brought with it. One of the effects of travel, however, over an extended period of time, was that each new displacement presented a minor ontological crisis, a feeling that was especially apposite here in San José. We could have been almost anywhere, provided it was a backwater. Market towns in Wales and Catalonia came to mind; places that, under other circumstances, or to other people, felt like home.

Later, inside the theatre, a modestly imposing building in the late colonial style, the lights failed, the sound system packed up, and for a full three minutes we were left in silence, and in the dark. Only then did I begin to feel at my ease; only then did I feel as though I'd arrived, before the invisible red, velvet curtain. "Who has not stood tense before his own heart's curtain?" asks Rilke in his *Duino Elegies*, reminding us not to be complacent, to always confront oneself at the deepest level; and this phrase echoed through my thoughts in the lengthy lacuna of nothing happening. Even if the electrical problem were to be resolved, the idea of pulling aside those symbolic curtains seemed like an unnecessarily dramatic intervention. I was more than content to remain in darkness, indefinitely, despite the agitation and impatience of those around me. When eventually the lights did come on, and the crimson curtain was drawn aside, I had become so attuned to my state of tranquil vacuity that what occurred on stage could only be regarded as an intrusion. Sure enough, the mayor, or some other local functionary, delivered a long speech about the importance of culture, and of poetry, here in a town of cattle ranchers.

That night I could not sleep. Outside my hotel, fortuitously located on Calle Borges, there was a commotion from the little bar across the way, that spilled out onto the road. I heard raised voices, and imagined a pair of loudmouthed but cowardly poets coming up against a group of rustic drunks, as might happen in a story by Borges himself, or indeed Bolaño – but then things quietened down, though the light on my balcony stayed on, and I was no more able to extinguish it than I could resist the restless insomnia that pursued me into the dawn.

    The next morning, back in Buenos Aires, the world was too loud and large inanimate objects moved around quickly, dangerously. Crossing the road from the ferry terminal with a pair of suitcases, trying to track down a taxi, demanded an exceptional degree of agility. The distilled lethargy of small town Uruguay now resembled the leftover dross of a dream from which you awaken and cannot quite piece together: the dream's debris holds you back from this raucous new world of cranes and office blocks and the relentless blasting of car horns. We eventually found a taxi that took us to Palermo and I checked into my regular hotel. There was a finality about this return trip to Buenos Aires, as though the chain of events brought into play by the making of the anthology had at last run its course.

> From time to time I walk backwards:
> it's my way of remembering.
>
> If I were to walk only going forward,
> I could tell you
> what forgetting is.
>
> Humberto Ak'Abal, 'Walking Backwards'.

The map on my bedroom wall proved prophetic. It had felt like a challenge of sorts, the intimation of a journey that might come about when the time was right. I had no idea it would take so long. And then, many years later, influenced by my reading, and by serendipitous meetings with Latin American writers, a number of whom became my friends, I had started out on this pilgrimage. I sometimes wonder if, by pasting that map to the wall, I had some secret knowledge of what was to come, knew already the inscribed trajectory of my life, as though guided by some daimon or guardian angel.

Or had the map simply been a metaphor, having little to do with an actual geography and more with an inner compulsion to go elsewhere, to be anywhere except where I was, which at that time was London, a place which, not many years later, I vowed to leave, never to return? When you are young, there is a tendency to make reckless declarations of intent. In my own youth, I was perpetually setting out, and never arriving. By the age of thirty-three, facing extinction in a Barcelona hospital, I was exhausted by the metaphor of the journey.

I remember a story by Kafka, 'The Departure', in which the narrator sets out on a journey, and when his servant asks him where he is going, he replies "I don't know, just out of here ... out of here, nothing else, it's the only way I can reach my goal." "So you know your goal?" the servant asks. "Yes," the narrator replies, "I've just told you. Out of here – that's my goal."

Perhaps a map need only be an imagined space on a white wall, and nothing more. But although my map of Latin America was a projection, and a trope for 'out of here', it was also a geographical space or destination, the source or origin of many of the works of poetry and fiction that engaged my imagination over decades, and of places that one day would become actualised on my travels in search of poems. My pilgrimage necessitated many journeys, and several maps, but the destination was never in doubt.

As a translator, I was a vessel or a channel, by which the thoughts and images contrived by others would be re-invented as thoughts and images in another language, and sent out into the world anew. Translation is a mysterious practice, and occasionally I forget that I do it, since it is what one is always engaged in, without option and at all times, from the very start of life. Early childhood is the acute phase of translation, and of being translated, comprising countless moments in which every gaze, every enraged reaction or response on the part of the infant meets with either incomprehension or else with a tentative, and then a more assured translation by its carers. By the time we come to consider translation as the transference of semantic content from one language to another, we have already acquired a specific set of linguistic skills, and these have determined our cultural and aesthetic choices to such a degree that they establish, in large part, who we are, and how we are perceived by others.

The roles or personae we accumulate can sometimes seem like traps for the unwary. Like almost everything else I've done, other than write, I became a translator by accident. But it seemed like a natural extension of what I was already doing, since writing itself is an act of translation – from silence, or from life itself.

★ ★ ★

It is almost a truism to say we live our lives surrounded by stories – ours and other people's – and interpret everything that happens to us in terms of those stories, even as we recount them. We might believe the story we tell about ourselves but that doesn't make it true; it doesn't even make it a story. The narrative impulse is unavoidable – we are storytelling creatures, *animals with ideas,* as Lowry's Consul would have it – and yet I find it difficult to comprehend life stories that cohere to evoke a single person or a consistent self (the essential person that is me). I have almost no identification with or understanding of the nineteen-year old I offered up at the outset of this chronicle. I do not consider the self that I inhabit now to be the same self I was then, nor any of the innumerable selves that emerged between.

According to the philosopher Galen Strawson, people who see themselves as the unchanging protagonist of their life's story can be contrasted with those who see their lives as a series of intrinsically separable events – and themselves as different people at the time of each event. His contention is simple: some people see their lives as the narratives of a single self; others see the events of their lives happening to the self that existed at that moment. Neither viewpoint is superior to the other; they're just different. However, Strawson suggests, there is a tendency among some of the former, who are motivated by a sense of their own importance or significance, to believe that unless a life is gathered together in the form of a cohesive narrative it lacks an ethical character, and he wonders *why on earth, in the midst of the beauty of being, it should be thought important to do this.* These words, on first reading them, brought about in me an overwhelming sense of release. I felt at once unburdened of any need to carry around with me a fully-formed and articulated narrative of my self, one which sustained a consistent identity.

It attracts and repels me in equal measure, this idea that we might lack an essential, identifiable self, and yet at the same time its absence does not seem to be an obstacle to contentment, or even serenity. "The thing I call my individuality is only a pattern or dance," wrote the physicist Richard Feynman. "The atoms come into my brain, dance a dance and then go out – there are always new atoms, but always doing the same dance, remembering what the dance was yesterday."

★ ★ ★

Four years after my father's death, I paid a visit to the village where I was raised. I needed to take a walk. It was nearly always while walking that ideas appeared to me, and especially here, on the red loam of my native patch, where I could walk without a map, or rather, rely on the map I carried inside my head. When walking in the nearby hills I am most at my ease, no doubt because here I find it impossible to tell where my self ends and the world begins; or to put it slightly differently, my sense of self ebbs away, dissipates, and merges with that larger consciousness we call 'nature' (as if nature were a thing apart from ourselves).

At times, grief for my father became confused with a kind of grief for the landscape, with the place he lived out his life, and where I grew up. My grief became absorbed by the hikes I took in the Black Mountains, especially one walk above the hermitage in the Grwyne Fechan valley that I associated most closely with my father. I can feel him in the landscape, and walking there brings me closer to him. I had never thought of my father as believing in a life beyond the grave, but I do remember him saying to me once that when we die what is left of us becomes absorbed into the soil, the plants and flowers, back into nature. I had always thought of him as an agnostic, if not an atheist, so it was strange to hear him describe a kind of regenerative animism.

On this May afternoon, the anniversary of my father's death, I visited my parents' final resting place; modest slabs of stone propped up against the church in which I was baptised by the Reverend H.G.H Griffths, the predecessor of the Reverend Cyril James, whom my father insisted be called upon to attend to the spiritual welfare of the crazed hippy axeman one Christmas Day, long ago, in this same graveyard. After laying down a potted plant and paying my respects, I went inside the church and sat in the old family pew, near the front, on the right, and sank into soft reflection amid a multitude of my childhood selves, which had occupied that seat on many occasions and I felt, yes, this is familiar, and began to reflect upon the billions of subatomic particles being displaced, replaced, of this dizzying life of heat and light and the granularity of time and matter, the solar energy that drives the wind, the heave and sway of the years, and was comfortable with the self I was in that moment, despite sensing a contiguity with an earlier self, who, however, made no demands of kinship, any more than did the carved stone salmon hidden by some crafty mason in the stonework of the ancient walls, and I would have stayed there indefinitely had the church warden not come in from the vestry – that room no doubt still smelling of damp rot, candle wax and camphor – who seemed surprised to see me there, and after some polite interrogation told me that she wanted to lock up. So I left, and drove down past the old family home, parked in the lay-by and walked through the Elvicta estate to the Usk, along the river, past the sewerage treatment plant to the metal bridge that had, during World War Two, connected the G.I. camp housing the 99th Infantry Division on the Glanusk estate with the army base at Cwrt-y-Gollen, and upon which, as a boy, I would stand and watch the fish, or catch them, if I was lucky, the sparkling silvery trout and the sleek sinewy eels. I crossed the road and skirted the now defunct military base, climbed up through the bluebell woods to Gypsy lane, so called because many years ago a man known as Gypsy Smith lived in a caravan at the bottom of the long and muddy track. As a child I was intrigued by the idea of living in such a way, and I make a mental note to ask my father what became of this Smith – for there was a time when my father knew practically everyone in this valley, and the inhabitants of most of the farms for miles around – and whether he had lived alone in the old caravan, or whether he had a spouse and children, for although I could not be certain, I seemed to recall a little Romany boy of my own age at St Edmund's primary school who was a Smith, a name otherwise uncommon in a village of Morgans and Gameses and Ralphs; and then it strikes me, with a dull shock, that I cannot ask my father, for the fact is that he is dead, and all I will ever remember of the man named Smith, who lived at the end of a country lane, is his walk, his way of proceeding through the world, which might accurately be described as purposeful, and which, in a literary context, might read: "He was a dark, unsmiling man who always walked intently towards a point invisible to anyone but himself," and though I write this now, I am unsure whether I am remembering correctly, or if this is merely the confabulation of the years that have passed between my act of remembering and the inciting incident, namely my younger self watching this Smith make his way down Llangenny Lane half a century ago on an autumn day, with his soldier's erect walk, his eyes straight ahead, as even now he strides out from oblivion into memory, and that is all I have, rather than a photographic imprint in the brain, as my memories settle in random order, just as randomly encountered as the memories of my father himself or of the lambs that gambolled in the adjoining field, as I made my way up the hill on my walk that day.

Emerging from the woods in golden evening light, a fox crossed the field in front of me. He spotted me soon after I saw him, must have caught my scent on the breeze, because he turned his head and stopped mid-step, one front paw raised in a characteristic pose, snout turned towards me, and we were so close I could see his long whiskers quivering, eyes alert and questioning. The passage of a few brief seconds as we assessed each other, before he set off on his way, seemed like time out of time.

I continued up the rough track and onto the lane that leads back towards the village, with a view over the Usk valley and the Llangattock Mountain beyond. My father took a walk up the lane almost every evening of his working life. "Anyone for a turn up the lane?" he would ask of the household in general, and a recurrent memory is of him, dressed for a walk in windcheater and hat – he was suspicious of hats and caps, as he was of beards, but in his later years would don a stiff tweed trilby – stepping toward the front gate and reaching for the latch. He walked with his head down, eyes to the ground, as though looking for something that he might have dropped but was never too hopeful of finding.

Perhaps, after all, the best way to tell a story is as though we didn't understand it, just as being unknown to ourselves may sometimes be the best way to live. We do not need to be attached to any of the fictions we have told ourselves along the way. Nor, on our journey, should we be surprised to find that the land is strewn with the tattered ruins of maps, and is inhabited by animals and beggars.

Notes

Books and articles cited in the main text appear below. A few notes expand on some of them. Unless referenced otherwise, all translations from Spanish are my own.

9 For more on the role of maps in the literary imagination, see Peter Turchi's intriguing study, *Maps of the Imagination: The Writer as Cartographer*, Trinity University Press (2009).

10 'On Exactitude in Science', J.L. Borges, *Collected Fictions*, Translated by Andrew Hurley. Penguin, 1998, p 325.

15 "God said . . ." Gioconda Belli, 'God said', in *The Other Tiger: Recent Poetry from Latin America*, Seren, 2016, p 99.

21 "I too dislike it . . ." Ben Lerner, *The Hatred of Poetry*, FSG Originals, 2016, pp 5-6.

22 "The outcome of all this . . ." Darío Jaramillo, in 'Contra los recitals de poesía', in SoHo magazine, 14 September, 2011.

24 Salman Rushdie, *The Jaguar Smile: A Nicaraguan Journey*, Vintage, 2007, pp 18-20.

27 "we began smelling it from Arambala . . .", from Alma Guillermoprieto's report in the *Washington Post*, January 27, 1982.

28 Mark Danner's report, 'The Truth of El Mozote' appeared in the *New Yorker*, November 29, 1993.

31 "criminals" and "vampires in search of blood" cited in the *Miami Herald*, May 2, 2018.

31 "My colleagues and I . . .", Alma Guillermoprieto, *New York Review of Books*, June 6. 2019.

35 "We have a house in South America . . ." Daniel Samoilovich, 'The House in Tigre', in *The Other Tiger*, p 45.

36 More on my niece's ordeal can be read in my memoir *The Vagabond's Breakfast*, Alcemi (2011) Chapter 36. Nicola's own account, 'I was abducted at gunpoint' can be found in the *Guardian*, October 20, 2006.

49 Cf: "When the beginnings of self destruction enter the heart, it seems no bigger than a grain of sand . . .' John Cheever, *Journals*, Vintage, 1991.

55 "I think that was the first time . . ." Juan José Saer, *The Witness,* translated by Margaret Jull Costa, Serpent's Tail, 1990, pp 31-32.

58 "I went out into the street in flames . . ." Julio Trujillo, 'Ten Tequilas', in *The Other Tiger,* p 227.

60 "The bound and gagged bodies of twenty-six men", CBS News, November 24, 2011.

65 "The days keep taking away the things . . ." Jorge Fernández Granados, 'Things' in *The Other Tiger,* p 213.

67 "I was either calling my past self a liar . . ." Leslie Jamison, *The Recovering: Intoxication and its Aftermath*, Granta, 2018, p 252.

71 "The man who tells you he has thought of everything has forgotten the hare." Anna Crowe, 'A Calendar of Hares', Scottish Poetry Library.

73 "Addicts often suffer from self-deception . . ." Peg O'Connor, *Life on the Rocks*, CRP, 2016, p 96.

80 "Translating poems that seem to be very straightforward . . ." Susan Bassnett, cited on the Stephen Spender Trust website (stephenspender.org): 'Poetry translation advice from the judges.'

81 "fear of the false . . ." and "Sand conquered all . . ." W.G. Sebald, *The Rings of Saturn*, translated by Michael Hulse, Vintage, 2002, pp 6-7.

83 "a translator is . . . very close reader . . ." J.L. Borges cited in Norman di Giovanni, *The Lesson of the Master*, Continuum, 2003, p 181.

83 "to translate is also to read, and to translate is to write . . ." Lydia Davis, 'To Reiterate' in *The Collected Stories*, Penguin Books, 2009, p 215.

84 "The beggars emerge from ancient catacombs . . ." Juan Manuel Roca, 'Landscape with Beggars', in *The Other Tiger,* p 227-9.

85 Juan Manuel Santos, *La batalla por la paz*, Península, 2019.

88 Juan Manuel Santos, in 'The Legacy of Peace' a talk delivered at the London School of Economics, November 2, 2016.

97 "Like the Britons . . ." Nick Miroff, the *Washington Post*, October 3, 2016.

99 "To walk is to advance . . ." Ariel Williams, 'Discourse of the teller of worms', in *The Other Tiger,* p 201.

104 "think Skegness on the edge of the Kalahari . . ." etc. Jon Gower, *Gwalia Patagonia,* Gomer, 2015, pp 106-8.

104 "To suppose for one second . . ." Jorge Fondebrider, *Versiones de la Patagonia,* Emece Editores, 2003, Chapter 14.

106 Bruce Chatwin, *In Patagonia* (1977), Introduction to 2006 Vintage edition by Nicholas Shakespeare, p xxiii.

107 "I can't stand it . . ." Nicholas Shakespeare, *Bruce Chatwin,* Vintage, 2000, p. 366.

107 Chatwin's request that Nita Starling wash his clothes is also cited in Shakespeare, 2000, p. 296.

108 "an object without real value, but desirable in great measure . . ." is also cited in Gower, 2015, p. 176.

108 "Never have I wanted anything as I wanted that piece of skin . . ." in W.G. Sebald, *Campo Santo,* Penguin, 2006, p. 184.

108 "When Chatwin strayed away from the truth . . ." Gower, 2015, p. 184.

109 "A country boy . . .", *In Patagonia,* p.17.

109 "How had he travelled from here to there?" Shakespeare, 2000, p. 294.

113 "Even though you walk barefoot . . ." Jorge Aulicino, 'A somewhat difficult syntax', in *The Other Tiger,* p 173.

114 "The landscape had a gaunt expression . . ." Paul Theroux, *The Old Patagonian Express,* Houghton Mifflin, 1979, p 403.

120 'Nazi' boys school outing story, reported in *Clarín,* August 25, 2016.

125 "Here they come . . ." María Rivera, 'The Dead', in The Other Tiger, pp 311-21.

126 Mariano Picón-Salas, *De la conquista a la independencia,* Fondo De Cultura Económica, 1944/1997, p 30.

132 "Another flower but the same . . ." Luis Felipe Fabre, "Xochicuicatl, in *The Other Tiger,* p 321.

133 Octavio Paz's views on 'the Mexican' have largely been rejected by Latin American commentators over the past seventy years. Emmanuel Orduñez Angelo, writing in the *New York Review* claims that 'It is considered bad taste to take Paz's

view of Mexico seriously these days' but goes on to question whether some of his conclusions are not still valid, especially with regard to witchcraft: 'Surely the culture Paz was describing must be extinct, we tell ourselves; Mexico has modernized substantially in the past seventy years. Yet murderers still blame demons for their crimes; journalists still present those crimes as stories about "possessed" men murdering "witches."' Deadly Myths: Magic, reality, and violence against women in Fernanda Melchor's *Hurricane Season*.' *NYRB*, 14.01.2021.

134 Juan Rulfo, *El llano en llamas*, Catedra, 1985.

134 "actions take place in a time that never stops recurring . . ." Juan Villoro, 'Pedro Páramo', in *Efectos Personales*, Ediciones Era, 2000.

135 "Nomads . . ." etc. Reina Roffé, *Juan Rulfo*, Forcola, 2017, p 155.

135 "the worst night of sweaty intoxication imaginable . . ." Carmen Boullosa, 'Dead Souls', essay in *The Nation*, May 18, 2006.

137 "We are always mapping the invisible . . ." Denis Wood, *The Power of Maps*, Guildford Press, 1992, p 5.

137 "The stories in *El llano en llamas* derive their power . . ." Juan Villoro, 2000.

137 Alastair Reid, 'On Being a Foreigner', in *Outside In: Selected Prose*, Polygon, 2008, pp 147-158

145 "In the mirror of midday . . ." Pedro Serrano, 'Dark Ages', in *The Other Tiger*, p 147.

146 Photo of Dylan Thomas by Francis Reiss, courtesy of Getty Images. Photo of Diego Rivera by Carl Van Vechten, courtesy of the Library of Congress, Washington, D.C.

148 Patrick Leigh Fermor, *The Broken Road*, John Murray, 2014, pp 112-19.

149 'Approximately ten women are murdered every day in Mexico . . .', Linnea Sandin, In CSIS (Center for Strategic & International Studies report, March 19, 2020, and KUT 90.5 radio (Austin, Texas), March 9, 2020.

150 Photographs of the Zapatista Generals Feliciano Polanco Araujo and Teodoro Rodriguez in Sanborns, Mexico City, are in the Public Domain.

154 "This building doesn't satisfy anyone . . ." Fabio Morábito, 'Time of Crisis', in *The Other Tiger*, p 51.

162 "Life is not what one lived . . ." Epigraph to Gabriel García Márquez, *Living to Tell the Tale*, translated by Edith Grossman, Vintage, 2004.

164 Pepe Ochoa interview, *Plumas libres,* September 2014.

170 "The spy reads as we read . . ." Luisa Valenzuela, 'The Wanderer', *The Brooklyn Rail* website.

170 "Writing . . ." Maurice Blanchot, *The Space of Literature,* University of Nebraska Press, 1982, p. 33.

174 "How, unless you drink as I do . . .", Malcolm Lowry, *Under the Volcano,* Penguin, 2000, p 55.

178 "You are interfering with my great battle . . .' etc, *Under the Volcano,* p 220.

178 David Ryan, *Malcolm Lowry's Under the Volcano,* Ig Publishing, 2017.

179 Lowry's fascination with mirrors, cited in Douglas Day, Malcolm Lowry: A Biography, OUP, 1973, p 383.

179 "his habit of slyly watching for audience reaction . . ." Gordon Bowker, *Pursued by Furies: A Life of Malcolm Lowry.* Flamingo, 1993, p xviii.

179 "I hate those bloody toffs who come to sea . . ." etc. Day, 1973, pp 92-3.

179 "What kind of man are you . . ." Day, 1973, p 462.

180 Photo of Malcolm Lowry courtesy of AP/Press Association.

181 "How many bottles . . ." Lowry, 2000, p 294.

181 "a nice good lovely glass . . ." Ernest Hemingway, in a letter to Archie MacLeish, 28 June 1957. *Selected Letters, 1917-61.* Scribner, 1981, p 877.

182 "But if you look at that sunlight there . . .' etc, Lowry, 2000, p 55.

182 "So I held on like a terrier . . ." Ronnie Duncan, 'A Journal of Crete' in *Aquarius* 25/26, 2002, p 150.

185 "The devil instilled in me a black acoustic fury . . ." Julián Herbert, 'Dark', in *The Other Tiger,* p 333.

185 "I spent my childhood . . ." Julián Herbert, *Tomb Song,* translated by Christina MacSweeney, Graywolf, 2018, p 72.

185 "My precocity . . ." Julián Herbert, 'Del hielo al abrigo: El Cerdo de Babel', 2014. On academia.edu website.

186 "in some dark corner of my consciousness . . ." *Tomb Song*, 2018, p. 75.

187 "all my friends . . ." 'Del hielo al abrigo: El Cerdo de Babel', 2014.

192 "We need translations. . ." Kate Briggs, *This Little Art*, Fitzcarraldo, 2017, p 58.

198 "those European bitches", Joanna Moorhead, in 'The surrealist muses who roared', the *Guardian*, 18 June, 2010.

198 "Leonora stays well away from Frida Kahlo . . ." Elena Poniatowska, *Leonora*, translated by Amanda Hopkinson, Serpents'Tail, 2015, p 267.

199 "a fluid, uncategorical mode . . ." Lorna Scott Fox, 'Swimming under cemeteries: Leonora Carrington: almost- forgotten, radical and an 'essential artist-thinker for our fragile time'.' *Times Literary Supplement,* May 5, 2017.

202 "Yet I am sure of this . . ." Alastair Reid, 'The Tale the Hermit Told', in *Inside Out: Selected Poetry and Translations,* Polygon, 2008, pp 46-8.

206 Although Alastair claimed that he hadn't read Borges or even heard of him when he arrived in New York in 1964, there is evidence elsewhere that he first encountered Borges' work in the 1950s. I can only imagine that he was misremembering the timing of this particular conversation with Vargas Llosa in London.

210 "*A fiction is any construct of language . . .*" Alastair Reid, *Outside In: Selected Prose,* Polygon, 2008, p 322.

211 Alastair Reid's translation of 'The Other Tiger' appears in *Inside Out: Selected Poetry and Translations*, Polygon, 2008, pp 181-3.

212 'The Tale the Hermit Told', in *Inside Out,* pp 46-8.

213 "Reid was never forgiven" *Guardian* obituary of Alastair Reid, by James Campbell, September 26, 2014.

217 "memory is fickle . . ." Catalina González Restrepo, 'Viaje', in *The Other Tiger*, p 247

220 The two Mexican poets referred to are Alí Calderón and Mario Bojórquez.

225 "Near the rocks, belly up, is God . . ." Rómulo Bustos Aguirre, 'Marbella Scene', in *The Other Tiger*, p 165

227 Thomas Pynchon, 'The Heart's Eternal Vow', *New York Times*, April 10, 1988.

256 "There is a ship . . ." Raúl Zurita, 'Inri', in The Other Tiger, p 353.

256 The 'Citizen of Nowhere' speech was delivered at the British Conservative Party Conference in October 2016. The full text, for those who can bear to read it, can be found online at *The Spectator*, 5 October 2016.

257 "No book is ever finished, however, even when it has gone to press and is done and dusted; it carries on reinventing itself in the heads of its readers, if not its creator." Perhaps, as Borges wrote somewhere, one publishes books so as not to continue correcting them endlessly.

259 "I have a vague suspicion . . ." Roberto Bolaño, 'Chilean Poetry under Inclement Skies' in *Between Parentheses: Essays, Articles and Speeches, 1998-2003*, translated by Natasha Wimmer, New Directions, 2011, p 95.

259 'Fragments of a Return to the Native Land', in *Between Parentheses*, pp 61-74

260 'The Corridor with No Apparent Way Out', in *Between Parentheses*, pp 75-83.

261 "Literature . . . has always been close to ignominy, to vileness, to torture." Roberto Bolaño in interview with Luis García-Santillán on *Crítica.cl* website, 13 April 2002.

261 "Zurita creates a wonderful body of work . . ." in Roberto Bolaño, 'Chilean Poetry under Inclement Skies', *Between Parentheses*, p 96.

262 "he would have liked to have 'had it out' with the 'hepatic' Bolaño . . ." Chiara Bolognese, 'Roberto Bolaño y Raúl Zurita: Referencias cruzadas.' In *Anales de Literatura Chilena*, 14 (Dec 2010): 259-272.

267 "Next to the river of these skies . . ." Jaime Luis Huenún, 'In the House of Zulema Hualquipán', in *The Other Tiger*, p 53.

270 "It is not possible that a place . . ." article by Marella Oppenheim, 'Excavations at Chile torture site offer new hope for relatives of disappeared', *The Guardian*, 2 May, 2018. The 2021 Netflix series, *A Sinister Sect: Colonia Dignidad* offers first-hand accounts by some of Schäfer's victims. Difficult watching, and impressionistic rather than detailed in its execution.

270 "Humboldt was the first . . ." Andrea Wulf, *The Invention of Nature: The Adventures of Alexander von Humboldt, the Lost Hero of Science,* John Murray, 2015, p. 5.

273 "that it reinforces, rather than challenges . . ." from 'Exhibit B, the human zoo, is a grotesque parody – boycott it' by Kehinde Andrews, in *The Guardian*, 12 Sep 2014. The response, by Stella Odunlami, and her exchange with Andrews, appeared in the same newspaper on 27 September, 2014.

274 Bruno Latour, *Down to Earth: Politics in the New Climatic Regime,* translated by Catherine Potter, Polity, 2018, pp 1-2.

281 "If they tell you that I fell ..." Beatríz Vignoli, 'The Fall', in *The Other Tiger,* p 231.

281 V.S. Naipaul, 'The Brothels Behind the Graveyard', *New York Review of Books,* September 19, 1974.

284 Roberto Bolaño, 'Scholars of Sodom', *NYRB,* April 12, 2012.

285 Ian Buruma, 'The Lessons of the Master, *NYRB,* November 20, 2008.

286 Margaret Murray, *NYRB* letters page, January 15, 2009. The full text of her letter is as follows: 'On Elizabeth Hardwick's advice, "Never ever speak to them dear. They always get it wrong," I did not cooperate with Patrick French's book [*The World Is What It Is: The Authorized Biography of V.S. Naipaul*]; nor have I read it. There are a number of things wrong in Ian Buruma's review of it [*NYRB,* November 20, 2008]. Gillon Aitken was not dispatched to Buenos Aires checkbook in hand. (I wish he had been.) There was one pregnancy and one that turned out not to be. I heard nothing about Pat raising the child. The majority of my letters to Vidia were written because he had a habit of saying "please write me a little letter." If he chose to leave them unopened, that was his business. Not mentioned in Ian Buruma's review is an error by Patrick French: no one has ever called me Margarita. Vidia [Naipaul] says I didn't mind the abuse. I certainly did mind.'

286 Paul Theroux, *NYRB* letters page, January 15, 2009.

292 "If I admitted to being an alcoholic ..." cf. Leslie Jamison, "I know I said I was an alcoholic and then took it back and said I wasn't really and then took that back and said I actually was but the thing is I'm really not, I promise." *The Recovering,* 2018, p 344.

294 "I am not sure if there is any such thing ..." Jorge Fondebrider, 'Closing up the House', in *The Other Tiger,* p 349.

301 Einstein/Besso story is cited, among many other places, in Carlo Rovelli's book *The Order of Time,* translated by Erica Segre and Simon Carnell, Allen Lane, 2018, p. 96.

302 Rommel story: I later discovered, while idly googling 'Rommel's tailor' that in 1999, the British editor of *GQ* magazine was sacked for placing the 'Desert Fox' on a list of the Best Dressed Men of the 20th Century.

304 'These fragments I have shored against my ruins', T.S. Eliot, *The Waste Land.* In every draft of this chapter prior to 2021 I had written 'against my ruin', in

the singular. It is the way I remembered the line, and it made sense to me that way. Then in May 2021, I was reading Brian Dillon's *Essayism*, and came across these lines: "Do you remember when you quoted *The Waste Land* – 'These fragments I have shored against my ruins' – and I was absolutely sure, without checking, that it ought to be 'ruin'? That is how I have heard the line in my head for more than half my life, and I was awfully sure of myself. I was wrong, of course – it is 'ruins'." Dillon continues: "It seems to me now that my version, the product of a decades-long mistake, sounds like evidence of some abiding anxiety: the fragments piled up to protect from disaster, 'against' understood as 'in case of', the whole line a crystallising of my anxious attitude to life and to writing alike. Something akin to: *these fragments I have written in the sure knowledge that my ruin is coming, and this is all I've got.* And your version of Eliot's line? It might I suppose mean the same thing, except that disaster has multiplied, the state of emergency become the norm. But unlike me you have properly heard 'shored' not as the erection of a barricade but as a *shoring up*, propping up, support: as if your first impulse is to learn to live with fragments, with ruins, with the aggregate, particulate, dusty motion between past and future.' Brian Dillon, *Essayism*, Fitzcarraldo, 2018, p. 136.

308 "The tiger leaps . . ." Pedro Serrano, 'Dark Ages', in *The Other Tiger*, p 147.

308 "When I saw your handwriting on the envelope . . ." John Berger, *and our faces, my heart, brief as photos*. Bloomsbury, 1984, pp 52-3.

309 "What has prompted me to write over the years . . ." John Berger, *Confabulations,* Penguin, 2016, p 7.

310 "True translation is not a binary affair . . ." Confabulations, p 4.

313 *"Would you rather have no bones or no skin?"* The question appears in Leslie Jamison, *The Recovering*, Granta, 2018, p 280.

323 "From time to time I walk backwards . . ." Humberto Ak'Abal, 'Walking Backwards', in *The Other Tiger*, p. 241.

323 Franz Kafka, 'The Departure', translated by Tania and James Stern, from *The Complete Short Stories*, Vintage, 1999, p 449.

325 "Why on earth, in the midst of the beauty of being . . ." Galen Strawson, 'Against Narrativity', in *Ratio* XVII, 4 December 2004, p 436. I acknowledge Strawson's distinction but cannot agree with the way in which the problem has been posed, as one of either/or. I believe that one may be both 'episodic' and the owner of a semi-continuous (and even semi-conscious) narrative identity, and nor do I see any contradiction in this way of being. Notably, Strawson goes some way to meeting the 'narrativist' viewpoint, as he calls it, in a later essay, 'The Unstoried Life', when he concedes that the sequence of recorded events might, "for some people in some cases" be important.

However, that does not alter his belief (which I share) that "for most of us . . . self-knowledge comes best (and only) in bits and pieces." Galen Strawson, *Things That Bother Me*, NYRB Books, 2018, p 201.

325 "The thing I call my individuality . . ." Richard Feynman, *What do you care what other people think?* Bantam, 1998, p 244.

328 " . . . just as being unknown to ourselves may sometimes be the best way to live." This sentiment finds an echo in some unlikely quarters. C.G. Jung, despite a lifetime following the maxim 'know thyself' ends his autobiography as follows: "Yet there is so much that fills me: plants, animals, clouds, day and night, and the eternal in man. The more uncertain I have felt about myself, the more there has grown up in me a feeling of kinship with all things. In fact it seems to me as if that alienation which so long separated me from the world has become transferred into my own inner world, and has revealed an unexpected unfamiliarity with myself." C.G. Jung, *Memories, Dreams, Reflections*, recorded and edited by Aniela Jaffé, Richard and Clara Winston, trans. London: Collins & Routledge, 1963, p 330. Some years later, Hélène Cixous would write: "I know that it's by being unknown to myself, that I live." Cixous, Hélène, and Mireille Calle-Gruber, *Rootprints: Memory and life writing*, Routledge, 1997, p 10.

Acknowledgements

Most of the chapters in this book are introduced by a few lines of poetry. With a few exceptions, these are taken from poems in *The Other Tiger: Recent Poetry from Latin America*, of which this book is the companion, or shadow volume, reflecting glimmers from the other side of the mirror.

I would like to thank the Arts Council of Wales for appointing me Creative Wales Ambassador for the year 2014, and am especially grateful to Sioned Puw Rowlands and Nikki Morgan, who suggested I apply for the award. The consistent support of Wales Arts International between 2011-2017 allowed me to gather much of the material for this book and for *The Other Tiger*.

Extracts from earlier drafts of *Ambassador of Nowhere* have appeared in *Southwest Review* (USA), *The Common* (USA), *Firmament* (USA), *Berlin Literary Review*, *PN Review*, *Wales Arts Review* and *New Welsh Reader*. I'd like to thank their editors. Other extracts have appeared on my own website, *Ricardo Blanco's Blog*.

It would be impossible to list all the people whose counsel and goodwill helped inform the journeys recorded in this chronicle, but I would like to thank the following for their kindness and hospitality, friendship and advice, or simply their company on this Odyssey of many twists and turns: Jorge Fondebrider, Pablo Braun, Inés Garland, Pedro Serrano, Carlos López Beltrán, Fabio Morábito, Lucrecia Orensanz, Jorge F. Hernández, Julián Herbert, Mónica Álvarez Herrasti, Mercedes Luna Fuentes, Fernando Rendón, Juan Manuel Roca, Darío Jaramillo, Rómulo Bustos Aguirre, Piedad Bonnett, Federico Díaz-Granados, Verónica Zondek, Menashe Katz, Paulo Slachevsky, Silvia Aguilera and Enrique Winter. I offer special thanks to my minders in Medellín and Guadalajara: Santiago Hoyos and Ivan Hernández.

Along the way, the book, or parts of it, have been read by many people. They include Patrick McGuinness, Tom Bullough, Jon Gower and my colleagues at the Reclamation Yard: Tristan Hughes, Abigail Parry, Ailbhe Darcy, Tim Rhys, Tyler Keevil, Meredith Miller, Susan Morgan and Bob Walton. Thanks to you all. My Latin American readers gave me invaluable advice and corrected a few errors: many thanks to Jorge Fondebrider, Inés Garland, Verónica Zondek, Juan Villoro and Andrés Neuman.

I'd like to thank all the poets who contributed to *The Other Tiger*. I also thank those I have omitted from this page through negligence or forgetfulness.

I want to thank Rose, my wife, not only for her incalculable kindness and support, but also in her role as my best critic, editor and proofreader.

Finally, many thanks to my agent, Anna Webber, for believing in this book, and to Sarah Johnson, Jamie Hill and the team at Seren, for getting the thing done.

Author Note

Richard Gwyn's novels include *The Colour of a Dog Running Away* and *The Blue Tent* and he has published four collections of poetry, most recently *Stowaway: A Levantine Adventure*. His memoir, *The Vagabond's Breakfast*, won Wales Book of the Year for non-fiction in 2012. He is the editor and translator of the landmark anthology, *The Other Tiger: Recent Poetry from Latin America* and his other translations include the poetry collections *Impossible Loves* by Darío Jaramillo and *Invisible Dog* by Fabio Morábito. He is the author of *Ricardo Blanco's Blog*.

Also by Richard Gwyn

"Richard Gwyn, the editor and translator of this wonderful anthology of contemporary poems from Latin America, has given us an incisive overview of recent, innovative writing we're not likely to find elsewhere in English. The preface is solid: informative, intelligent, and immensely useful to both novices and old hands; the thematic organization is revelatory and moves us far from the rather pedantic, strictly historical or geographical focus of so many other anthologies; and the translations are beautiful and to the point.

This is a book that belongs in every library, private or institutional, that has shelf-space for volumes of poetry. I think Alastair Reid, to whom the book is dedicated, would have been very happy with the tribute." – *Edith Grossman*

www.serenbooks.com